LOUISIANA STATE UNIVERSITY STUDIES
MAX GOODRICH, General Editor

*Humanities Series*
DONALD E. STANFORD, Editor

Number Fifteen
*Nine Essays in Modern Literature*

# Nine Essays
# in
# Modern Literature

~·~·~·~·~·~·

*Edited by*
Donald E. Ṣtanford

*Louisiana State University Press*

BATON ROUGE
MCMLXV

Copyright 1965 by Louisiana State University Press
Library of Congress Catalog Card Number: 65–12840
Printed in the United States of America. Price $3.00.

Second Printing, 1966

# PREFACE

THIS COLLECTION OF nine essays—seven by members of the Department of English and two by members of the Department of Foreign Languages of Louisiana State University—is indicative of the cosmopolitan nature of twentieth-century literature. Of the eleven writers here examined, five are American, two are English, one is Irish, one Spanish, one French, and one Greek. And in most instances, the authors of these essays have found it appropriate to examine their writers in relation to European antecedents or to Western civilization as a whole. *Finnegans Wake* by the Irish writer James Joyce is shown to have affinities with a number of epics: *Paradise Lost*, the *Divina Commedia*, the *Aeneid*, the *Chanson de Roland*, and *Beowulf*. The Greek poet Constantine Cavafy is examined with reference to his Alexandrian-Hellenistic background and with reference to his influence on the British novelist Lawrence Durrell. The work of the American John Dos Passos was deeply affected by the Spanish novelist Pío Baroja and the problems of the Spanish masses in the modern industrialized and mechanized age. Although William Faulkner's most notable fiction usually deals with a restricted area of the American South, an analysis of his two important character creations, Isaac McCaslin and Temple Drake, demonstrates his concern with the spiritual crisis of the entire Western world. The American Lawrence Ferlinghetti's nonconceptual, visually conceived poetry is in the tradition of the French symbolists Rimbaud and Mallarmé, of the American expatriate Ezra Pound, and of the Spanish poet García Lorca. Techniques developed by

v

the French novelist Alain Robbe-Grillet have had far-reaching influence in Europe and America. Some of the techniques he employed in his novel *Jealousy* are here examined. The work of the British novelist Muriel Spark is shown to have as its frame of reference the Catholic moral universe. Her novels are discussed with wide-ranging allusions to English and European literature. The poetry of the American Southerner Allen Tate, as the essay devoted to him demonstrates, cannot be adequately discussed without frequent recourse to ancient, medieval, and modern European philosophies and literatures. And although the essay on the American critic Yvor Winters is chiefly concerned with critical theory, these theories were formulated by Winters after a thorough immersion in English and European literatures, particularly the French.

The essays of this volume are representative of the intellectual and aesthetic interests in the field of modern literature of the faculty and graduate school of Louisiana State University. It is hoped they will advance in some measure our understanding of one of the most difficult and complex periods in the history of world literature—our own twentieth century.

DONALD E. STANFORD
Louisiana State University

# CONTENTS

*Nine Essays in Modern Literature*

*BERNARD BENSTOCK*

# HERE COMES EVERYBODY
## *Finnegans Wake* as Epic

As a "NOVEL" dealing with a vast cross-section of the contemporary world, *Finnegans Wake* corresponds in various particulars with the many epics of other cultures and eras, and there are suggestions in the *Wake* that Joyce meant for a definite affinity between his work and the classical epics to be noted—with *Paradise Lost* primarily, and to a lesser extent with the *Divina Commedia,* the two Homeric works, the *Aeneid,* the *Chanson de Roland,* and *Beowulf.* Employing the familiar conventions prevalent in most instances in these epics, he often found that they naturally fit with convenience into the framework of his *Wake,* and as often that they could be used in mock form to differentiate between the heroic material of classical epics and the nonheroic aspects of contemporary society. The familiar method of alternating and combining parallels and parodies, which had already reached a dazzling peak in *Ulysses,* is further exploited here, and a glance at the outline for a prose comic epic envisioned by Henry Fielding in his *Joseph Andrews* preface over two hundred years ago—almost at the genesis of the English novel—indicates that such an ideal was probably close to Joyce's interests during the construction of *Finnegans Wake.* The vast comic elements and the poetic prose language (both expanded and augmented since *Ulysses*) suggest the plausibility of an investigation of the use of epic conventions, of Joyce's acknowledgments to other epics and their creators, and of his attempts to telescope the history of mankind into a single multifaceted project through a contemporary perspective. Even if Joyce had not consciously sought to create

3

a work which would generally be termed an epic, he must have been aware that the history of the form has witnessed the creation of both "authentic" (unconscious) and "literary" (conscious) efforts—the *Iliad, Odyssey,* and anonymous *Beowulf* and *Chanson de Roland* classified in the former group; Virgil's, Dante's, and Milton's works in the latter. As such, the *Wake* is a literary epic, although there are significant implications in the text to indicate that Joyce's awareness of Jung's concept of the collective unconscious allowed him to anticipate the mysterious appearance in his masterpiece of elements of the natural epic.

A basic list of various traits commonly associated with the epic is easily agreed upon: mythical, legendary, and historical material usually underlie whatever plot exists; a tradition of oral recitation often pervades the work; and an element of monumental conflict— among the gods, between men and gods, among heroic mortals— seems vital to the epic scheme. A secondary consideration may well involve *types* of epics: the odyssey of search or discovery, the genesis of a new world, or heroic warfare. Joyce, an avid reader of the established primitive and literary epics of Western civilization, must have been influenced by these characteristics, for he blends that which is history, that which is myth, and that which must be termed legend, in order to construct a timeless cosmos in which Finn MacCool, Eamon de Valera, and Kathleen ni Houlihan are contemporaries. Napoleon and Wellington are no more real in the *Wake* than Castor and Pollux, nor more historically accurate than Gog and Magog. The common denominator of prototype levels the legendary Cadmus, the mythical Bladud, and the literary Master Solness, all builders of cities. Joyce is aware that no clear-cut distinction between history and legend can always be achieved: a literal acceptance of biblical material makes it history, while the skeptic views it as legend. Joyce accepts Cain as the first builder of the City of Man—"And that was how framm Sin fromm Son, acity arose" (94) [1]—but he is equally aware that within his own lifetime Baron G. E. Haussmann was at work rebuilding parts of Paris: "This is the Hausman all paven and stoned, that cribbed the Cabin that never was owned" (205). This fragment repeats the theme of city-building in terms of the oft-repeated rhyme of "The House That Jack Built," while Shem is Joyce's re-creation of Cain as the city-builder: "He fould the fourd; they found the hurtled stones; they fell ill with the gravy duck: and he sod town with the roust of the meast" (224).

The town that is being founded here is Dublin of course (Bailé átha Cliath, the Irish name for the city, means "Town of the Hurdle Ford"), and all references to the founding of cities and the building of towers and walls return us to this universal city in *Finnegans Wake.*

Joyce, then, is attempting to encompass a vast amount of historical and legendary material and fuse it through a timeless concept with the basic mythical patterns in order to create a work which deals essentially with that which is universal. His own narrative structure, on its most obvious literal level, concerns the story of his Chapelizod publican and family; this narrative forms the fictional details the author supplies. But the huge mass of amorphous material which underlies this iceberg cap of fiction is the accumulation of the many cultural levels of experience which give dimension in time and space to his localized series of events and personages.

Conscious of the "authentic" epic, the ancient work of folk origin, often of collated myths (although *Finnegans Wake* is the conscious product of a sophisticated mind, a calculated literary effort), Joyce is nonetheless striving to achieve a work that absorbs in its universality those aspects of the collective unconscious which have a primitive basis for existence in our culture. The *Wake* is after all, as critics have frequently asserted, an aural book, and re-echoes often the facets of an oral recitation: it is the oration of an impersonal bard who sometimes surrenders his function to other commentators, like the pedantic Professor Jones, the narrator of the Mookse and Gripes fable and the Burrus-Caseous episode (149–168). The rhetorical devices of character speeches also add to the "aural" aspect of *Finnegans Wake,* and Joyce seems to envy the fresh naïveté with which the ancients could naturally approach the creation of an epic—the Icelandic *Eddas,* the Anglo-Saxon *Beowulf* and French *Roland,* the *Kalevala* of the Finns, and the *Iliad* and *Odyssey* of "our homerole poet" (445)—and he apparently seeks to reproduce the unconscious elements of pre-sophisticated man in the *Wake.* Much of the first chapter of the *Wake,* therefore, is reproduction of primitive sounds and qualities of early epical poems: "So, how idlers' wind turning pages on pages, as innocens with anaclete play popeye antipop, the leaves of the living in the boke of the deeds, annals of themselves timing the cycles of events grand and national, bring fassilwise to pass how" (13).

Nor are the elements of epic conflict missing from *Finnegans*

*Wake.* "What clashes here of wills gen wonts, ostrygods gaggin fishygods!" (4), the epical introduction to the *Wake* announces. The haves against the have-nots comprise the economic struggle, the class war; one's *will* against one's *wants* form the inner struggle of the individual; pagan Goths will be warring against each other, while those who worship other gods combat the God of the Christian ("fishygods"). This struggle in *Finnegans Wake* is primarily the same as that which concerns Milton in *Paradise Lost;* the difference between the two works is that Joyce has tampered with the *dramatis personae* of the events to arrive at a new central figure, the Adam whose fall creates Man, *"Père Adam"* (124). Man, however, is the synthesis of this war in heaven, the synthesis of Shem and Shaun, who represent Lucifer and the Archangel Michael respectively— "mikealls or nicholists" (113) and "Mitchells *v.* Nicholls" (147). That union of the two sons happens both before and after the battle, of course: Earwicker is their father and combines the antithetical elements of both; the sons eventually are fused into the Earwicker figure, and that fusion may well suggest that the antithetical elements have finally been assimilated by the individual. The epic battle in heaven, however, concerns us throughout the work and is described in the introduction as:

Where the Baddelaries partisans are still out to mathmaster Malachus Micgranes and the Verdons catapelting the camibalistics out of the Whoyteboyce of Hoodie Head. Assiegates and boomeringstroms. Sod's brood, be me fear! Sanglorians, save! Arms apeal with larms, appalling. Killykillkilly: a toll, a toll. What chance cuddleys, what cashels aired and ventilated! What bidimetoloves sinduced by what tegotetabsolvers! What true feeling for their's hayair with what strawng voice of false jiccup! O here here how hoth sprowled met the duskt the father of fornicationists but, (O my shining stars and body!) how hath fanespanned most high heaven the skysign of soft advertisement! (4)

The war in heaven is simultaneously taking place on earth as well; the pattern has been divinely fixed and repeats itself throughout life—the wars of religious fanaticism are being constantly fought and are reflections of the epic struggle among the angels. Joyce again accepts the convention of interweaving gods and men, angels and men, in the epical tapestry, but does so to the extent of having them lose their divine identities with the mortals who personify their actions on earth. The hooded "White Boys" spread religious violence in Ireland as a microcosmic re-enactment of the macrocosmic struggle in heaven; it is immaterial to Joyce whether they are followers of

Michael or Old Nick—the sides have become confused with each other, and like the Kilkenny cats, they have nothing left to show for their struggle but their tails. The pattern becomes one of permanence and change; the regeneration that follows the wars is a sexual one rather than a religious resurrection: "The oaks of ald now they lie in peat yet elms leap where askes lay. Phall if you but will, rise you must: and none so soon either shall the pharce for the nunce come to a setdown secular phoenish" (4).

Although the *Wake* contains aspects of all three types of epic, it is essentially concerned with the creation myth. Joyce recognizes contemporary society as verging on chaos, a chaos from which, like Milton, he re-creates the world. After the statement of themes and "epical introduction" of the classic struggle, the "wake" motif is sounded: the battle in heaven is over, and the women wail for the dead, while the earth remains in chaos awaiting creation. But no sooner have the party of demons been "hurtleturtled out of heaven" (5) than the epic invocation is heard: "Stay us wherefore in our search for tighteousness, O Sustainer, what time we rise and when we take up to toothmick and before we lump down upown our leatherbed and in the night and at the fading of the stars!" (5). And suddenly we find ourselves in the midst of a bustling metropolis of our modern technological age; an epic listing of its characteristics is presented:

the wallhall's horrors of rollsrights, carhacks, stonengens, kisstvanes, tramtrees, fargobawlers, autokinotons, hippohobbilies, streetfleets, tournintaxes, megaphoggs, circuses and wardsmoats and basilikerks and aeropagods and the hoyse and the jollybrool and the peeler in the coat and the mecklenburk bitch bite at his ear and the merlinburrow burrocks and his fore old porecourts, the bore the more (5).

The city is the Dublin Joyce knew, but it is also the Pandemonium built by the outcast angels. The world suddenly emerges full-grown (the ancient cities are incorporated into the building of the modern: Stonehenge is combined with engine to form *stonengens*, but it will someday return to stone again). This is Joyce's superfetation theme of one world burrowing on another, of a new world growing out of the old. And the city is that which Cain built, for since the fall from heaven and Adam's fall from grace are happening simultaneously— "so sore did abe ite ivvy's holired abbles" (5)—Satan and Cain find themselves building the same city, but only to find it fully built before them.

Creation in the *Wake* is a multileveled affair; actually it is the world which is being born and finally heralded as created in the Recorso chapter: "The old breeding bradsted culminwillth of natures" (593). But the creation myth has its microcosmic proportions as well as its macrocosmic: the birth of the world—"A hand from the cloud emerges, holding a chart expanded" (593)—is parallel to the building of the city and the erection of a wall and a tower. It is from this edifice that Tim Finnegan (like Ibsen's Bygmester Solness before him) falls: "(There was a wall of course in erection) Dimb! He stottered from the latter. Damb! he was dud. Dumb! Mastabatoom, mastabadtom" (6). Meanwhile, wave after wave of invaders were discovering, conquering, colonizing new lands, lands which had their own inhabitants and cultures; each invasion of one civilization conquering another and merging its culture with the existing native culture re-echoes the superfetation theme. Sir Almeric Tristram arrives with Strongbow's forces in 1169 and settles in Dublin, founding Howth Castle: "Sir Tristram, violer d'amores, fr'over the short sea, had passencore rearrived from North Armorica on this side the scraggy isthmus of Europe Minor to wielderfight his penisolate war" (3); Jonathan Sawyer is simultaneously founding the city of Dublin in the state of Georgia (in Laurens County): "topsawyer's rocks by the stream Oconee exaggerated themselse to Laurens County's gorgios" (3); and St. Bridget is being created out of the goddess Brigit, while St. Patrick through baptism is creating Christians out of heathens: "avoice from afire bellowsed mishe mishe to tauftauf thuartpeatrick" (3), and Christ is creating the Church upon "the rock which is Peter." All creation is therefore happening at once: the stone is hurled into the lake, and the successive waves of ripples are each a manifestation of the other; the growth of the individual repeats the growth of the species; the most minute event of creation reflects the major aspect of world creation which has already occurred, and nonetheless begins to build up a series of events (a snowballing of creations, invasion, founding, building, integrating) which will finally result in the one vast world-creation which is yet to come. The creation myth in the *Wake* is its major epical aspect in terms of scope and significance.

But although primarily an epic of the establishment of world order, *Finnegans Wake* may just as easily be interpreted in terms of its heroic warfare; the opening battle is just a foreshadowing of the heroic struggles which take place throughout the *Wake*. Joyce is dealing with man's wars of expansion and colonization, and utilizes the Crimean War of the mid-nineteenth century as the prototype of such conflicts. He seems to select this particular war for several interesting reasons: because it was typical of imperialistic England's "necessary" conflagrations, because it was fought on the flimsiest of pretexts (England's concern for Turkey's rights violated by Russia's "aiding" Christians persecuted in that country), because so many Irishmen were conscripted to fight for England, and because the word "crime" is coincidently incorporated into the name of the war. Also, the Crimean War produced a genuine heroine, Florence Nightingale, the nurse who became more famous than any of the opposing generals, because she wrought apparent miracles saving lives. After the battle is over, the radio in Earwicker's pub broadcasts an on-the-spot transcription of a nightingale's song (such broadcasts were apparently quite common in London during the thirties), but the bird's song is recognized by the customers to be Earwicker's guilty stammer: "(floflo floreflorence), sweetishsad lightandgayle, twittwin twosingwoolow" (360). Nurse Nightingale is instrumental in recording H.C.E.'s guilt because, as the single woman against the backdrop of men at war, she symbolized for Joyce the cause of the war—woman tempting man to strive for her protection and comfort. She subdivides here into the two temptresses, being both Florence Nightingale, and her equally famous contemporary Jenny Lind, the "Swedish nightingale." These two sing their *twosingwoolow,* a "wooing" song of "woe" to bring men "low." But they also return to heal the wounded, to mourn for their lovers, to piece together the body of Osiris, to bequeath to their children the attributes of the father. Miss Nightingale, wandering across the battlefield to tend to the wounded, echoes the role of the banshees in Celtic mythology—like the washerwomen of the final chapter of Book One of the *Wake,* they wash the blood from the raiment of the heroes *before* the battle (another aspect of the cyclical pattern). Florence Nightingale reappears in *Finnegans Wake* during a flood scene, and again she symbolizes the banshees at the river: "Flood's. The pinkman, the squeeze, the pint with the kick. Gaa. And then the punch to Gaelicise it. Fox. The lady with the lamp" (514). Here she is again the temptress who ruined the great man; she is Kitty O'Shea, Parnell's mistress, as the reference to "Fox," one of Parnell's aliases in the affair, indicates.

The events of this "heroic warfare" in the *Wake* are hardly epical;

Joyce has managed to reduce the Crimean War to the lowest level of absurdity: it is being broadcast by a pair of radio comedians named Butt and Taff (again, Shaun and Shem), who eventually unite to become someone named Buckley. It is Buckley who has the distinction of shooting the Russian general, and the episode depicts "How Burghley shuck the rackushant Germanon" (338). Actually, this fictitious bit of nonsense is an Irish pub tale concerning the mythical Buckley spotting a Russian general in the process of defecating during a lull on the front lines. Although strongly tempted to shoot him, Buckley finds himself united by a common human bond with the general, and desists until the general uses turf for toilet paper; it is then that the irate "budly shoots thon rising germinal" (354). This event becomes the deciding incident in Joyce's treatment of his "epic" battle, since the Russian general once again is the stuttering Earwicker, and he is once again beset by the soldiers and deposed by his sons. There is little doubt that Joyce here is commenting upon the stupidity of war, upon the common heritage which would ordinarily unify all mankind regardless of country, until the patriotic symbol is raised, and the Irishman is once again goaded into serving his oppressors and shooting his fellow man. Also, the events of the shooting of the general are again an aspect of the Crucifixion: the Russian general is being sacrificed in order to unite the antithetical elements of mankind, the Butt and the Taff aspects of himself. But this Christ figure is far from a sinless man; he is the Earwicker who carries the entire burden of man's guilt upon his back because he has *committed all sins.* Joyce's implication here is that it is useless for a sinless man to assume mankind's guilt and die for those sins; the task requires the composite sinner, and one by one Earwicker, Shem, and Shaun re-enact the Crucifixion—Earwicker in the person of the Russian general, Shaun as Haun being interred (473), Shem as Glugg being beaten by his brother at the end of the Mime when the dirge is heard:

Home all go. Halome. Blare no more ramsblares, oddmund barkes! And cease your fumings, kindalled bushies! And sherrigoldies yeassymgnays; your wildeshaweshowe moves swiftly sterneward! For here the holy language. Soons to come. To pausse (256).

In echoes of *Cymbeline* and *The Tempest* (twilight is twilight, whether Shakespearean or Celtic) the descendant of the great Irish writers is laid to rest; the Hebrew word for peace (*shalom*) antici-

pates the Hebrew prayer for the dead, *kaddish*—"Kidoosh!"
(258)—and Shem's final "gttrdmmrng" (258).

Like all heroic warfare in *Finnegans Wake,* the Butt-Taff version
of the Crimean War is merely another tavern brawl in Earwicker's
Bristol Bar—so named because it was to the city of Bristol that
Henry II gave the charter for Dublin, causing all subsequent Irish
wars for independence—and Earwicker as the general is once again
"crowned" with a "buttle" at the "Inns of Dungtarf where Used awe
to be he" (16). The radio war is being broadcast in the "Tavern"
chapter (Book II, Chapter III), and it is when Earwicker rises to
defend the fallen general that the real brawl takes place. The
Crimean War then is merely a prelude to the real "heroic warfare"—a tavern brawl!—as it was merely a "reflection" of the epic
struggle in heaven. No one affair of combat is any more important
than another in the *Wake,* since they are essentially all the same
war; no historical event is any more real than the fictional counterpart invented by Joyce or the legendary warfare recorded by bibles.

As an epic of a search or voyage of discovery *Finnegans Wake*
contains its parallel with the *Odyssey* and *Divina Commedia:* in its
broadest pattern the *Wake* is a long night's groping for light and
form; the Recorso episode brings the voyage of discovery to an end
as dawn illumines the chaos, brings the world out of the void, and
synthesizes the opposites into a coherent but still contradictory
whole. The Odysseyan Everyman, who had by day wandered
through the streets of Dublin in *Ulysses* in search of a son, a family,
a home, repeats his odyssey in his nightmare; the search for himself
becomes a quest for the assimilation of the antithetical elements of
himself, a synthesis of sons Shem and Shaun. As Dante, Joyce
wanders through the human purgatory he discovers on earth and
comes to the realization that this earthly *purgatorio* is a composite of
all aspects of heaven and hell; the historical, legendary, and mythical dead are present before him as they were for Dante in his
wanderings through the strata of the three worlds. Joyce has destroyed that iron-bound stratification in the *Wake,* and seeks to
combine all his personages into one universal man who can be
neither damned nor blessed, since he is everyman.

But, on the specific level, Joyce has created an odyssey story
within the framework of the *Wake*: the fourth chapter of Book II
records the voyage of Tristram's ship bringing Iseult from Ireland.
As such, the voyage is sexual, as is Leopold Bloom's search for a

family of his own in *Ulysses;* and like Bloom, Earwicker is the universal aspect of his wife's lover. The voyage is Gulliver's to the land of the Houyhnhnms—"the whole yaghoodurt sweepstakings and all the horsepowers" (387). It is also Moses' Red Sea crossing— "and then there was the drowning of Pharaoh and all his pedestrians and they were all completely drowned into the sea, the red sea" (387). The drowned man in the myth is Mark of Cornwall, destroyed by his nephew Tristram and his bride Iseult; as such, he is also the Martin Cunningham of "Grace" and *Ulysses* whose real-life model was drowned off Kingstown: "and then poor Merkin Cornyngwham, the official out of the castle on pension, when he was completely drowned off Erin Isles, at that time, suir knows, in the red sea and a lovely mourning paper and thank God, as Saman said, there were no more of him" (387). Other sea voyages are re-enacted by the Joycean bride-ship: Sir Roger Casement's landing by submarine near Dublin in 1916—"then there was the official landing of Lady Jales Casemate, in the year of the flood 1132 S.O.S." (387)— the landing of the "Plymouth brethren" (389), the sailing of Noah's ark—"The Frankish floot of Noahsdobahs" (388)—and the Spanish Armada—"the Flemish armada, all scattered, and all officially drowned, there and then, on a lovely morning, after the universal flood, at about aleven thirtytwo was it?" (388). This Tristram-voyage of discovery results in the sexual union of Tristram and Iseult: "whoever the gulpable, and whatever the pulpous was, the twooned togethered" (396).

As an epic, however, *Finnegans Wake* lacks two important classical elements: as poetic as Joyce's language is, its form is nonetheless that of prose; and as serious as Joyce's purpose is in the *Wake,* his subject matter is decidedly comic. This returns us to the specifications for a comic epic in prose set down by Henry Fielding in his preface to *Joseph Andrews:*

The EPIC, as well as the DRAMA, is divided into tragedy and comedy. HOMER, who was the father of this species of poetry, gave us a pattern of both these, though that of the latter kind is entirely lost; which Aristotle tells us, bore the same relation to comedy which his Iliad bears to tragedy. . . .
And farther, as this poetry may be tragic or comic, I will not scruple to say it may be likewise either in verse or prose: for though it wants one particular, which the critic enumerates in the constituent parts of an epic poem, namely metre; yet, when any kind of writing contains all its other parts, such as fable, action, characters, sentiments, and diction, and is

deficient in metre only, it seems, I think, reasonable to refer it to the epic. . . .[2]

Fielding, looking ahead, described the qualities of the new art form as it was developing under his pen, and as he expected it to develop thereafter. The history of the English novel, however, despite its varied characteristics and its attainment of a high level of sophistication, has rarely engendered the prose comic epic that Fielding predicted; as an art form the novel has developed away from the broad novels of epical significance, which the eighteenth century sought to produce, to highly specialized developments of a handful of characters and a small series of carefully analyzed events. With *Finnegans Wake,* as perhaps with his earlier *Ulysses,* Joyce seems to have attempted to write the culminating work embodying the varied aspects of the contemporary novel: symbolism and naturalism, the psychological as well as the sociological approach, the novel of character and the novel of prototypes.

That Joyce was an admirer of Fielding is apparent from the parallels drawn from *Joseph Andrews* and *Finnegans Wake:* Joseph's parents, Gaffer and Gammer Andrews, become the epical parents of all of us in the *Wake*—"Gammer and gaffer we're all their gangsters" (215)—and Earwicker as the pub-keeper is given the generic name of innkeepers (his guilt and shame punned into it), "Burniface" (315), echoing the call for refreshments from the innkeeper in *Joseph Andrews: "Je voi* very well, *que tuta e pace,* / So send up dinner, good Boniface." [3] That Joyce was conscious of the epic as a form throughout the composition of *Finnegans Wake* is equally apparent from the vast list of classical epics sprinkled throughout the work. As he so often does, Joyce might well be hiding the hint that *Finnegans Wake* is to be viewed in terms of Fielding's definition in his references both to *Joseph Andrews* (in what other English novels is an inn so much the scene of action as in these two?) and to the history of the world epic.[4]

The epic most significant in the *Wake* is *Paradise Lost* by "Milltown" (71), since the events of Earwicker's fall parallel those of Adam in "Milton's Park" (96), and the cast of Joyce's epic fits Milton's *dramatis personae.* But the fall of Dublin also parallels the fall of Troy in the epics of "homeur" (34), and Joyce compares the battle for Troy and the funeral games following the death of Achilles with the Easter Rising in Dublin: "I want you, witness of this epic struggle, as yours so mine, to reconstruct for us, as briefly as you can, inexactly the same as a mind's eye view, how these funeral games, which have been poring over us through homer's kerryer pidgeons, massacreedoed as the holiname rally round took place" (515). This re-enactment of the *Iliad* follows upon Joyce's version of Homer's other epic, and echoes of the *Odyssey* are heard in the *Wake* as well: "nobodyatall with Wholyphamous" (73); Odysseus represents Everyman again for Joyce, especially since he embodies the ultimate negative side of Everyman when he declares himself to be Noman: "Noeman's Woe, Hircups Emptybolly!" (321). The H.C.E. of Here Comes Everybody is here depicted in its converse as the Odysseyan Noman, the two sides of Earwicker's universal personality. Some critical comparison has been made between the two "blind poets" in reference to Joyce's *Ulysses*, but what Joyce learned from the Greek epic poet in writing *Ulysses* is not discarded in the composition of *Finnegans Wake*. In the earlier novel Joyce utilized Homeric parallels throughout, as Stuart Gilbert's study has proved, emphasized, and belabored, in instances where contemporary parallels were logical with the ancient, or where—as in the case of his perfidious "Penelope"—the parallels were ironic. The same technique can be found in the *Wake*: Earwicker is no more a heroic Ulysses than was Leopold Bloom, yet the struggles throughout remain as epic in proportion as those in Homer.

Other epics and epic writers are mentioned in the *Wake*; for example: "pious Eneas" (185), and a reference to the first line of the *Aeneid*, "If all the MacCrawls would only handle virgils like Armsworks, Limited!" (618), the implication being that Roman Catholics have been unable to write as great an epic about their basic myth— the Virgin—as had pagan Virgil; *MacCrawl* puns Finn MacCool and mackerel—the symbol of the fish of early Christianity. Dante figures throughout the *Wake* in various aspects: he has written the Catholic epic, *"Through Hell with the Papes* (mostly boys) by the divine comic Denti Alligator" (440), and was one of Joyce's favorite authors. Throughout the *Wake* Joyce calls upon the greatest of ancient poets to witness his epic: "Daunty, Gouty and Shopkeeper" (539) and "Suffoclose! Shikespower! Seudodanto! Anonymoses!" (47). But Dante, like the males in *Finnegans Wake*, is also the victim of a young girl's unwitting temptation; he had been tempted into the creation of an epic: "Still he'd be good tutor two in his big armschair lerningstoel and she be waxen in his hands. Turning up and fingering over the most dantellising peaches in the lingerous longerous book of the dark" (251). The hero Roland is celebrated often in the *Wake,* since he is the prototype of the fallen hero, a man of epic stature, and since his friendship with Oliver becomes another parallel of the friendship motif which assimilates the antagonistic brothers: "while olover his exculpatory features, as Roland rung, a wee dropeen of grief about to sillonise his jouejous, the ghost of resignation diffused a spectral appealingness, as a young man's drown o'er the fate of his waters may gloat, similar in origin and akkurat in effective to a beam of sunshine upon a coffin plate" (56). Echoing Byron, Joyce interweaves Roland with another epic figure, Finn's son, Ossian—"Rolando's deepen darblun Ossian roll" (385) —into a pattern of epic figures which gives *Finnegans Wake* the appearance of a summation of epic literature. Joyce's use of myth allows him constantly to weld hero after hero into a single epical mold, and he draws from the literatures of many civilizations available to him.

It might be well to suggest in this connection that Joyce consciously attempted to create a "bible" of sorts from his contemporary summation of world myth, since the various bibles are in themselves epic summations of their cultures. This seems hardly unlikely when one realizes that the proof Mohammed offered to justify his contention that his *Koran* was divinely conceived was that no mortal man could have written such a work; he challenged any other mortal to duplicate the effort—and Joyce accepted the challenge. And as Mohammed claimed that the *Koran* superseded the Old and New Testaments because he absorbed the older bibles and surpassed them, so might Joyce claim the same for the *Wake.* Joyce's work obviously is based upon both Old and New Testament material as well as the *Koran*—the "alcohoran" (20)—and the Egyptian *Book of Amenti*—"the house of Amanti" (237), "our Amenti in the sixth sealed chapter of the going forth by black" (62). Also present in the *Wake* can be found an acknowledgment of debt to Hindu religious material—"Bhagafat gaiters" (35)—and Confucian doctrine— "master Kung's doctrine of the meang" (108). Joyce's approach, as such, is intrinsically an aspect of the twentieth century: only through a realization of contemporary anthropological investigation could a concept of the basic myth underlying these various religious texts be postulated. Joyce fuses the material of these texts, arrives at his own version of a common denominator of mythical prototypes, and creates his synthetic "bible" of twentieth-century civilization.

Joyce provides his own indications that the *Wake* is being constructed to rival the bibles of the world: Shem is creating "his farced epistol to the hibruws" (228), "a most moraculous jeeremyhead sindbook for all the peoples" (229). *Farced* and *jeer* indicate the comic tone of the book, while *moraculous* contains the Gaelic word for ancient (*mor*)—*culo* is gratuitous—*hibruws* refers not only to the Old Testament, but also to Joyce's select audience of highbrows.

It is in the conscious use of epic conventions, however, that Joyce indicates that his *Wake* is to be interpreted in the light of an all-inclusive view of contemporary times as seen through the perspective of the ancient epics of other civilizations. The epic imitations of the first chapter have already been discussed, but they are only an opening clue to the epic conventions employed throughout the work; in many instances Joyce will duplicate certain touches of style or technique to enforce their significance upon the reader's mind. The opening sentence of the *Wake* indicates that we are beginning the cycle of life in the middle; the last sentence of the book ends without a final mark of punctuation and is meant to be read directly into the first; and Joyce offers *"The Suspended Sentence"* (106) as a suggested title for Anna Livia's "mamafesta." The macrocosmic study of the establishment of world-order is being told from the middle, but at every instance within that macrocosm the various component elements (like the microcosmic incident of the life of one pub-keeper Earwicker) follow the pattern as well. This technique of duplicating in the miniature what he is attempting in the entire structure carries over to Joyce's handling of the epic as a poetic convention in *Finnegans Wake*: not only is the *Wake* itself to be viewed as a composite epic, but individual parts are minor epics of sorts within the larger framework. Since several heroes occupy the same domain in the work, Joyce indicates that each is deserving of an epic for himself. The actual epic hero is Finn MacCool, and therefore it is the first chapter, dealing with the legendary giant, that is primarily written in epic language; Earwicker as Finn's replacement is already a middle-class sham-hero, as is the Shaun-demagogue who deposes him. Earwicker is introduced in apologetically epic language; unlike Finn, ("Of the first was he to bare arms and a name: Wassaily Booslaeugh of Riesengeborg. His crest of huroldry, in vert with ancillars, troublant, argent, a hegoak, poursuivant, horrid, horned"—5), Earwicker is heralded forth at the opening of Chapter II with:

Now . . . concerning the genesis of Harold or Humphrey Chimpden's occupational agnomen (we are back in the presurnames prodromarith period, of course just when enos chalked halltraps) and discarding once for all those theories from older sources which would link him back with such pivotal ancestors as the Glues, the Gravys, the Northeasts, the Ankers and the Earwickers of Sidlesham in the Hundred of Manhood or proclaim him offsprout of vikings who had founded wapentake and seddled hem in Herrick or Eric, the best authenticated version, the Dumlat, read the Reading of Hofed-ben-Edar, has it that it was this way. We are told how in the beginning it came to pass that like cabbaging Cincinnatus the grand old gardener was saving daylight under his redwoodtree one sultry sabbath afternoon (30).

Although hardly ignominious, the presentation of Earwicker is not the heroic trumpeting which sounded for the pagan hero Finn; this introduction is humble and biblical: it presents Adam in the garden (the Hill of Howth—*Ben Adair* in Celtic—is combined with Eden) and the source is the *Talmud* (*Dumlat* read backwards). He is compared with Cincinnatus, the Roman who twice left his plow to fight for his country and twice returned to it; but behind this humble figure stand the lusty Vikings who comprise Earwicker's heritage ("discarded" heritages are not to be dismissed in the *Wake*). The change from the first to the second signifies the change from the divine age to the heroic age in Vico's cyclical pattern: the settling down of the giants to the agricultural life after the voice of God in the thunderclap had driven them into the caves, and their ungoverned sex under the skies is converted into marriage and family.

The next stage is even less heroic, as the oligarch Earwicker is upended by his son, the spokesman of the "people." Actually, this is Shaun, the demagogue, but the Viconian situation is complicated by Joyce's use of Bruno's concepts of antagonistic opposites: Earwicker has two sons, Shem and Shaun. It is Shem who destroys the old ruler: he embodies the three soldiers who have observed Earwicker's indiscretion in Phoenix Park ("some woodwards or regarders, who did not dare deny, the shomers, that they had, chin Ted, chin Tam, chinchin Taffyd, that day consumed their soul of the corn"—34); he is killer Cain as well as the Ham who observed his drunken father, Noah; that the soldiers were drunk identifies them again with Shem, whose drinking habits are legion: "he had

gulfed down mmmmuch too mmmmany gourds of it retching off to
almost as low withswillers" (171). The son destroys the father when
he has become aware of the Garden of Eden incident; he becomes
his father's heir when he has become aware of sex—when he reaches
puberty. This is Ham's sin, and in the *Wake* it becomes apparent at
the dawn scene in which the parents have awakened to comfort little
Jerry (Shem), who cries in the night when he wets his bed; Anna
Livia comforts him, and Jerry, looking past her, sees his father
standing naked in the doorway: "Gauze off heaven! Vision. Then. O,
pluxty suddly, the sight entrancing!" (566). It is this sight which
leads into the lewd criminal court scene (572–574), and it is Shem's
traumatic experience. As Glugg (the "Nick" of the Mime) he is
beaten by his brother Chuff when, during the games, he has proven
incapable of guessing the girls' riddles and lost their favor to Chuff
(an odd instance of the victor adding injury to the vanquished's
insult). The significance of this late beating becomes apparent from
Glugg's baby-talk petulance when the girls scoff at his wounds:
"Split the hvide and aye seize heaven! He knows for he's seen it in
black and white through his eyetrompit trained upon jenny's and all
that sort of thing which is dandymount to a clearobscure" (247).
Shem knows the sexual secret because he has the intelligence to
correlate his remembrance of his parents in their bedroom with what
he has read in black and white, and may well have reached puberty
also; Shaun lacks the knowledge and the ability, and already re-
sents what he doesn't understand and can't accomplish.

In the situation in the *Wake*, the younger son displaces the older:
Shaun has found the letter dug up by Biddy the hen; the letter was
dictated to Shem by Anna Livia, and contains of course the sexual
secret of life. With the letter Shem can replace his father, but Shaun
steals the letter, claims it as his own; he is Shaun the Post delivering
the letter to the people; thus he is Richard Piggott (at this instant at
least), forging the letter to destroy the true leader, Charles Parnell.
Shaun succeeds, and is heralded before the people in the opening
chapter of "his" Book (III); he is Earwicker's chosen successor,
however, although Anna Livia favored Shem. Here Joyce is utilizing
the Jacob-Esau biblical story for his own purposes in the *Wake*; he is
toying with biblical legend to suit his immediate purposes at any
given point: Shem is Esau, "this Esuan Menschavik and the first till
last alshemist" (185), when he is the older son deprived by the
enterprising younger, and now an outcast; he is Jacob when he

represents the deposer of the father, the cunning son, the mother's favorite, the villain who is Cain, Lucifer, Loki, even the Prometheus who rebelled against the gods:

Shem is as short for Shemus as Jem is joky for Jacob. A few toughnecks are still getatable who pretend that aboriginally he was of respectable stemming (he was an outlex between the lines of Ragonar Blaubarb and Horrild Hairwire and an inlaw to Capt. the Hon. and Rev. Mr Bbyrd-wood de Trop Blogg was among his most distant connections) but every honest to goodness man in the land of the space of today knows that his back life will not stand being written about in black and white (169).

The description of Shem which follows is hardly in keeping with the physical traits of an epic hero; twice removed from the heroic lineage of the great Finn, Shem is a freak. The "epic catalogue" of his

bodily getup, it seems, included an adze of a skull, an eight of a larkseye, the whoel of a nose, one numb arm up a sleeve, fortytwo hairs off his uncrown, eighteen to his mock lip, a trio of barbels from his megageg chin (sowman's son), the wrong shoulder higher than the right, all ears, an artificial tongue with a natural curl, not a foot to stand on, a handful of thumbs, a blind stomach, a deaf heart, a loose liver [etc.] (169).

This freakish Shem is a far cry from his popular brother, the contemporary epic hero. Proclaimed by the populace as the savior, Shaun is the embodiment of Earwicker's dream; if the father had somewhat fallen short of the epic hero, his dream representation of himself as his favorite son lacks nothing. In fact, the opening of Shaun's chapter (Book III, Chapter I) is a minor epic in itself; Earwicker is finally in bed after the tavern brawl and his dream is nothing less than Dante's *Divina Commedia:*

And as I was jogging along in a dream as dozing I was dawdling, arrah, methought broadtone was heard and the creepers and the gliders and flivvers of the earth breath and the dancetongues of the woodfires and the hummers in their ground all vociferated echoating: Shaun! Shaun! Post the post! with a high voice and O, the higher on high the deeper and low, I heard him so! And lo, mescemed somewhat came of the noise and somewho might amove allmurk (404).

The epic hero is then introduced; items of his sartorial attire are enumerated in such a fashion as to indicate the convention of the putting on of armor in the Homeric and Virgilian epics:

dressed like an earl in just the correct wear, in a classy mac Frieze o'coat of far suparior ruggedness, indigo braw, tracked and tramped, and an

Irish ferrier collar, freeswinging with mereswin lacers from his shoulthern and thick welted brogues on him hammered to suit the scotsmost public and climate, iron heels and sparable soles, and his jacket of providence wellprovided woolies with a softrolling lisp of a lapel to it and great sealing-wax buttons, a good helping bigger than the slots for them, of twentytwo carrot krasnapoppsky red and his invulnerable burlap whisk-coat and his popular choker, Tamagnum sette-and-forte and his loud boheem toy and the damasker's overshirt he sported inside, a star-spangled zephyr with a decidedly surpliced crinklydoodle front (404).

As elegant as this apparel seems to be to the proud father, it is actually strictly a comic theatre costume; Shaun is dressed like Sean the Post in Dion Boucicault's *Arrah-na-Pogue*. Here he represents the international politician: he has donned the political armor for every country and political occasion; he is able to vary his dialect to suit constituents everywhere, and his attire is composed of articles from every corner of the Empire. As such, Shaun is not only the British demagogue attempting to appeal to the Welsh, Scots, and Irish (the Irish collar, the Welsh brogues—shoes and accent—the Scottish suit), but an American politico (*a starspangled zephyr*), a Russian (*krasnapoppsky red*), and an ecclesiast (*surpliced crinkly-doddle front*).

The epic describing of a hero's armor is a common device in *Finnegans Wake*; in the epic Crimean War scene, Earwicker as the Russian general is properly attired in "his raglanrock and his mala-koiffed bulbsbyg and his varnashed roscians and his cardigans blousejagged and his scarlett manchokuffs and his treecoloured camiflag and his perikopendolous gaelstorms" (339). Joyce here has managed to pun into these articles of "armor" the names of three British commanders in the Crimean War, a Russian leader, and a fortification: Lord Raglan, the Earl of Cardigan, Sir James Yorke Scarlett, Prince Menchikov, and the Malakoff fort. (It is concomitant with Joyce's "cult of coincidences" that Raglan and Cardigan have given their names to such sartorial innovations as the raglan sleeve and the cardigan jacket and sweater.) The constant repetitions of articles of clothing through the *Wake* are aspects of Joyce's use of Carlyle's *Sartor Resartus* (of clothes as the surface coverings hiding the basic truth of the body), of Swift's *Tale of a Tub* (the coat which is willed by the father to his three theologically squabbling sons), and of a reference to the biblical Joseph, who owned a coat of many colors and was proficient in interpreting dreams. This theme of clothing becomes prominent in the tavern yarn of the Norwegian

Captain and Kersse the Tailor (311–332) and the Prankquean-van Hoother incident (21–23).

Following his putting on of armor, we finally meet the epic hero himself; in the eyes of his father he is every inch the hero, and in the brogue of his father we hear him described:

that young fellow looked the stuff, the Bel of Beaus' Walk, a prime card if ever was! Pep? Now without deceit it is hardly too much to say he was looking grand, so fired smart, in much more than his usual health. No mistaking that beamish brow! There was one for you that ne'er would nunch with good Duke Humphrey but would aight through the months without a sign of an err in hem and then, otherwise rounding, fourale to the lees of Traroe. Those jehovial oyeglances! The heart of the rool! And hit the hencoop. He was immense, topping swell for he was after having a great time of it (405).

This portrait of the hero is of course the jaundiced view of Earwicker identifying with his popular son, and should be viewed in direct contrast with the author's "objective" view of H.C.E. In the sixth chapter of Book I, Joyce presents twelve riddles through which he identifies his *dramatis personae;* the first is a lengthy description of the central hero of the novel, and despite the fact that the answer to the description is "Finn MacCool" (139), it becomes obvious that it is also Earwicker. Joyce has now compressed his epic hero with the bourgeois successor: as Everyman, Finn and H.C.E. have finally merged into a single individual, since enough time has now passed to allow us to render all the events of the first four chapters (dealing with Finnegan and Earwicker) into history and myth. What emerges is the single hero who retains some of the heroic aspects of the giant: "What secondtonone myther rector and maximost bridgesmaker was the first to rise taller through his beanstale than the bluegum buaboababbaun or the giganteous Wellingtonia Sequoia" (126), but it is also "Dook Hookbackcrook" (127), the humble Earwicker. Joyce's portrait of our contemporary epic hero harks back to the Leopold Bloom of *Ulysses,* and the nonhero is characterized in the *Wake* as the typical burgher: "business, reading newspaper, smoking cigar, arranging tumblers on table, eating meals, pleasure, etcetera, etcetera, pleasure, eating meals, arranging tumblers on table, smoking cigar, reading newspaper, business; minerals, wash and brush up, local views, juju toffee, comic and birthdays cards; those were the days and he was their hero" (127).

But in the minor epic of Shaun the "Savior," Earwicker presents the hero he might have been had he, like Finn, lived in an heroic age; he imagines for his favorite son all the splendor he would like to have had for himself, a typically bourgeois reaction. Shaun is therefore depicted as the perfect hero of the epics, but since he is Shaun, the glutton, the description of the epic hero is followed by an epic feast. An encyclopedic list of food follows, describing Shaun's daily meals: breakfast consists of "a bless us O blood and thirsthy orange, next, the half of a pint of becon with newled googs and a segment of riceplummy padding [etc.]" (405); then dinner: "half a pound of round steak, very rare, Blong's best from Portarlington's Butchery, with a side of riceypeasy and Corkshire alla mellonge and bacon with (a little mar pliche!) a pair of chops" (406), and so on through lunches and suppers and midnight snacks. And having finished "gormandising and gourmeteering" (407), Shaun is now ready to speak to the people; Earwicker launches into another epic introduction of his hero: "When lo (whish, O whish!) mesaw mestreamed, as the green to the gred was flew, was flown, through deafths of durkness greengrown deeper I heard a voice, the voce of Shaun, vote of the Irish, voise from afar" (407), and the epic boasting follows. Shaun apologizes with false humility that he is unworthy of the honor of being the Royal Mailman and discloses his envy of his brother, while patronizingly claiming that he feels sorry for the "game loser!" (408). His boasting is an unctuous collection of campaign promises; he advocates "no five hour factory life with insufficient emollient and industrial disabled for them that day o'gratises" (409), while he himself, the politician, is prevented from working by the fact that he is a cleric: "Forgive me, Shaun repeated from his liquid lipes, not what I wants to do a strike of work but it was condemned on me premitially by Hireark Books and Chiefoverseer Cooks in their Eusebian Concordant Homilies" (409). The Shauniad epic moves from his campaigning and apologetics to the tale of the Ondt and the Gracehoper, a further vilification of Shem, and the complete disintegration of the hero before he reappears in the next chapter as Jaunty Jaun.

The epic convention of cataloguing is a basic feature of *Finnegans Wake*; the list of hundreds of rivers in the Anna Livia Plurabelle section, the lists of items of clothing throughout—usually in groups of seven articles to comprise the Seven Mystic Sheaths—"pouch, gloves, flask, bricket, kerchief, ring and amberulla" (24), and "in his grey half a tall hat and his amber necklace and his crimson harness and his leathern jib and his cheapshein hairshirt and his scotobrit sash and his parapilagian gallowglasses" (387)—and the lists of titles for various occasions: names that the American hog-caller bellows at Earwicker through the prison-cell keyhole: *"Firstnighter, Informer, Old Fruit, Yellow Whigger, Wheatears, Goldy Geit, Bogside Beauty* [etc.]" (71); titles for Anna Livia's "mamafesta": *"The Augusta Angustissimost for Old Seabeastius' Salvation, Rockabill Booby in the Wave Trough, Here's to the Relicts of All Decencies, Anna Stessa's Rise to Notice* [etc.]" (104); lists of children's games: *"Thom Thom the Thonderman, Put the Wind up the Peeler, Hat in the Ring, Prisson your Pritchards and Play Withers Team, Mikel on the Luckypig, Nickel in the Slot, Sheila Harnett and her Cow* [etc.]" (176); and the list of essay titles used by Kev and Dolph during their lessons: "Duty, the daughter of discipline, the Great Fire at the South City Markets, Belief in Giants and the Banshee, A Place for Everything and Everything in its Place [etc.]" (306). These catalogues are an integral part of the *Wake*, and serve the dual purposes of repeating the basic themes in succinct form and of parodying contemporary song-titles, slogans, epithets, clichés, key words, which are bandied about every day until they lose their significance and become mere catch-phrases. Joyce is rebelling against attempts at classification and pigeon-holing; his characters remain elusive throughout; they exchange their masks with the utmost of abandon. They represent essentials not particulars, prototypes not stereotypes. Joyce's use of details, of minute characteristics, of clichés and song titles, suggests the timelessness of the essential qualities of human existence, as well as the immediacy of each age's "names" for those qualities.

The epic characteristics already enumerated are each repeated often in *Finnegans Wake*. The battles are numerous: the war in heaven, the tavern brawl, the Crimean War—each is fought over and over again, never the same twice. The initial struggle can be compared with a later version:

That it was wildfires night on all the bettygallaghers. Mickmichael's soords shrieking shrecks through the wilkinses and neckanicholas' toastingforks pricking prongs up the tunnybladders. Let there be fight? And there was. Foght. On the site of the Angel's you said? Guinney's Gap, he said, between what they said and the pussykitties. In the middle of the garth, then? That they mushn't toucht it (90).

The war in heaven again dissolves into the battles of temptation in the Garden of Eden, and yet a vast amount of time, the space between eons, has elapsed (*Guinney's Gap* re-echoes "ginnandgo gap" [14] of the *Eddas*). Time is fluid: all wars are being fought consecutively in time, as well as simultaneously, yet the gap persists between wars. Earwicker is both the victor and the victim: he has won the battle but is slain, he has been beaten but will be resurrected:

were he chief, count, general, fieldmarshal, prince, king or Myles the Slasher in his person, with a moliamordhar mansion in the Breffnian empire and a place of inauguration on the hill of Tullymongan, there had been real murder, of the rayheallach royghal raxacraxian variety, the MacMahon chaps, it was, that had done him in. On the fidd of Verdor the rampart combatants had left him lion with his dexter handcoup wresterected in a pureede paumee bloody proper (99).

Man's fate in *Finnegans Wake* is to outlive his heroism; killed in the prime of his heroic life the hero is resurrected to achieve old age and ignominy. They who had been Tristrams become King Marks; like Arthur cuckolded by Lancelot and Guinevere, and like Finn cuckolded by Diarmait and Grainne, Earwicker lives too long to remain a hero.

As in the *Iliad*, the death of the hero calls forth the funeral games in the *Wake:* Earwicker's demise in the tavern scene is, in fact, accomplished through a series of athletic contests. Having already taken place as soon as the battle has begun, it is recorded in tomorrow's morning papers—on the Sports page: "You'll read it tomorrow, marn, when the curds on the table. . . . Screamer caps and invented gommas, quoites puntlost, forced to farce! . . . One hyde, sack, hic! Two stick holst, Lucky! Finnish Make Goal!" (374). (The battle in heaven had already been described as a football match in Shem's chapter: "All Saints beat Belial! Mickil Goals to Nichil! Notpossible! Already?" [175], the last two words expressing the "reader's" dismay at the strange chronology of events.) As befits Joyce's time-compression, these funeral games are also the cause of the hero's funeral; he himself is killed in the contests which are fought because of his death, and in keeping with still another violation of chronological time, he is already reading about it in the Sports section. This compression of time is inherent in the portmanteau words which describe the events; the shooting of the Russian general is again taking place, in a rugby match in the morning papers: "Good for you, Richmond Rover! Scrum around, our side! Let him have another between the spindlers! A grand game! Dalymount's decisive. Don Gouverneur Buckley's in the Tara Tribune, sporting the insides of a Rhutian Jhanaral" (375).

*Finnegans Wake* (like the *Odyssey*, the *Aeneid*, the *Divina Commedia*, and Joyce's *Ulysses*) also takes us down to Hades, on a journey into the underworld, where the dead heroes parade by. The vision of Pandemonium which we have already seen as modern Dublin (5) is magnified into many views of hell: after Earwicker's trial the epic fall and resurrection motif is heard: "The house of Atreox is fallen indeedust (Ilyam, Ilyum! Maeromor Mournomates!) averging on blight like the mundibanks of Fennyana, but deeds bounds going arise again" (55). And the drunken Earwicker goes off pub-crawling through seven Dublin taverns, taverns which are various versions of heaven and hell (and old Dublin pubs at that!): "to drink in the House of Blazes, the Parrot in Hell, the Orange Tree, the Glibt, the Sun, the Holy Lamb and, lapse not leashed, in Ramitdown's ship hotel" (63), the latter an Egyptian tomb (the tomb of Rameses) which again echoes the Book of the Dead. Earwicker is entombed as an Egyptian monarch, "first pharaoh, Humpheres Cheops Exarchas" (62), Cheops, ark, and ship's hotel suggesting the method of burial employing a funeral ship. The *Amenti*'s "Chapters of the Coming Forth by Day in the Underworld" is repeated in "the sixth sealed chapter of the going forth by black" (62). In imitation of Homer, Joyce describes his own exile in Trieste (which he likens to a journey into the underworld), as well as Earwicker's death: "For mine qvinne I thee giftake and bind my hosenband I thee halter. The wastobe land, a lottuse land, a luctuous land, Emeraldilluim" (62). Here the marriage vows are parodied as an approach to death, while shades of Eliot's "Waste Land," Homer's island of the lotus-eaters, Lot's Sodom, and Ireland are combined to present Hades.

Actually, H.C.E. has been buried in Lough Neagh, "the Lake of Healing" in Northern Ireland, which thus becomes a symbol of resurrection. The healing lake returns the hero to life; the coffin in which he had been buried suddenly disappears: "The coffin, a triumph of the illusionist's art . . . had been removed from the hardware premises of Oetzmann and Nephew, a noted house of the gonemost west" (66), and Earwicker has descended into the underworld. The funeral pomp provides another catalogue of "show coffins, winding sheets, goodbuy bierchepes, cinerary urns, liealoud blasses, snuffchests, poteentubbs, lacrimal vases [etc.]" (77). Earwicker is "buried burrowing in Gehinnon, to proliferate through all his Unterwealth" (78); his journey is made by "coach, carriage, wheelbarrow, dungcart" (79)—a suggestion of the hen digging in the refuse pile (the Hebrew Gehenna, originally the valley of Hinnon where refuse was burned) again suggests the finding of the letter as a resurrection motif.

Hell is again seen as a series of Dublin pubs when Patrick brings Christianity (and consequently the Christian concept of heaven and hell): "Byrne's and Flamming's and Furniss's and Bill Hayses's and Ellishly Haught's, hoc . . . stiff or sober" (289). But the full-scale descent into the underworld does not take place in the *Wake* until the third chapter of Book III. Shaun, as Yawn, lies exhausted on a hill in County Meath; the four judges arrive to question him, but as the interrogation proceeds Yawn disintegrates completely, and from the mound of his decomposed body rises a series of voices, resulting in the final voice, that of H.C.E. Under interrogation Yawn fondly remembers, "I used to be always overthere on the fourth day at my grandmother's place, Tear-nan-Ogre, my little grey home in the west" (479)—a reference to Tir-na-nOg, the land of eternal youth in Celtic mythology. And the ghostly voice from deep beneath Yawn's carcass is heard declaiming, "saouls to the dhaoul, do ye. Finnk. Fime. Fudd?" (499), a ghostly version of the Tim Finnegan vaudeville ballad: "Bad luck to your souls. D'ye think I'm dead?" This resurrection line Joyce renders elsewhere in Gaelic—"Anam muck an dhoul! Did ye drink me doornail?" (24)—and in Latin—"Animadiabolum, mene credidisti mortuum?" (74).

But he need not have his protagonist descend into the underworld to bring forth his parade of dead heroes; the entire *Wake* is of course such a parade: the combatants in heaven, Napoleon and Wellington, the Irish defenders and foreign invaders, the Crimean contestants, historic and mythological, all appear and reappear throughout the course of the flow of the book. Shem, while drunk at the Earwicker trial, conjures up "Helmingham Erchenwyne Rutter Egbert Crumwall Odin Maximus Esme Saxon Esa Vercingetorix Ethelwulf Rupprecht Ydwalla Bentley Osmund Dysart Yggdrasselmann" (88). Norse gods, Gallic defenders, Saxon kings, Roman emperors, German princes, Puritan invaders—and a healthy group of as yet unidentifiable personages—they provide another epic list of heroes parading through the underworld of Shem's drunken unconscious. But most significant are the initials of all their names, which spell

HERE COMES EVERYBODY, and again the ghostly garner of heroes equals the totality of Earwicker himself.

Like many another epic, *Finnegans Wake* contains a significant series of digressions; like *Beowulf*, the *Wake's* plot-line is rather thin, and actually more is discerned of its significance from the important digressions. Joyce is less concerned with the events than with the recording of these events, the various circumstances under which they are reported; his epic best resembles the epic events of the Fenian Cycle or the Tristram-Iseult saga (both of which are heavily drawn upon for the plot of the *Wake*), where many conflicting versions are available because of manuscript discrepancies. As such, *Finnegans Wake* reverts to the "authentic" epic which accumulates its material with the passing of years. Like the mysterious letter found by the hen in the midden heap, it bears the ravages of time and tells its story in fragments; the important trial which attempts to get to the bottom of the epic event of Earwicker's fall is constantly being replayed, each time amassing new evidence on top of evidence already obscured. Never do the events wholly coincide, never is there a complete version of the important incident: each age interprets the significance of the epic fall in its own terms to satisfy its own needs and desires. In the short span of time which elapsed between the incident and the initial trial, many of the participants have already died: Peter Cloran, the scoundrel who divulged the news of the incident (40), has died in jail as Paul Horan (49)—born as St. Peter, he dies as St. Paul, representing the duality of self in the *Wake*; the Hosty who wrote the ballad has been drowned (quite probably in Lake Neagh): "passed away painlessly after life's upsomdowns one hallowe'en night, ebbrous and in the state of nature, propelled from Behind into the great Beyond by footblows coulinclouted upon his oyster" (49). Again in miniature fashion the fall has been repeated; Lucifer has once again been "booted" out of heaven.

But despite the loss of the entire cast of principals, the trial takes place; substitutes for each of the accusers quickly appear—"by the coincidance of their contraries reamalgamerge in that indentity of undiscernibles" (49–50)—and the trial goes on. The events are so thoroughly obscured that the trial begins to revolve around a false report of an encounter with a masked assailant (62–63), and finally the suggestion that Earwicker has been arrested for banging on his own door (64); the "authentic" version comes to light, and we now learn that Earwicker has put a lock on his gate to keep out donkeys, but has been locked in himself for his own protection (69). This series of reports on the happenings of the epic fall continues under a haze of time-obscured hearsay; there is never a single accurate account of the important occurrence. This handling of the material of the *Wake* attempts to present the contemporary epic as a version of the past as seen by the present; the non-heroic age retells the heroic story in its own versions; what Myles Dillon in his history of *Early Irish Literature* tells us about the Fenian Cycle applies equally as well to *Finnegans Wake*: "The temper of the Fenian Cycle might be characterized as romantic rather than epic. The heroic tradition is, for the most part, preserved not in the vivid narrative which brings the reader close to the action, but rather as the record of a glorious past, the fierce joy of paganism as it was remembered in a rather melancholy Christian present." [5] It is significant that much of the story of Finn MacCool comes to us in a version in which a descendant is relating the tales of past heroism to St. Patrick (in *The Colloquy of the Old Men*), since one of the last significant incidents of the *Wake* is the 432 A.D. arrival of St. Patrick and his encounter with the Arch-Druid. Here the cyclical pattern again is obvious if we accept the possibility that the entire *Wake* is a romantic version of the heroic past (the age of Vico's giants), reported in chaotic fashion to Patrick (Vico's patriarch of the succeeding age).

These digressions are not the only Beowulfian aspects of *Finnegans Wake;* many instances in the *Wake* echo the alliterative verse form of Anglo-Saxon heroic poetry. Joyce often suggests a return to the heroic age with the sudden interjection of "that dark deed doer, this wellwilled wooer" (246) into a passage concerning heroic warfare, celestial and terrestrial:

Arranked in their array and flocking for the fray on that old orangeray, Dolly Brae. For these are not on terms, they twain, bartrossers, since their baffle of Whatalose when Adam Leftus and the devil took our hindmost, gegifting her with his painapple, nor will not be atoned at all in fight to no finish, that dark deed doer, this wellwilled wooer, Jerkoff and Eatsoup, Yem or Yan, while felixed is who culpas does and harm's worth healing and Brune is bad French for Jour d'Anno. Tiggers and Tuggers they're all for tenzones. Bettlimbraves (246).

The Chuff-Glugg battle of the Mime is already over (but is of course also taking place, as well as *about to* take place), and the Shem figure has been beaten; Lucifer has once again been kicked down the stairs ("the devil took our hindmost"), and the Eden incident has already been observed ("felixed is who culpas does"), the two events compressed into a single action. The word "painapple" refers both to the forbidden fruit and the World War One euphemism for hand-grenade, a pineapple. The brother dichotomy of Jacob and Esau (as well as the oriental principles of interlocked opposites, Yin and Yang) is evident from the day of their birth; "Jour d'Anno" not only implies the birth of the "twains," but reiterates the cause of the conflict—Anna Livia, the eternal woman. Joyce thus employed the alliterations of "arranked" and "array" and "flocking for the fray" and "that dark deed doer, this wellwilled wooer" to suggest the heroic poetry of the Anglo-Saxon, as well as the Germanic prefix in "gegifting."

During the tale of the Norwegian captain, Joyce launches into many passages of alliteration, Beowulfian rhythms, and kennings; the setting throughout the tale is Viking and heroic—like the Prankquean, the Norse captain sails three times into Dublin Bay, only to sail away without paying his tailor or his inn bills. The sacking of the mainland by the Scandinavian seamen is a frequent theme in the *Wake*—"Fuvver, that Skand, he was up in Norwood's sokaparlour, eating oceans of Voking's Blemish" (157)—and here the Norse captain is again the guilty Earwicker:

But old sporty, as endth lord, in ryehouse reigner, he nought feared crimp or cramp of shore sharks, plotsome to getsome. It was whol niet godthaab of errol Loritz off his Cape of Good Howthe and his trippertrice loretta lady, a maomette to his monetone, with twy twy twinky her stone hairpins, only not, if not, a queen of Prancess their telling tabled who was for his seeming a casket through the heavenly, nay, heart of the sweet (had he hows would he keep her as niece as a fiddle!) but in the mealtub it was wohl yeas sputsbargain what, rarer of recent, an occasional conformity, he, with Muggleton Muckers, alwagers allalong most certainly allowed, as pilerinnager's grace to petitionists of right, of the three blend cupstoomerries with their customed spirits, the Gill gob, the Burklley bump, the Wallisey wanderlook, having their ceilidhe gailydhe in his shaunty irish (312).

What begins as a Norse saga of seafaring soon dissolves into a theological dispute; the sailing of the Vikings for plunder is joined with the sailing of the Pilgrims ("pilerinnager's grace") for safety from religious persecution. But since all this is happening on several levels at once, such theologians as John Gill, George Berkeley, and

John Wesley ("Gill," "Burklley," and "Wallisey") are also the war-
riors Goll (slayer of Finn MacCool's father), the Buckley who shot
the Russian general, and the Duke of Wellington—a merging of the
mythical, the fictional, and the historical heroes. It is also significant
that the first line of this paragraph ("But old sporty, as endth lord, in
ryehouse reigner") is a re-echo of the rhythms of the introduction of
the epic hero Finnegan: "Bygmester Finnegan, of the Stuttering
Hand, freemen's maurer" (4). The paragraph ends with an alliterative enumeration of twelve trades, ending significantly with that of
the weaver, suggesting the twelve apostles and the twelve customers present in Earwicker's pub during the telling of the saga of
the Norwegian captain: "Lorimers and leathersellers, skinners and
salters, pewterers and paperstainers, parishclerks, fletcherbowyers,
girdlers, mercers, cordwainers and first, and not last, the weavers"
(312–313). The sea battle that follows again evokes images of heroic
verse: the Norse captain's ship is about to be overtaken, Earwicker is
at the cash register in his tavern, and Finnegan is about to fall again:
"Thus as count the costs of liquid courage, a bullyon gauger, stowed
stivers pengapung in bulk in hold (fight great finnence! brayvoh,
little bratton!) keen his kenning, the queriest of the crew, with that
fellow fearing for his own misshapes" (313).

   The epic convention of repeating key phrases and stock epithets is
duplicated by Joyce in his use of recurring sounds in various individual ways in *Finnegans Wake*. Joyce's use of repeated leitmotifs
(of names, numbers, and sounds) is the binding element of his
narrative, and his technique of catch-phrases and rhythmic patterns
adroitly ties the myriad motifs together. Ten one-hundred-lettered
"words" specifying the roll of thunder mark the end of a stage of the
cycle and punctuate Earwicker's dream, each fitting into the particular series of events being enacted at the instant (3, 23, 44, 90,
113, 257, 314, 332, 414, 424). In counterpoint to these thunderclaps
the chimes of church bells toll the hours of the night throughout
Earwicker's sleep. The major statement of the motif is heard during
the washerwomen's episode as "Pingpong! There's the Belle for
Sexaloitez! And Concepta de Send-us-pray! Pang! Wring out the
clothes! Wring in the dew!" (213), while secondary soundings are
heard at various instances (32, 58, 268, 327, 379, 528), allowing for
over seven hours of sleep. Equally important are the reiterations of
the Viconian theme as they appear under their various guises, most
succinct in the washerwomen's portion also: "Teems of times and

happy returns. The seim anew. Ordovico or viricordo. Anna was, Livia is, Plurabelle's to be" (215), but unlike the external phenomena of thunder, church bells, and branches rasping against the bedroom windowpane, this theme is exclusively literary. It has its closest repetition in Anna Livia's closing soliloquy, "Themes have thimes and habit reburns. To flame in you. Ardor vigor forders order. Since ancient was our living is in possible to be" (614), and is complete in somewhat scattered form during the lessons: "For as Anna was at the beginning lives yet and will return. . . . We drames our dreams tell Bappy returns. And Sein annews . . . of order and order's coming" (277). But in most cases in the *Wake* only portions of this four-part statement are echoed (18, 226, 510, 620). Other such recurring patterns are derived from songs like "The Man That Broke the Bank at Monte Carlo" (71, 90, 105, 232, 274, 514, 538) and "The Wild Man from Borneo Has Just Come to Town" (130, 331, 345, 382, 415, 481, 502), and nursery rhymes like "This Is the House That Jack Built" (8, 18, 80, 106, 205, 271, 274, 369, 375, 439, 476, 511, 580). The repetitive use of sounds, noises, leitmotifs, and titles also includes the recurring riddle (a traditional device in such diverse literary pieces as *Oedipus Tyrannus* and "Rumpelstiltskin"), the most important ones being "why do I am alook alike a poss of porterpease?" (21), re-echoed throughout the Prankquean tale and later (96, 187, 191, 224, 260, 274, 372, 397, 417, 493, 511, 520, 623), "when is a man not a man?" (170; also: 231, 307, 356, 495, 586, 607), and "Was liffe worth leaving?" (230; also: 12, 143, 199, 269).

Its all-inclusive attempt to present the scope and dimensions of human life establishes the *Wake* as a conscious effort to create an epic of the thought of twentieth-century humanity. Joyce transcends the boundaries of Western culture to include aspects of other cultural patterns which have begun to become infused into the stream of contemporary thought during the past centuries; at once psychological and sociological, it is an epic of an era which has had its thinking shaped by Marx and Darwin, Freud and Frazer, Planck and Einstein. Joyce availed himself not only of the advances in various technological areas already made during his lifetime, but was equally capable of incorporating such prophetic experiments as the world-wide use of television (in public houses at that!) and the splitting of the atom, both of which figure prominently in the *Wake*. At many instances Earwicker's dream is visualized in his sleeping

mind on a television screen: Television kills telephony in brothers'
broil. Our eyes demand their turn. Let them be seen!" (52); elsewhere the marriage of the Norwegian captain is seen in a cinematic
newsreel: "With her banbax hoist from holder, zig for zag through
pool and polder, cheap, cheap, cheap and Laughing Jack, all augurs
scorenning, see the Bolche your pictures motion and Kitzy
Kleinsuessmein eloping for that holm in Finn's Hotel Fiord, Nova
Norening" (330). Conscious of the technological contrivances of the
age, *Finnegans Wake* is at once a "fadograph of a yestern scene"
(7), a "tolvtubular high fidelity daildialler, as modern as tomorrow
afternoon and in appearance up to the minute . . . equipped with
supershielded umbrella antennas for distance" (309), and a "non-
day diary, this allnights newseryreel" (489).

The splitting of the atom is a vital point in *Finnegans Wake*; it
occurs during the shooting of the Russian general (reported on the
"up to the minute" radio presented to Earwicker by the customers at
the tavern) and is an aspect of the destruction of the father by the
son, the mysterious Buckley. Actually Joyce is not only anticipating
the world-shaking explosion which leveled Hiroshima six years
after the publication of *Finnegans Wake*, but is explaining that even
this modern phenomenon has occurred before:

The abnihilisation of the etym by the grisning of the grosning of the
grinder of the grunder of the first lord of Hurtreford expolodotonates
through Parsuralia with an ivanmorinthorrorumble fragoromboassity
amidwhiches general uttermosts confussion are perceivable moletons
skaping with mulicules while coventry plumpkins fairlygosmotherthem-
selves in the Landaunelegants of Pinkadindy. Similar scenatas are pro-
jectilised from Hullulullu, Bawlawayo, empyreal Raum and mordern
Atems (353).

This new explosion-detonation was heard in Eden when Adam fell,
and by the giants in God's thunderclap; it is all within the Viconian
concept ("by the grisning of the grosning of the grinder of the
grunder"), the four stages of the cycle punctuated by the thunderclaps. This new thunder which "would split an atam" (333) is
expected to cap the realm of contemporary chaos. Since Adam was
first split into his many descendants, every new annihilation of the
atom is a repetition of the cycle of life. *Finnegans Wake* thus
endeavors to summarize the redundant elements of contemporary
life, to boil down all the aspects of our civilization and its complex
roots into a single environment which can be analyzed: pagan

Borneo, Imperial Rome, and Modern Athens are all present in the Dublin which is Joyce's world focus.

Like all expansive works which may vie for the title of epic, *Finnegans Wake* strives for scope and universality, and attempts to portray its own times in terms of timelessness. Joyce selected his characters in terms of history, myth, and legend, and individualized them in the light of the many prototypes available to him in world literature. There is astonishingly little in the *Wake,* despite its heavy reliance upon coincidence, that is accidental. With microscopic accuracy Joyce hunted the "coincidental" element down to its most basic root in repetitive, spiraling, evolving history, and relied upon his intimate knowledge of the Irish milieu (and particularly Dublin) for his "manufactured" coincidences. The Phoenix Park setting for the Earwicker misdemeanor is a case in point: whereas St. Stephen's Green exists in Dublin for Stephen Dedalus's convenient walks in *A Portrait,* the coincidence lies in Joyce's choice in naming his hero; conversely, Phoenix Park exists, and is so called because of historic accident. Joyce need only utilize the place for his purposes once he realized the significance of the resurrection motif in his epic fabric. In a letter to Harriet Shaw Weaver, dated 14 August 1927, Joyce comments: "As to 'Phoenix'. A viceroy who knew no Irish thought this was the word the Dublin people used and put up the mount of a phoenix in the park. The Irish was *fiunishgue*= clear water from a well of bright water there." [6] In the Fenian Cycle we learn that Finn (whose original name was Demne) received his name once he had eaten of the salmon of wisdom from the river, and was therefore termed "fair" or "white." The various linguistic accidents involved precede Joyce's tampering with language for his own purposes in the *Wake*; Joyce utilized the Anglo-Gaelic Fionn-Uisge–phoenix pun as readily as he used Christ's pun—"thuartpeatrick" (3)—as it naturally fit his framework. Fionn is the legendary MacCool; Uisge is the river, Anna Livia (as well as the source for the English word, whiskey); together they are the rebirth motif of the phoenix.

Perhaps, then, there remains only the necessity of defending *Finnegans Wake* from the too-easy assertion that it is mock-epic after all. It is as ill-fitting a term for the *Wake* as it is for *Don Quixote* or *Huckleberry Finn,* since all three achieve epic stature and grandeur by their scope, fullness of development, and all-inclusiveness in design. What Pope was able to do in *The Rape of*

*the Lock* was *reduce* epic pretensions in his society to their basic
absurdity; what Joyce sought to achieve was an augmented view of
the basic elements in his material. He developed his figures as
archetypes, as characters, and, on occasions when necessary to his
design, as stereotypes. Each of the primary participants of the *Wake*
is realized on all three levels, each exists allegorically, realistically,
in exacting literalness, and in sketchy caricature. Every device
chosen by Joyce earmarks the careful selection practiced by the
artist to accumulate a totality of experience in an all-inclusive plan.
The choice of the dream setting (perhaps a newly discovered source
of psychological information for Freud and followers, but certainly
an ageless source for poets and prophets for many civilizations)
achieves for Joyce what it achieved for the creators of the *Divina
Commedia,* the *Romance of the Rose, Pilgrim's Progress,* and *Piers
Plowman:* a frame through which both the literal and the symbolic
can harmoniously exist. The much-discussed question of "Who is the
dreamer in *Finnegans Wake*?" seems so easily answerable in the
light of the epic material in the work. On the symbolic level it is of
course Everyman dreaming the history of his existence; on the literal
level it is Earwicker (*our* microcosmic Everyman) recounting in
disguised form his misadventure in Phoenix Park; and on the creative level it is Joyce himself giving form to what he has experienced
and learned and understood (in the same way in which the Demi-
urge, creating the universe, dreams away its cycles of evolution).

Having carried the modern novel to an ultimate point in *Ulysses*
with a fusion of naturalistic and symbolic elements, Joyce goes even
a step further in the *Wake* by creating a novel which defies definition as a novel while yet containing the basic story line. Having
critically and judiciously consumed the existing literary epics available to our civilization, Joyce sets out to duplicate their most significant elements for his own age. Like the *Iliad,* and *Odyssey* and
*Aeneid, Finnegans Wake* presents the most fabulous aspect of its
age, while managing to reproduce its most natural aspects; like the
*Divina Commedia* and *Paradise Lost,* it represents the morality of
its age without moralizing; and like *Beowulf* and the *Chanson de
Roland,* it holds a mirror to its times and shows the dual image of the
age as it sees itself, as well as where the self-deception lies. In
choosing his cumulative title for his many-sided work, Joyce arrived
at *Finnegans Wake* because it signified the many levels of his epic:
allegorically it was the awakening of the legendary giant, Finn

MacCool; literally it was the wake for the hod carrier Tim Finnegan; and prophetically it was the arising of the "Finnegans" of the world. Within the confines of the *Wake* exist many an alternate title concomitant with its epic theme and treatment. One such would be: "the humphriad of that fall and rise" (53).

*PETROULA KEPHALA RUEHLEN*

# CONSTANTINE CAVAFY
## A European Poet

ON THE TWENTY-NINTH of April 1933, Constantine Cavafy died on his seventieth birthday. A few days before, he had jotted down for a friend to read—cancer of the throat had deprived the poet of the ability to speak—"And I had twenty-five more poems to write!"

In 1963 Greece, the world, celebrated the centennial of Cavafy's birth and the thirtieth anniversary of his death. A tasteful new edition of his poems, by G. P. Savidis, has marked the occasion.[1] This new edition follows (for the first time) the scheme set out by the poet himself for an arrangement of his poems in a thematic rather than in a chronological order.[2] Apart from this fine tribute, the most exciting landmark of the Cavafy Year was the release—by the poet's heir—of the rich collection of Cavafy papers, which up to now had been closed to the public. The collection, containing approximately five thousand papers—personal and family papers, essays, notes, as well as unpublished poems—was entrusted to Mr. Savidis for eventual editing and publication.

I had the good fortune to be in Athens during the summer of 1963, where Mr. Savidis very kindly allowed me to look at the Cavafy material. I suppose every lover of literature who has ever had the chance to find himself among long-hidden and unexplored papers of his favorite author has experienced the awe I felt that summer afternoon when for the first time I was able to touch and examine the yellowish pictures and manuscripts of Cavafy. There they were, neatly filed—first the family pictures, where one could only guess which of the grave-looking boys was Constantine; then the pictures

of the young man, dressed and combed with extreme care, with the
features of an unmistakable personality and a deep somewhat
troubled look in his dark eyes; and the more recent pictures of the
poet's maturity, most startling pictures of an intellectual who had
been through agony of body and spirit and who had not come out
unscathed. Then there were the pictures of the house on Rue
Lepsius, half-lit rooms with oriental furnishings, heavy draperies,
low sofas, carved furniture, tables inlaid with mother-of-pearl, elaborately wrought brass chandeliers, huge mirrors in heavy gilt
frames, old-fashioned china lamps. And suddenly I could see the
figure of the tragically isolated old man walking once more in those
empty rooms where he had lived alone for so many years, working
over those exquisite verses of utter lucidity, which have the power to
evoke a world.

> Half past twelve. Time has passed quickly
> since nine o'clock when I lit the lamp,
> and sat down here. I have been sitting without reading,
> and without talking. With whom could I talk
> all alone in this house.[3]

It was here, in Alexandria—the old capital of the Ptolemies, the
crossing-path of East and West, the melting-pot of races, cultures,
and religions—that the scholar spent his nights studying ancient
documents until the past was present and alive and those troubled,
confused, tragic figures of history were caught once again in the
whirlwind of our passions and came back to repeat the pathos of
their lives among us.

> Ah, here, you came with your undefinable
> fascination. In history few
> lines only are found about you,
> and so more freely I molded you in my mind.
> I molded you handsome and emotional.
> My art gives to your face
> a dreamlike attractive beauty.
> And so fully did I vision you,
> that late last night, as my lamp
> was going out—I deliberately let it go out—
> I thought you came into my room,
> you seemed to stand before me as you must have been
> in conquered Alexandria,
> pale and weary, ideal in your grief,
> still hoping they would take pity on you
> the foul ones—who were whispering, "Too many Caesars." [4]

There is magic in those lines in Greek, and only he who has attempted to translate poetry—that part of the meaning which lies in the suggestive quality that words have acquired through the centuries—will understand the frustration that is involved in the task.

To an international audience Cavafy is accessible only through translation, because he had the disadvantage to be writing in a language which, of however glorious a past, is little known today outside Greece. This is especially unfortunate because one of the most important features of Cavafy's originality lies in his unique use of words and in effects achieved through elements intrinsic to the Greek language. A great many of Cavafy's stylistic innovations are due to the fact that he was writing at a period when Greece was creating a new language out of a confused and divided past. In English there is nothing comparable to the conflict between purist and demotic Greek. Purist Greek at the time Cavafy began to write was the official language of the state; yet it was mostly a written language, which had lost contact with the mass of the people and the life of the nation and consequently had become artificial and dead. However, it was a language with a vast tradition; through ages of theological controversies it had developed if not a power for lyrical expression of feeling—except perhaps in church hymns—yet a remarkable synthetic power, subtlety, precision, concreteness, density of expression, and a certain austere beauty. Demotic Greek, on the other hand, was the language of the people, mostly a spoken language, with practically no pretentions of erudition or sophistication, yet with a rare freshness and inventiveness which had already found expression in folk literature in the mainland of Greece during the long years of Turkish occupation, and which had proved its potentialities by achieving excellence in more sophisticated treatment in some of the Greek islands which were free of Turkish rule and able to follow the European literary trends of the time.

In the second half of the nineteenth century and in the beginnings of the twentieth, the poets of the newly freed Greece were ambitious to establish demotic Greek as the language of literature, the only language fit to express the spirit of the new nation. The poetic movements of the time were discovering and exploiting popular and folk materials, especially folk songs, and they were exhibiting a dominant lyrical tone. Although he adopted the cause of demotic Greek, Cavafy's loyalties in language were divided. As a son of a well-to-do family of merchants related to the tradition-minded

Phanariot circles on his mother's side, he was brought up and educated in the formal purist tradition. Moreover, since early youth he was an avid scholar showing great interest and erudition in Greek history and language. His early poems, which he later abandoned and which are not usually included in the collections of his verse, are written in the stiff, formal, purist Greek of the "Romantic" tradition in vogue at that time in Greece. However, in Alexandria he became involved with a group of young demoticists and came to be an enthusiastic supporter of the demotic movements of his time in poetry. He embraced the movement, but not its narrow-minded fanaticism. Cavafy, by temperament and upbringing, was a traditionalist. Although capable of expressing strong lyrical sentiment, as seen in some of his most evocative erotic poems, Cavafy was the heir of the long-forgotten art of austere economy and perfect balance of the ancient Greek epigrammatists and of the precision and meticulousness of the Byzantine theologians and scholars. However, these were qualities which could not be abstracted from the language in which they had been achieved; Cavafy was mature enough not to reject the past but to try to preserve it, build upon it, and make it a part of the present life of the nation. Four hundred years had created a dividing gap in the Greek sensibility and letters—I do *not* mean a loss of national feeling or of a sense of identity—and Cavafy knew that unless Greece bridged it, the literature, the history, and the great civilization of its ancestors would become those of a foreign people. "I am not a Greek, I am Hellenic," he used to say, trying to encompass the totality of the physical and intellectual expansion of the race through the ages.

Cavafy knew, of course, that language changes and that the conditions of our life change too. He had no illusions about restoring ancient Greek or something close to it, as some of the most fanatical purists seemed to have. But he knew also that a nation which denounces its past has no hope for the future. Taking his cue perhaps from the idiom spoken in Alexandria, which was something of a mixture of purist and demotic elements, Cavafy developed his own personal style—a perfect amalgamation of the life and emotive power inherent in demotic Greek and of the dignity, density, and suggestive and illusory possibilities of purist Greek. His language is full of turns of expression and words borrowed from the entire Greek linguistic tradition since classical times. And so perfectly could he integrate his diverse material that in poems like "In the

Month of Athyr," or in "Come, O King of the Lacedaemonians," he achieves the perfect *tour de force* by integrating whole ancient Greek passages in the modern Greek context while being not only perfectly clear and intelligible, but absolutely natural too. He did not employ or try to bring back to use archaic expressions long forgotten or belonging to the province of the literary historian or the linguist. Although comparable to Joyce's and other modern writers' attempts to break down the linguistic frontiers, Cavafy's experiment—although equally bold—was, I believe, more successful, for every archaic or unusual word in his poems is within the modern Greek linguistic consciousness and is perfectly clear to the average educated Greek.

It took a vast knowledge of the language and an unusual sensitivity and power over words to perform the task; for, as I said, Cavafy's language is not demotic Greek sprinkled with purist or archaic expressions, or vice versa, but an ideal fusion. "I have tried to blend the spoken with the written language," he wrote to his friend Pericles Anastasiades; "I have called to my help in the process of mixture all my experience plus as much artistic insight as I possess in the matter—trembling, so to speak, over every word. . . ." The result was a style of deliberately prosaic quality, simple, concentrated, almost dry, economical, unadorned, divested of every element which would cause it to deviate from the strictest austerity—at its best, inevitable. Cavafy's poetry is highly intellectual; yet it is deeply suggestive and characterized by strong emotive power. "A more elaborate style and a less controlled imagination would have destroyed Cavafy's subtle and special charm," remarks C. M. Bowra.[5]

Since they can hardly be rendered in translation, these features are necessarily restricted to the appreciation of the people of the poet's own race and language. What is it then that survives translation in Cavafy? Eliot said that great poets are more translatable than minor writers because, although just as much of the original significance is lost as is lost when we translate lesser poets, "there is also more saved—for more was there."[6] Obviously much is saved in Cavafy's case. His poetry does not appeal to the wider public; except for a few lyrical pieces, it is a difficult kind of poetry, demanding a certain degree of erudition, sophistication, and ability for abstract thought if it is to be fully appreciated. Yet Cavafy's reputation abroad has been steadily growing. His complete poems have been translated into French and twice into English, not to mention several translations of individual poems in various languages. There is something in Cavafy, apparently, which is capable of transcending national limits. Auden, who doesn't know one word of modern Greek, defines this element as Cavafy's unique tone of voice. He has read translations of Cavafy made by different hands, he says, but every one of them was immediately recognized as a poem by Cavafy. Nobody else could have written it; it revealed a person with a unique perspective on the world.

Discussing Great Europeans, Eliot said that in figures like Dante, Shakespeare, and Goethe, the quality which survives translation and which "is capable of arousing a direct response as of man to man, in readers of any place and any time," is wisdom.[7] I am not going to plead Cavafy's greatness or wisdom here, for both have to be tested by time. The point I want to make is that for a poet to appeal to a wider audience than that of his place and time, and for that appeal to be not the transient one of a passing fashion but a deeper and more permanent relationship between himself and his readers, he should share in some degree in the qualities which make a poet transcend the limits of his country and become, if not a Great European—at least a *European* poet. He should have, if not the wisdom of the great sages—for those are few—the relative wisdom of the serious artist who has something significant to tell to his fellow men. In this respect I believe that Cavafy is not only a Greek poet but a European poet too, for even in translation his poetry remains highly relevant and significant to the European reader, arousing that "direct response as of man to man" that Eliot was talking about.

By "European" audience I do not mean an audience strictly confined within the limits of Europe, but one which emotionally and culturally is within the European, or Western, tradition. A part of this essay will be devoted to the examination of the qualities which are essential for a poet to be called European, and the way these criteria can be applied to Cavafy. Eliot, in his discussion of what is a classic, what is a universal classic, and what is a Great European, has given us a set of values by which the greatness of a poet can be established. The criteria in this discussion will in part be an adaptation and combination of Eliot's values as they apply to Cavafy as a European poet.

My first criterion is a quality which can best be termed as *maturity*. As Eliot has said, maturity cannot be defined. We cannot make its meaning apprehensible to the immature; if we are mature we will recognize maturity when we encounter it, either in a civilization, or in a literature, or in a personality. However, in order to make my point clear, I shall distinguish four qualities which a poet should exhibit in order to be recognized as properly mature; or rather, since these qualities do not exist independently from each other, I shall call them four aspects under which maturity is revealed in poetry. These aspects are a sense of history, maturity of mind, maturity of manners, and maturity of language.

There is no doubt that one of Cavafy's most important features is his use of history. "I am a historical poet," Cavafy used to say. By that he did not mean his erudition in classical, Hellenistic, and Byzantine history; he did not mean that he used those eras as settings for many of his poems either; nor did he mean that a great many of the characters in his poems are personalities we read about in history books. What he meant was that he felt in himself that particular consciousness which makes us aware that we are not living in an isolated present in a vacuum of time; that the past is not the special domain only of museums, historiographers, or antiquarians; and that our present experience would be a succession of meaningless facts unless seen in relation to parallel human experiences in the past.

It is the European poet especially who cannot turn his back upon the past and hope to bring order in the present experience or find a meaning in it. It is not only because European history has been too long and too complex, or because too many countries and civilizations rose and fell, that we cannot ignore the destiny they have traced for us; other civilizations besides the European have had a long and bloody history. But it is that the experience of all these ages of our history has been made *meaningful* to us through a body of historical knowledge and literature which we cannot afford to pass over. The fact that Mark Antony and Cleopatra have existed, loved, lost a kingdom of half the world, and died for that love; and the fact that Shakespeare has created through them his immortal symbols of great romantic love in the name of which a man has been able to say, —"Let Rome in Tiber melt, and the wide arch / Of the ranged empire fall! Here is my space"—have forever changed our concept of love. No man will sacrifice the world for the love of a woman again, no poet will immortalize the sacrifice or bewail the death of the capacity for it, but the line or the work of art will bear a relation to the myth of Antony and Cleopatra. At the present time, when modern man is confused and lost in a chaotic universe because he feels that his life and his experience are so radically different from those of his forefathers that the wisdom he has gained through the ages cannot help him to find order and meaning and catharsis in his existence—at the present time it is incumbent on the artist to rejoin the broken threads of human experience and assert once again the common destiny of man.

> Home is where one starts from. As we grow older
> The world becomes stranger, the pattern more complicated
> Of dead and living. Not the intense moment
> Isolated, with no before and after,
> But a lifetime burning in every moment
> And not a lifetime of one man only
> But of old stones that cannot be deciphered [8]

said Eliot, who in so many ways has stressed the importance of the historical consciousness in modern literature.

In that still very significant article of his on Joyce in 1923, Eliot made the statement, "In using the myth, in manipulating a continuous parallel between contemporaneity and antiquity Mr. Joyce is pursuing a method which others must pursue after him. . . . It is simply a way of controlling, of ordering, of giving a shape and a significance to the immense panorama of futility and anarchy which is contemporary history. It is a method already adumbrated by Mr. Yeats, and of which I believe Mr. Yeats to have been the first contemporary to be conscious." [9] At the time Eliot was writing those words I do not believe he knew of the existence of Cavafy. As far as I know, the first time Eliot came across Cavafy's poetry was through E. M. Forster about 1928, which resulted in Eliot's publishing two of Cavafy's poems in the *Criterion*. I do not know whether Eliot would have modified that statement about Yeats had he had a chance to be earlier or more intimately acquainted with Cavafy's poetry; Eliot's and Cavafy's personalities were too different for a liking at first glance, and we must not forget that it took Eliot many years to find an interest in Yeats. But my point is that it was not Yeats only who was the first contemporary to feel the need for the mythical method. Although probably at that time not aware of each other's existence, Yeats and Cavafy started developing the mythic method almost simultaneously—Cavafy some years earlier, as a matter of fact. The two poets were almost exactly contemporaries—Yeats being two

years younger and dying six years later than Cavafy. Both belonged
to small but proud countries engaged at the time in strong nation-
alistic movements, a fact which might partly account for both poets'
strong sense of the past. Both had an aristocratic attitude towards
life and their art, being perhaps the last patrician poets of our times.
Both started publishing poetry in the late eighties—in neither case
considered their most representative work. Both were poets of middle age, achieving their major work in their fifties and later. It was
only when they saw experience in retrospect that its manifold significance was revealed to them; it was only in later maturity that they
both attained the impersonality that Eliot sought in art—the impersonality of the poet "Who, out of intense and personal experience, is
able to express a general truth; retaining all the particularity of his
experience, to make of it a general symbol." [10] And it was at the time
of their full maturity that they started using the historical past in its
cyclic recurrence or in its timeless presence as their major theme and
method of symbolism. The fact that two poets of distant and different backgrounds have followed parallel courses of artistic development points perhaps to the most significant fact that the
development of the mythic method was not generated by happy
coincidence but by something deeper in the need of the times.

Even in poems written around 1904–1906, like "Expecting the
Barbarians," "Trojans," or "King Demetrius," Cavafy has shown a
conscious and mature use of history. By 1911 he had reached an
advanced enough stage of development to produce a poem like "The
God Forsakes Antony," which apart from its being a very good poem
in itself, is the poem where Cavafy's myth of Alexandria found its
first distinct formulation.

> When suddenly at the midnight hour is heard
> an invisible company passing
> with exquisite music, with voices—
> your fortune that is now yielding, your works
> that have failed, the plans of your life
> that have all turned out to be illusions, do not mourn
>     uselessly.
> As one prepared long since, as one courageous,
> say farewell to her, to Alexandria who is leaving.
> Above all do not deceive yourself, do not say that it was
> a dream, that your hearing has been mistaken;
> do not stoop to such vain hopes.
> As one prepared long since, as one courageous,
> as it befits you who have been worthy of such a city,

firmly approach the window,
and listen with emotion, but not
with the coward's entreaties and complaints,
as a last enjoyment listen to the sounds,
to the exquisite instruments of the mystic company,
and say farewell to her, to Alexandria you are leaving.[11]

The characterization is mature. The poem is an address to Antony, yet the speaker's voice is not overbearing. Although he utters no word, Antony emerges from the poem a distinct personality, three-dimensional, effortlessly carrying on his shoulders the tremendous burden of Plutarch and Shakespeare—not refuting them, not ignoring them, not even trying to supersede them, but silently acknowledging his debt to them while being himself, an Antony whom only Cavafy could have created. What remains when we read the poem is Antony—no, it is ourselves whom we see sadly but firmly approaching the window in doomed Alexandria to hear the voices of the invisible followers of the god who are abandoning us alone to face the destiny we ourselves have shaped. The image of Alexandria we get from the poem is enriched and partly modified by the idea and myth of Alexandria developed more fully in Cavafy's later poetry. In a body of work with rare unity like Cavafy's this is to be expected. Yet "The God Forsakes Antony" can stand perfectly on its own. Even if we had never read poems like "Alexandrian Kings," "Tomb of Ignatius," "Myres: Alexandria, A.D. 340," still we could not fail to understand what Alexandria stands for. For Alexandria does not exist in the far past; Alexandria is here around us—our greatest, most exquisite, and most destructive destiny.

In "Theodotus" the point can perhaps be made clearer. The first stanza is addressed to Julius Caesar and it refers to the incident described in Plutarch where Theodotus, King Ptolemy's teacher of rhetoric, advised the Egyptians to kill Pompey when he landed and present his head to Caesar. The second stanza is addressed directly to the reader and constitutes one of the most earnest and powerful admonitions one could find in poetry.

If you are one of the truly elect,
watch how you obtain your dominance.
However much you are renowned, your achievements
in Italy and in Thessaly
however much the cities do acclaim,
however many honorary decrees
your admirers have issued for you in Rome,

neither your joy, nor your triumph will last,
nor superior—superior in what way?—person will you feel,
when, in Alexandria, Theodotus brings to you,
on a bloody platter,
wretched Pompey's head.

And do not trust that in your life
limited, regulated, and prosaic,
such spectacular and dreadful things do not take place.
Perhaps this very hour into some neighbor's
orderly house he is entering—
invisible, incorporeal—Theodotus,
bringing such a frightful head.[12]

There is a strong didactic element in this kind of poetry; as a matter of fact one could argue the point that Cavafy is basically a didactic poet.[13] But so are Milton and Dante and Eliot, yet the fact does not detract from the greatness of their poetry. Not many poems can claim a more sustained level of poetic feeling. Not only the didactic intention, but the same admonitory address to the reader that Cavafy uses in "Theodotus" can be seen in the following three lines in "Death by Water":

Gentile or Jew
O you who turn the wheel and look to windward,
Consider Phlebas, who was once handsome and tall as you.[14]

These lines always bring into my mind the last lines from Cavafy's "Tomb of Iases," a dead youth's last appeal to the living through his epitaph,

Traveler,
if you are an Alexandrian, you will not condemn. You know
the passionate force
of our life; what ardor it has; what supreme pleasure.[15]

"As you," "if you are an Alexandrian"—these are the connecting links which make the lives of the Phoenician sailor and the young Alexandrian youth, both dead so long ago, relevant to us and to our destiny. There is a strong similarity of tone in the two apostrophes—the same pathos of the voices of the dead trying to reach us from the underworld and speak to us, explain to us, warn us. There are so many dead in Cavafy's poems that even a collection of titles is impressive: "Tomb of Lysias Grammaticus," "Tomb of Eurion," "Tomb of Iases," "For Ammones who died 29 years old, in 610,"

"Tomb of Ignatius," "Tomb of Lanes," "Epitaph of Antiochos, King of Commagene," and many others. I do not believe that there exists elsewhere a congregation of dead so very alive.

There is one more poem of Cavafy's which I would like to discuss in connection with his sense of history. The poem has the title "Those Who Fought for the Achaean League," and it is an epigram in the best tradition of Simonides and the other famous epigrammatists of the Greek Anthology.

> Valiant you who fought and fell in glory;
> fearless of those everywhere victorious.
> Blameless you, if Diaeus and Critolaus have erred.
> Whenever the Greeks want to pride themselves,
> "Such men our nation brings forth" will they say
> about you. So wonderful your praise will be.
> Written in Alexandria by an Achaean;
> the seventh year of Ptolemy Lathyros.[16]

Although it was easy to perceive the purity of style and the excellence of structure—unfortunately lost in the translation of such a tightly wrought form as an epigram—I always felt there was something eluding me in the meaning and the significance of the poem, especially of the last two lines. They did not seem to add anything; yet I refused to believe that a poet like Cavafy, who constructed his poems with such care and accuracy and who cultivated such an economy of style, could ever allow two insignificant lines—which sounded like a poor device for "antiquing" the poem—to bring an anticlimax to a brilliantly constructed epigram. I had let the matter rest at that, until a very acute suggestion by Mr. Seferis came to illuminate the subject for me and transform the poem into one of Cavafy's most significant achievements.[17]

The epigram refers to the battle near Corinth in 146 B.C., the last desperate effort of the Achaeans before they succumbed to the "everywhere victorious" Romans. In that battle, the fate of Hellenistic civilization was decided; all hope was lost. In order to find the key to the particular emotional situation which prompted this tribute to those who fought for the Achaean League, we must turn, as Mr. Seferis has suggested, to the date of its composition, 1922. That was the year of the destruction of the Greek army in Asia Minor. One should be a Greek to realize the full emotional significance of the destruction to Greece. It meant the irrevocable loss of all hope for recovering from the Turks the old Greek colonies in Asia and for recreating the old glory that was the Byzantine Empire; it was the destruction of the dream of the "Great Idea," as it was called, which had been nourished for four hundred years in the breasts of the Turkish-occupied Greeks and bequeathed from generation to generation in the folk songs and the tales about the last emperor of Byzantium, who would wake up from his long sleep and restore Constantinople and St. Sophia and all they represented to their rightful heirs. But the offensive launched in Asia in 1921 was a failure. The leaders had erred in their ambition, in their inner conflicts, and in their judgments about the help of the Allied forces and especially England, just as Diaeus and Critolaus, the leaders of the Achaean League, had erred in their ambition, in their conflicts, and in their judgments about Rome. The task of the poet was to pay the tribute which is thought meet for heroic sacrifice—an epigram to the valiant and blameless ones who fought and fell in glory. The tribute was paid by an Achaean in Alexandria, the seventh year of Ptolemy Lathyros. That was a time of trouble, political corruption, and degradation in the kingdom of the Lagides. Cavafy's time also was a time of gradual decay and disintegration in the Greek settlement of Alexandria, which since the advent of the English had fallen from an economically, politically, and socially flourishing and ruling class to the pitiable state of fight for survival. Alexandria could not last long after Corinth—after Asia Minor. The anonymous Achaean, Cavafy, knew it. The modest identification, the bitterness and despair hidden in the last line about the destiny of his people, yet the quiet resignation to fate which is felt as an undertone to the whole poem, are almost insurpassable in their simplicity.

> Written in Alexandria by an Achaean;
> the seventh year of Ptolemy Lathyros.

Transcending the personal and the local, the poet's tribute in its almost classical dignity and controlled emotion attains universal significance to all those who fight a lost battle in order to maintain an ancient ideal.

This awareness of history is indispensable, says Eliot, in order to attain maturity of mind. "There must be the knowledge of the history of at least one other highly civilized people, and of a people whose civilization is sufficiently cognate to have influenced and entered into our own." [18] Such was the case with Cavafy and the Hellenistic and Byzantine civilizations, which although of his own people, were sufficiently removed in time to be distinct from the one he was part of. It is only through the recognition of the relation between two cultures, between the past and the present, that we can hope to develop that particular sense of value which makes us able to distinguish the permanent from the ephemeral, the universal from the local. This all-important consciousness of history Cavafy had, and it enabled him to condense all human experience in a single statement:

> Traveler,
> if you are an Alexandrian, you will not condemn.

This is what I mean by maturity.

The third way maturity is exhibited by a poet is in maturity of manners. By maturity of manners I do not mean only those ways in which Eliot says that Congreve's society was more mature than Shakespeare's—not only the elegance, the refinement, the sophistication of life, the wit and beauty of Cavafy's Hellenistic world, an over-refined civilization towards its end.[19] By maturity of manners I also mean that refinement of manners which springs from a mature conscience, an awareness of values in life, a delicate sensibility. In his discussion of maturity of manners, Eliot refers to the story of Aeneas and Dido, and especially to that scene in Book VI of the *Aeneid* in which Aeneas cannot forgive himself for his behavior towards Dido although he is aware that his destiny is governed by powers beyond himself, as a *locus classicus* of maturity of manners in European society. It is this maturity of manners which I believe Cavafy does not lack.

Cavafy's myth of the Hellenistic world with its culture, sophistication, hedonism, and exquisite aesthetic sense, is one of the best expressions in modern literature of the over-refined society of a civilization towards its end. Cavafy portrays not only the elegance of life, the refinement of pleasure, or the enchantment of the soft perfumed nights of Ionia; nor only the vanity, the corruption, the vice, the impotence, and the weakness of an aging civilization. What impresses us most, what finally the reader carries within him, is that from amidst this corruption, this impotence, and this weakness, man does not emerge a failure. I believe that paragraphs like the following describing Cavafy's world are rather misleading, not because they misinterpret it, but because they miss some of its most important aspects.

It was in this Hellenistic Alexandrian world, then, that Cavafy found the "landscape" through which he could express himself with pertinence and urbanity. Out of it he was to build his "myth" of a personal and at the same time perennial human condition, that of the tired, rapacious, over-refined man who is the generic hero of his poems, *homo Europaeus*, as we might call him, of our not so late humanist period. For that after all is the principal figure that emerges from behind the many masks which Cavafy gives him: the sick guest of an aesthetic city, of a Greco-Roman asylum, full of selfish desires and absurd vanities, ageing into impotence and ugliness, purified by every longing, sapped by every depravity, all sentiment and all fatigue, devoted to fate and pain as the morphinist to his drug, lonely, hollowed out, old as the ages, all nostalgia, animal and sage, all bare, with no ambitions, gnawed by the dread of death, by the relentless dance of time that sweeps all that he loves into oblivion, and finding relief only in his art where he can watch with something approaching a detached irony the spectacle of a life of pleasure, folly, misfortune, vice, and sybaritic elegance which he now can never again enjoy.[20]

The picture we get here is of a world wholly negative and decadent, with a sensibility if not completely dead, then certainly very restricted. This is one aspect of Cavafy's world, but not the whole story. Among the things the critic missed are the lyrical feeling of the perfection of beauty, the strength of sensual pleasure, the fight between asceticism and self-indulgence, the conflict of races and religions, the clash of values of different cultures. Cavafy's man is certainly the *homo Europaeus*, but the *homo Europaeus* is of a more complex nature and of a grander stature than the critic would have us believe. Cavafy's world is not a heroic world; nor is it a peaceful or healthy world either. Failure, misfortune, and an overpowering destiny of inevitable doom constitute the scene in which his figures move. We cannot expect them to exhibit heroic virtues. However, there is a grandeur in the way the Cavafy man accepts his destiny and bears his fate. In the fact that the man who created Alexandria for himself is able firmly to approach the window and say farewell to her, we see a maturity of manners which, in the frame of its world and situation, can be compared to that of Aeneas. As an instance of that quality by which man surpasses self-pity and asserts his dignity even in failure, I would quote the thoughts of Demetrius, son of Seleucus, when he heard that Ptolemy had arrived in Rome poorly dressed and on foot so that he might beg with greater success:

> That in fact they have become
> some sort of servants to the Romans
> the son of Seleucus knows; that those are who give to them

and those who take from them their thrones
arbitrarily, as they please, he knows.
But at least in their appearance
let them maintain some majesty;
let them not forget that they are kings still,
that they are still called (alas!) kings.[21]

That is why Demetrius sent to Ptolemy purple robes, jewels, a
diadem, and many servants and horses, so that he might go to Rome
"like an Alexandrian Greek monarch" and not like a beggar. It is the
spirit of this thought and gesture that counts, not the fact that
Ptolemy refused the presents and chose to beg. King Demetrius of
Macedonia showed something of the same spirit when, having lost
his throne, he took off his golden robes and purple shoes, dressed
simply, and left.

> Doing like an actor
> who when the performance is over,
> changes his clothes and departs.[22]

Plutarch, whom Cavafy is quoting in an epigraph to the poem, found
the action beneath a king. Cavafy, a child of the age in which
Demetrius had lived, knew better—he knew the kind of courage it
required.

In discussing the aspects under which maturity is reflected in a
poet's work, we have examined so far a sense of history, maturity of
mind, and maturity of manners, and we have seen how these criteria
apply to Cavafy's poetry. The fourth aspect under which maturity is
exhibited is maturity of language. We have already discussed
Cavafy's innovations and contributions to the Greek language. We
have seen how he has been able to use creatively a language old and
seemingly exhausted—purist Greek—though uniting it to the present by the most powerful coalescence of two idioms, asserting the
essential continuity of the Greek language from the past to the
present just as he asserted the continuity of life and experience.
Ancient and purist Greek were not dead languages for Cavafy, no
more than Alexandria and Antioch and Byzantium were a dead
experience.

Maturity of language cannot exist except as a vehicle for the
expression of the mature mind. It was in order to attain the precision
necessary for the expression of a more complex reality and the
subtler feelings that it involved that Cavafy resorted to the synthetic
powers of purist Greek. Demotic Greek had not yet developed those

terms of abstract thought and of a more sophisticated set of emotions—terms indispensable to the intellectual trend of Cavafy's nature—nor a more complex sentence and period structure, all of which are characteristics of a mature language. A single poet, however great, cannot create a mature language overnight; it takes the gradual enrichment of thought and emotion that marks the growth of a people and a culture—which gradually finds its expression in language—to accomplish the task and prepare the ground for the poet who will absorb the achievements of his predecessors and give them forth together with his own contribution as the perfect expression of the full potentialities of the language at that time. No poet writing in an immature language—and no poet unless in his full maturity of thought and art too—could have written the stanzas:

> And from the wondrous panhellenic expedition,
> the victorious, the all-illustrious,
> the all-celebrated, the glorious
> as none has been glorious before,
> the incomparable: we emerged;
> a Greek world new, great.

> We, the Alexandrians, the Antiochians,
> the Seleucians, and the numerous
> other Greeks of Egypt and of Syria,
> and those in Media and those in Persia, and all the rest.
> With the extensive dominations,
> with the various action of reflective adaptations.
> And the Common Greek Language
> as far as the heart of Bactria we brought, as far as the
> Indians.[23]

Here the line, "with the various action of reflective adaptations," seems to sum up and contain all his other work, all the problems of the Hellenistic world with its racial, religious, and cultural conflicts that the burden of continuing the heritage of the Greek civilization in Asia and Africa involved, especially in view of the added complications that the two tremendous new powers of Rome and Christianity presented. It was through "the various action of reflective adaptations" that the small Greek group managed to absorb all forces and counterforces without losing its essential identity. The "various action" of adaptations of thought, of feeling—Julian, and Myres, and that Christian convert mourning his dead pagan father, who was priest in the Serapium, and all those other confused and torn figures of the Greco-Roman world can be seen in their inner struggle of compromises, of reconciliations, of adaptations in a complex world of conflicting ideals and values. And one is led to think of the "various action of reflective adaptations" of our time.

It took maturity of mind and the genius of Cavafy to reach a line of such tremendous force and comprehensiveness. But it certainly did take also that maturity of language that we can get only through tradition. Cavafy had behind him one of the richest traditions a poet could hope for. Perhaps its very richness would have intimidated a lesser poet in the use of a language which seemed to have realized all its potentialities, run its full course, and finally reached a dead end. Yet Cavafy succeeded in attaining a perfect balance between individuality and uniqueness on the one hand and tradition on the other. He comes as the last and one of the best poets of a great period of the Greek language, yet as an innovator too, uniting the past with the present and opening the road for the future poetic generations of Greece to a more mature and fruitful exploitation of all the resources of one of the richest languages in the world.

The first criterion in calling a poet "European" has been maturity, and we have discussed the four aspects under which it is revealed in a poet. The second criterion will be *comprehensiveness*. When I call a poet comprehensive, I mean that he does not restrict himself to one aspect of man's nature or to one phase of his life; to be comprehensive a body of art need contain, within the limits of its dominant theme or themes, a variety of human interests and emotions, and cover a wide range of sensibility. Cavafy's myth of the aesthetic city of Alexandria has misled some critics into placing too much emphasis on the theme of corruption and decadence and sensual pleasure in Cavafy to the exclusion of some of the most important aspects of his world—aspects which transcend the narrow limits of the sensibility of the "aesthete" and make his world significant in a larger sense. Although influenced, especially in his earlier years, by the aesthetic movement of the late nineteenth century in France and in England, Cavafy's aestheticism has a distinct quality of its own. It has neither the morbidity of Baudelaire, nor the dilettantism of Wilde. If there is a similarity, it is with Pater, because in both Cavafy and Pater the idealization of beauty has something of the classical spirit in it. In refuting the view of a critic of Cavafy, I used above the expression "lyrical feeling of the perfection of beauty." What I meant was that in the corruption and weakness and degrada tion of Cavafy's world, beauty retains an undefiled purity which

somehow atones for all the ugliness which surrounds it. What remains from the weakness, and the greed, and the miserable failure
of the life of Orophernes is a tetradrachm on which he has left

> a charm of his lovely youth,
> of his poetic beauty a light,
> an aesthetic memory of an Ionian boy. . . .[24]

Despite all her vices, I think that Cavafy's Alexandria has something
of the same quality that Cavafy ascribes to the youth of the following poem:

> It was this in him that was distinctive,
> that in all his dissoluteness
> and his great experience in love,
> despite the usual
> harmonious accord of attitude and age in him,
> there happened to be moments—of course
> very rare ones—when he gave the impression
> of a flesh almost untouched.
> The beauty of his twenty-nine years
> so tested by pleasure,
> at moments strangely recalled
> a youth who—somewhat clumsily—to love
> for the first time his pure body surrenders.[25]

Throughout Cavafy's work we can sense those ambivalent feelings
that the speaker of his poems has towards the Alexandrian world—
admiration for the perfection of its beauty, pride and exultation in
its daring, deep nostalgia for its sensual pleasure, enjoyment of its
wit, its elegance, and its artistic skills, pity for its degradation and
weakness, irony towards its petty vanities and lack of ideals and
political corruption—and above all we can feel the sense of identification with it, of belonging to it, yet of being able to view it with
artistic detachment.

It is because of his comprehensiveness that Cavafy is able to give
this variety of tone and evoke this multiplicity of emotions. For
Cavafy's world is not simple or one-dimensional; it is rich and
manifold, and it encompasses a whole panorama of humanity.
Within the narrow limits of one hundred fifty-four short poems,
Cavafy succeeded in giving to us the picture not only of the decadence of a European civilization, but also its religious problems, its
politics, its philosophy and art, its aspirations and failures, the tragic
doom of its existence. His poems span a period of more than two
thousand years, from Homeric times to the present; yet while each

poem is historically true and representative of the spirit of its time
and place, Cavafy's world has a rare unity of tone and spirit. While
each historical period is distinctly delineated, and the characters in
it, whether actual or fictitious, are alive not only as individuals but
also as representatives of their races, cultures, social levels, and
times; while the problems they confront are as diverse as life itself
and as various as the people who face them; and while the people
themselves range from artists and clerks and perfume sellers to
politicians and Emperors and gods, we have the feeling that they all
belong to the same world, and that in a strange way they breathe the
same air and share the same destiny. In its variety, then, Cavafy's
work is unified—each poem not only contributing to the understanding and enjoyment of the rest, but modifying and enriching
them, adding new dimensions and depth to every word. Most of the
poems are deceptively simple, small vignettes related in a dry,
matter-of-fact voice. But the more times you read them, the more
audible that voice becomes, haunting you with the faces of youths of
exquisite beauty and the subdued voices coming from the epitaphs
and the eyes of Byzantine queens and the old men forgotten in
lonely houses and the white flowers on the graves of dead lovers—
haunting you until you too seem to be walking the streets of the
city:

> New lands you shall not find, nor shall you find another sea.
> The city shall be following you. The streets you will be roaming
> the same. And in the same neighborhoods you will be growing old;
> and in these same houses you will be growing white.
> You shall always be reaching this city. As for another—abandon
>     hope—
> there is no ship for you, there is no road.[26]

This point leads us to our next criterion in calling a poet "European," and that is *universality*. When we read lines like the ones
quoted above, our appreciation and enjoyment of them do not
depend on whether they are written by a Greek or an Englishman or
a Frenchman: besides their significance to the people of the poet's
own country and language, their relevance is universal. Not that a
poet should renounce his national characteristics and become an
abstract "European"; "to be human is to belong to a particular
region of the earth, and men of such genius are more conscious than
other human beings. The European who belonged to no one country
would be an abstract man—a blank face speaking every language

with neither a native nor a foreign accent." [27] But to be "European" a poet should be free of provinciality of thought and temperament; he should have that sensibility which, while being part of the particular sensibility of his country, would also be representative of that wider sensibility and culture which we have termed "European." And of this sensibility Cavafy is representative in the same way that Eliot himself is: his poetry reflects the emotions, the spiritual agony, not only of his own place but of the whole world his place is part of. By being most local, Cavafy has given us a myth not of Greece, but of the whole Western world—an Alexandria which is personal yet universal, temporal yet timeless.


## II


Since the first translations into English of isolated poems, Cavafy has had an increasingly wide audience, which includes E. M. Forster, C. M. Bowra, Robert Lidell, Kimon Friar, Philip Sherrard, and other distinguished writers and critics. "Ever since I was first introduced to his poetry by the late Professor R. M. Dawkins over thirty years ago," says W. H. Auden, "C. P. Cavafy has remained an influence on my own writing; that is to say, I can think of poems which, if Cavafy were unknown to me, I should have written quite differently or perhaps not written at all. Yet I do not know a word of Modern Greek, so that my only access to Cavafy's poetry has been through English and French translations." [28] I do not know if I am right in finding in the turn of the sentence in Auden's "Musée des Beaux Arts," and especially in the opening lines, something which reminds me of Cavafy's use of language and situation. In a poetic work so very unlike his own, whatever influence Cavafy had on Auden is bound to be fully assimilated and not easily detectible. However, the testimony of a poet of Auden's caliber proves that Cavafy can not only be read and enjoyed outside Greece, but also exert an influence on non-Greek writers. The latest example of Cavafy's influence on a non-Greek work of literature can be seen in the fiction of Lawrence Durrell. Although assimilated not in a work of poetry but in a novel—which might be one of the reasons why the assimilation has been more perfect and fruitful—Cavafy is a great shaping force behind Durrell's The Alexandria Quartet.

Alexandria is the setting of a good number of Cavafy's poems and of the series of the four novels which constitute *The Alexandria Quartet*. In both cases Alexandria is a mythical city, hovering "between illusion and reality, between the substance and the poetic images" which its name arouses.[29] This mythical city is the main symbol of both Cavafy's and Durrell's worlds, the symbol of the inescapable human predicament.

Although Durrell's Alexandria is not a replica or imitation of Cavafy's capital of the Hellenistic world, it could not have existed without it. What Durrell developed from Cavafy is the basic idea of Alexandria—the "evocative outlines" of his Big City Poem, the outlines of a city which stands for and contains all the big cities of the world.[30] In Durrell's twentieth-century Alexandria, we find Cavafy's Hellenistic Alexandria with its glitter and luxury and materialism, with its sensuality and its explorations of the byways of sexual passion; here is again the combination of races, religions and philosophies in "the only city left where every extreme of race and habit can meet and marry, where inner destinies intersect," [31] and whose child is Justine—"neither Greek, Syrian nor Egyptian, but a hybrid: a joint." [32] Durrell's characters are given to the exploration and enjoyment of sexual relationship—whatever its nature—naturally, without self-consciousness and without shame, just as that youth in Cavafy's poem had given himself to sensual gratification, "without any ridiculous shame for the kind of pleasure. . . ." [33] Love in Cavafy is obsessive and corrosive; so is love in Durrell. Cavafy's sovereigns of the Hellenistic kingdoms are thirsty for power; so are Justine and Nessim. And above the whole scene reigns the sense of doom, the "deracination and failure"—the inescapable destiny that the city imposes on its inhabitants.[34] For Durrell, as for Cavafy, Alexandria is not a mere setting for the action of the human will, but the true creator and protagonist of the drama of its world, a living organism with a will of its own, a will "too powerful and too deliberate to be human—the gravitational field which Alexandria threw down about those it had chosen as its exemplars. . . ." [35]

"Capitally, what is this city of ours? What is resumed in the word Alexandria?" the narrator asks in the first page of *Justine*.[36] The idea of the city is explored all through the four books that form *The Alexandria Quartet*. It is the city that should be judged although her inhabitants—her children—must pay the price, says the speaker in *Justine*, reminding us of Cavafy in "Tomb of Iases." Nessim asks whether the disorder of their lives is not "a measure of the anxiety which they had inherited from the city or the age." [37] Finally, the idea is summed up in *Clea:*

> It is not hard, writing at this remove in time, to realise that it had all *already happened,* had been ordained in such a way and in no other. This was, so to speak, only its "coming to pass"—its stage of manifestation. But the scenario had already been devised somewhere, the actors chosen, the time rehearsed down to the last detail in the mind of that invisible author —which perhaps would prove to be only the city itself: the Alexandria of the human estate. The seeds of future events are carried within ourselves. They are implicit in us and unfold according to the laws of their own nature.[38]

All the citizens of Alexandria, at some point of their lives, feel the urge to leave the city and escape the bondage of their destiny. "I will go to another land, I will go to another sea," said the speaker in Cavafy's "The City." [39] The same despair makes Darley accept a new post in Upper Egypt and makes Nessim tell Justine that they should "seek an atmosphere less impregnated with the sense of deracination and failure." [40] But there is no escaping from one's own self; into Nessim's mind came Cavafy's answer, "pressed down like the pedal of a piano, to boil and reverberate around the frail hope which the thought had raised from its dark sleep." [41]

> New lands you shall not find, nor shall you find another
> sea. The city shall be following you.[42]

Finally, the children of Alexandria realize that there is no choice for them, that the city begins and ends in themselves, and that their qualities and values are determined by the city, of which they themselves are an integral part. They finally see "their history and the city's as one and the same phenomenon," [43] and although their feeling toward her is ambivalent—a sense of bond with the place of one's most painful experiences despite the hate for the pain it inflicts—at last they surpass "despairing self-pity" and they attain the "desire to be claimed by the city, enrolled among its trivial or tragic memories—if it so wished." [44] This is the final assertion of identification with the city—an assertion of belonging which so often comes out in references to Alexandria as "our city" and to Alexandrians as "we." It is this feeling of supreme identity that is expressed in the last stanza of that Cavafy poem in which an Alexandrian is asking a poet called Raphael for an epitaph for the young poet Ammones.

> Raphael, your verses let them be written so
> that they have, you know, of our life in them,

that both the rhythm and each sentence may tell
that of an Alexandrian an Alexandrian is writing.[45]

The same unmistakable pride that we detect in the last line of the
stanza—the pride of recognition of the separate identity of Alexandrians and of the unparalleled quality of their life—can be found
throughout *The Alexandria Quartet,* from the first question, "What
is this city of ours?" to the strong assertion in *Balthazar:* "I see all of
us not as men and women any longer, identities swollen with their
acts of forgetfulness, follies, and deceits—but as beings uncon-
sciously made part of place, buried to the waist among the ruins of a
single city, steeped in its values. . . . All members of a city whose
actions lay just outside the scope of the plotting or conniving spirit:
Alexandrians." [46]

In Durrell, as in Cavafy, man is seen as "an extension of the spirit
of the place," as a "responsive subject" through which the city
expresses "the collective desires, the collective wishes, which in-
formed its culture." [47] And since the spirit of the city is unified and
eternal, man is not seen from the perspective of historical time, but
from a timeless point of view; the past is not really past, and the
dead are not really dead, and reality becomes like Nessim's historical dreams, in which his friends and acquaintances walked among
the ruins of classical Alexandria, existing in an "amazing historical
space-time as living personages." [48] The living are at ease among the
dead, like Darley and Clea peacefully swimming among the familiar
and friendly figures of the dead sailors standing upright under the
waters of the bay as "appropriate symbols of the place." [49] It was in
that same place that Clea thought she had discovered the very islet
to which Antony was said to have retreated after his defeat in
Actium. The music Antony hears in Cavafy's poem bidding him say
farewell to Alexandria becomes a dominant theme throughout the
book, returning in the song of a whore at night, merging with the
wild music of the festival of *Sitna Mariam,* or serving as an
Eliotesque ironic parallel to another recurrent musical motif in the
novel, the popular hit of the time in Alexandria, "Jamais de la vie," to
which Melissa dances clumsily at the cabaret and to which her
dying middle-aged former lover listens in his death-bed as his last
music bidding him to say farewell to life.

But foremost among the dead in Durrell's Alexandria is Cavafy
himself, the poet of the city—close enough in time to be Balthazar's
friend and to frequent the small cafes of the city with him, yet

already a legend, one of Alexandria's great "exemplars" in whom the spirit of the city has found its most powerful expression. His poems are quoted throughout the four books of *The Alexandria Quartet*, paralleling the action of the characters and investing the most casual gestures and words with a deeper emotional significance and symbolic meaning. For the reader who has been moved by Cavafy, there is a strong evocative feeling in the part where Justine recites Cavafy's verses—"touching every syllable of the thoughtful ironic Greek with tenderness"; when she reaches the place where the poet —presuming the first person in the poem stands for the poet's own voice—goes sadly to the balcony to find relief by looking at the beloved city, she herself repeats the old motion and pushes back the shutters and stands on the dark balcony above the lighted city.[50]

In *Justine,* Darley gives a lecture on Cavafy. "But it was painful to me," he says to himself, "feeling the old man all around me, so to speak, impregnating the gloomy streets around the lecture-room with the odour of those verses distilled from the shabby but rewarding loves he had experienced—loves perhaps bought with money, and lasting a few moments, yet living on now in his verse—so deliberately and tenderly had he captured the adventive minute and made all its colours fast. What an impertinence to lecture upon an ironist who so naturally, and with such finesse of instinct took his subject-matter from the streets and brothels of Alexandria! . . . I remember saying only that I was haunted by his face—the horrifyingly sad gentle face of the last photograph." [51] Not only the poems, but the personality of the old poet himself echoes in the memory and consciousness of Durrell's Alexandria. He lives in the words of his fellow-student and close friend Balthazar—"I sometimes think I learned more from studying him than from studying philosophy. His exquisite balance of irony and tenderness would have put him among the saints had he been a religious man"; his verses return in old recordings, in Pursewarden's reciting "The City" in a bar, or in Darley's trying to recapture a lost afternoon with Melissa.

Durrell, like Cavafy, is haunted by the past. Through Darley in *Justine* he says that he is "a poet of the historic consciousness." [52] All four parts of *The Alexandria Quartet* are permeated and obsessed with the idea of Alexandria and the destiny it represents and imposes. No character, no action, is seen as an independent and separate phenomenon. Everything is part of the life of the city in her timeless existence, which encompasses the past, the present, and the future. The dead dominate the scene, impregnating life with the sense that everything has been experienced ". . . the dead are everywhere. They cannot be so simply evaded. One feels them pressing their sad blind fingers in deprivation upon the panels of our secret lives, asking to be remembered and re-enacted once more in the life of the flesh. . . . The simplest of these kisses we exchanged had a pedigree of death. In them we once more befriended forgotten loves which struggled to be reborn." [53]

Although the similarities between Cavafy's and Durrell's Alexandrias are significant, their differences should not be overlooked. The means the authors employ in the creation of their respective mythical cities, as well as the final effects they achieve, are widely different. Some of those differences are due to the use of different genres, but most are not.

Their use of language is diametrically opposed. Durrell uses rich and luxurious and colorful words with a profligacy which we would expect to find in poetry rather than in prose, especially after a steady diet of Hemingway; Cavafy, on the other hand, employs a medium of almost Doric simplicity and restraint which we would ordinarily call prosaic.

Within the wide range of material and the expansive possibilities that his medium offers, Durrell has created a world which is both rich and alive. Yet, as George Steiner noticed, *The Alexandria Quartet* leaves one "with a suspicion of triviality" and the sense that "at the center of this magnificently wrought fable of life" there is "a certain undeniable hollowness." [54] Steiner attributes this mainly to the privateness of Durrell's vision. Although Durrell's characters exhibit a wide range of sensibility, they are keyed to a higher pitch of awareness than the ordinary man. Their vision is introverted and esoteric, and despite the close and multiple view of them that the reader gets through the complex technique of narration and of space-time relationship that Durrell has devised, they remain distant and strange. There is no sense of identification and sympathy between Durrell's characters and the reader. Although highly interesting, Durrell's Alexandria is a foreign and exotic city whose citizens we shall never become. There is an hysteric brittleness in her love and a harshness in her beauty which we do not recognize as ours. Her wars, her politics, are not real; they do not concern us, they do not touch us, they are not our own. Although undeniably alive, Durrell's world has not achieved the timeless relevance and finality which is the mark of the great work of art. We are allowed to gain a view of the multiplied reflections of Alexandria in a complicated system of mirrors; but when we try to come closer to them—Justine, Nessim, Mountolive, Pursewarden, Darley, Melissa, and all the other fascinating figures of Durrell's world—they retreat further and further from us, and their voices which we had heard so many times now become inaudible and confused and indistinguishable, and their features we thought were so familiar to us become dim and distant. And in their place, the figures of another Alexandria approach and merge with us; although we have seldom heard them talk, their voices sound familiar in our ears, and although we have never seen them or had them described in detail to us, we recognize them at once. Myres, Ignatius, Cleon, Leukius, Demetrius Soter—the timeless figures of ourselves return among us more real than ever. They whisper to our ears their grievances and their failures and their wars and loves and disappointments, and as we listen to the tale of our lives, suddenly there is a universal pattern and order brought on the world, and we are able to feel the supreme catharsis that true art can achieve.

*WALTER BORENSTEIN*

# THE FAILURE OF NERVE
## The Impact of Pío Baroja's Spain on John Dos Passos

THE INFLUENCE OF Spain on the American writers of the "lost generation" is perhaps one of the most extraordinary examples of a literary
assumption that has been accepted almost without qualification and
without any truly perceptive analysis of the hypothesis.[1] The mention of Hispanic influence has been excessively vague and general,
and we may attribute this to the obvious lack of familiarity of many
critics of American letters with the precise character of the literature
of Spain during the past half-century. The presence of Spain in
Hemingway's *The Sun Also Rises* or *For Whom the Bell Tolls*, in
Dos Passos' *Rosinante to the Road Again* or *Adventures of a Young
Man,* and in Waldo Frank's *Virgin Spain* is only too apparent. The
more subtle and penetrating influences, however, have never really
been studied and have only been intimated by the American critic
Alfred Kazin[2] and the Hispanic scholar John T. Reid.[3] A further
example of this unquestioning acceptance—almost as if by faith—of
apparent Hispanic influence can be found in Ernest Hemingway's
confession of his great literary debt to the aging Pío Baroja in
October, 1956, when he called himself a disciple of Don Pío. Hemingway added: "Allow me to pay this small tribute to you who
taught so much to those of us who wanted to be writers when we
were so young. I deplore the fact that you have not yet received a
Nobel Prize, especially when it was given to so many who deserved
it less, like me, who am only an adventurer."[4] The Spanish political
philosopher Salvador de Madariaga likewise demonstrates this subjective evaluation of Hispanic dominance when he says that Hem-

ingway's two Spanish novels "blossomed out of this implantation of
the roots of that powerful American tree into Iberian soil."[5] The
current conviction that Hemingway's preoccupation with the concept of *nada* can be traced to the ideas of Baroja's contemporary
Miguel de Unamuno lends further evidence for the argument that
the question of Spanish influence has been treated in a perfunctory,
uncritical fashion and that further investigation of specific influence
may lead to serious doubts as to the validity of the theory.[6]

In an attempt to demonstrate a more obvious and apparent contribution of a Spanish writer to the formative literary years of one of
the Americans of the "lost generation," I have chosen the early Dos
Passos and the impact of Baroja's Spain on his philosophical concepts as related to his creative efforts in the novel. Not only is it far
simpler to establish these influences which have been discussed at
length by Dos Passos, but the tracing of these relationships may offer
new insights to those who have speculated about Baroja's influence
on Hemingway and have failed to observe the more apparent impact on Dos Passos. It is interesting to note that Dos Passos' novel of
1925, *Manhattan Transfer*, represents a mid-point in a circle that
began with Baroja and the members of his generation in Spain[7] and
was closed in 1951 with the publication of *La colmena* by Camilo
José Cela, one of Spain's leading contemporary novelists.[8] Cela drew
from Dos Passos certain novelistic concepts that the American author had originally found in Spain. Torrente Ballester in his recent
history of contemporary literature writes: "Es *La colmena* como un
gran friso en que las amontonadas figuras se repitiesen periódi-
camente en actitudes distintas. No hay entre ellas jerarquía. No
existe, por tanto, composición arquitectónica, sino *montaje*, ex-
actamente el mismo usado por John Dos Passos en *Manhattan
Transfer*."[9] It is the contemporary critic's comparative unawareness
of the work of either Baroja or Cela that may be responsible for the
vagueness of the references made to the Spanish experience of
certain American writers. These complex relationships offer the
modern critic a vast reservoir of material and a possible explanation
for many of the influences which have been casually accepted
without analysis or contradiction for so many years. Such names as
Benito Pérez Galdós, Juan Valera, Angel Ganivet, Ramón Pérez de
Ayala and Azorín might take their places along with the more
popular and often less meaningful figures as Federico García.Lorca,
José Ortega y Gasset and Miguel de Unamuno, and America would

not have to wait for Juan Ramón Jiménez to win the Nobel Prize for Literature before he might be recognized as one of the most important poets of the twentieth century.

Dos Passos first makes reference to "the failure of nerve" when he speaks of Gilbert Murray's use of the concept in one of his essays.[10] Murray writes:

> Any one who turns from the great writers of classical Athens, say Sophocles or Aristotle, to those of the Christian era must be conscious of a great difference in tone. There is a change in the whole relation of the writer to the world about him. The new quality is not specifically Christian: it is just as marked in the Gnostics and Mithras-worshippers as in the Gospels and the Apocalypse, in Julian and Plotinus as in Gregory and Jerome. It is hard to describe. It is a rise of asceticism, of mysticism, in a sense, of pessimism; a loss of self-confidence, of hope in this life and of faith in normal human effort; a despair of patient inquiry, a cry for infallible revelation; an indifference to the welfare of the state, a conversion of the soul to God. It is an atmosphere in which the aim of the good man is not so much to live justly, to help the society to which he belongs and enjoy the esteem of his fellow creatures; but rather, by means of a burning faith, by contempt for the world and its standards, by ecstasy, suffering and martyrdom, to be granted pardon for his unspeakable unworthiness, his immeasurable sins. There is an intensifying of certain spiritual emotions; an increase of sensitiveness, a failure of nerve.[11]

Murray goes on to point out that there are two roads that man can follow, the direction of the good citizen who lives in the world or the road of the ecstatic vision of the saint who rejects the world. He finds that "most Christians are inclined to believe that without some failure and sense of failure, without a contrite heart and conviction of sin, man can hardly attain the religious life." [12] Murray, like Dos Passos or Baroja, deplores this failure of nerve and the religious attitudes that rise from the belief in revelation. His final words of caution are very reminiscent of Baroja's ultimate hopes for man and reveal the dichotomy which brought about the essential contradiction in the works of both novelists. Murray concludes:

> The Uncharted surrounds us on every side and we must needs have some relation towards it, a relation which will depend on the general discipline of a man's mind and the bias of his whole character. As far as knowledge and conscious reason will go, we should follow resolutely their austere guidance. When they cease, as cease they must, we must use as best we can those fainter powers of apprehension and surmise and sensitiveness by which, after all, most high truth has been reached as well as most high art and poetry: careful always not to neglect the real needs of

men and women through basing our life on dreams; and remembering
above all to walk gently in a world where the lights are dim and the very
stars wander.[13]

This concept of "the failure of nerve" has taken many forms and is
the essential aspect of a great part of Western literature. George
Steiner, in his comprehensive analysis of world drama in *The Death
of Tragedy* concludes that the "metaphysics of Christianity and
Marxism are anti-tragic. That, in essence, is the dilemma of modern
tragedy." [14] The Christian hope for the salvation of man can be
equated with the Marxist ideal of the inevitable perfectibility of
man. Steiner feels that modern man is incapable of a truly tragic
concept. Both Dos Passos and Baroja come to the same conclusions
as Gilbert Murray when they use their novel as a kind of stage of life
into which they place the heroes they have fashioned of the clay of
their pessimistic philosophy. Dos Passos' heroes fail to resolve the
dichotomy which their creator had himself been unable to reconcile,
and these same American heroes are kinsmen of the broken heroes of
Baroja's Spain, the *héroes fracasados* of all his novels. Baroja, as a
member of the pessimistic "Generation of '98," lived at a time when
the disenchantment with the possibilities of reason was bringing
about a new philosophy in Spain replete with contradiction and
despair. Even Baroja, trained as a physician and imbued with the
objectivity of positivism and rationalism, was doomed to fall into the
inevitable pit of futility as a result of the struggle within him
between the power of science and his acceptance of the Darwinian
"struggle for life" on the one hand, and on the other, the humane and
antirational sensitivity that denied what he did not wish to be so.

Dos Passos, in an article concerning his Spanish experience, wrote
in 1920 of this same theme and its relationship to the Spanish
antiheroes of the picaresque novels:

These loafers and wanderers of Baroja's, like his artists and grotesque
dreamers and fanatics, are all the descendants of the people in the *Quijote*
and the *Novelas ejemplares* (of Cervantes), of the rogues and bandits of
the *Lazarillo de Tormes*, who with Gil Blas invaded France and England,
where they rollicked through the novel until Mrs. Grundy and George
Eliot packed them off to their reform school. But the rogues of the seventeenth century were jolly rogues. They always had their tongues in their
cheeks, and success always rewarded their ingenious audacities. Perhaps
the moulds of society had not yet hardened as they have now, or there
was less pressure of hungry generations. Or more probably, pity had not
come in to undermine the foundations.[15]

It is precisely this feeling of compassion—of pity—that underlies the whole of Dos Passos' concept and which tends to explain his idea of "the failure of nerve." We can readily see the strong influence of his Spanish experience and his reading of the novels of Pío Baroja on the formation of this attitude, which was already nascent in the young and impressionable Dos Passos. He continues on the same theme:

> The corrosive of pity, which had attacked the steel girders of our civilization even before the work of building was completed, has brought about what Gilbert Murray, in speaking of Greek thought, calls the failure of nerve. In the seventeenth century, men still had the courage of their egoism. The world was a bad job to be made the best of, all hope lay in driving a good bargain with the conductors of life everlasting. By the end of the nineteenth century, the life everlasting had grown cobwebby. The French Revolution had filled men up with extravagant hopes of the perfectibility of this world, humanitarianism had instilled an abnormal sensitiveness to pain, to one's own pain, and to the pain of one's neighbors. Baroja's outcasts are no longer jolly knaves who'll murder a man for a nickel and go on their road singing 'Over the Hills and Far Away'; they are men who have not had the willpower to continue in the fight for bread, they are men whose nerve has failed, who live furtively on the outskirts, snatching a little joy here and there, drugging their hunger with gorgeous images.[16]

John H. Wrenn, in what is one of the few comprehensive studies of the work of Dos Passos, points out the absence of any truly critical analysis of the work of one of America's major contemporary authors.[17] The stereotyped nature of much of the criticism of Dos Passos both as an artist and as a man has obscured the true picture of both, and Wrenn's work is a major contribution to the attempt to find some objective substance within all the vague and subjective commentary. The shock of Dos Passos' apparent political conversion to extreme right-wing conservatism has only added to the confusion. Thus the alienation of the "liberal" critics has been as much a deterrent to objectivity as has the literary ignorance of many of the more "conservative" commentators. Mr. Dos Passos, modern-day Goldwater Republican, who once served as a "contributing editor" to the *Daily Worker* according to an advertisement in the *New Masses* by the *Daily Worker,* has become an enigma that has baffled those who felt that they clearly understood the man through his work.[18] It is my hope that an analysis of some of the complex forces which contributed to his early concepts may throw some light on this extraordinary change.

Wrenn, in his exhaustive study, first tries to destroy the stereotype of Dos Passos by extricating him both from the "lost generation" of Gertrude Stein and the "exiles" of Malcolm Cowley.[19] He does this by listing some of the essential characteristics of Dos Passos' strangely integrated career: "the artistic bent, an interest in both Spain and America, a sense of responsibility, the loss of a father, and the desire to participate in events of his time." [20] He then adds:

> Some of these elements were common to others of his generation whose careers Malcolm Cowley chronicled in *Exile's Return;* but Dos Passos lacked the one essential element of Cowley's thesis—the process of "deracination," of being uprooted from his natural environment and set adrift as an "exile." And the fact that he was never an exile in any true sense of the word has been one of the controlling factors of his career. For Dos Passos was born unrooted to any plot of ground; and his life has been dedicated, therefore, to a search for congenial soil and climate— for "new ground on which to stand" or in which to grow.[21]

From 1912—when Dos Passos entered Harvard at the age of sixteen—until 1916—when he graduated *cum laude* and decided to find a field of action for himself as an ambulance driver in France [22] and thereby participate in the events of his time—he belonged to that small group of esthetes and intellectuals referred to as "a lost generation" by Gertrude Stein, as "exiles" by Malcolm Cowley, as "a queer bunch of . . . self indulgent brats" by Westbrook Pegler, as a "cult of disillusion" by another recent critic.[23] This early spirit of rebellion was to bring him to Spain in 1916 as a compromise with his desire to go to France, and this same spirit had been a part of the development of his formative years. In "The Camera Eye Twenty-five" in *U.S.A.,* the author recounts a part of his recollection of his Harvard days:

> . . . haven't got the nerve to break out of the
> bellglass four years under the ethercone breathe
> deep gently now that's the way be a good boy one
> two three four five six get A's in some courses
> but don't be a grind be interested in literature
> but remain a gentleman don't be seen with Jews
> or socialists
> . . . sit looking out into the twilight of the
> pleasantest four years of your life
>    grow cold with culture like a cup of tea
> forgotten between an incenseburner and a volume
> of Oscar Wilde
> . . . four years I didn't know you could do what

you Michaelangelo wanted to say
            Marx
                to all
the professors with a small Swift break all the
Greenoughs in the shooting gallery
. . . . and I hadn't the nerve
            to jump up and walk out of doors and tell
them all to go take a flying
                Rimbaud
                at the moon.[24]

John Dos Passos, born the illegitimate son of a wealthy lawyer and
an aristocratic Southern gentlewoman,[25] near-sighted from birth,
carted around as a child in Mexico, England, and the Continent,
constantly with governesses and friends of his family, longing for the
influence of a home and a family, without security of any kind,
without even a legitimate name until he was sixteen,[26] shy and
self-conscious, highly sensitive to human relationships, and ready to
respond intuitively and empathically to those with whom he had
any community of thought or feeling, wanted to escape from the
rootless existence of his childhood. He wanted desperately to belong, to find something in which he could believe. His trip to Spain
in October of 1916 was to open his eyes to a possible alternative and
to introduce him to a Spanish writer with whose ideas and personality he could find a community of thought and feeling. This was to
be the sensitive, lonely, and wandering figure of the Basque novelist
Pío Baroja.

How much the young Dos Passos had already been influenced by
the Spanish writers of his time, in the original or in French and
English translation, is a question that may be difficult to answer but
simple to surmise. Perhaps the most influential work of Baroja for
Dos Passos was the trilogy *La lucha por la vida,* published originally
in Spain in 1904 and translated into English by Isaac Goldberg and
published by Alfred Knopf in 1922, 1923, and 1924. The earliest
English translation of Baroja was made in 1919 by Jacob S. Fasset,
Jr., of the novel *La ciudad de los discretos.* The Spanish contemporaries of Baroja were probably unknown in the United States until
after the First World War. Although Maxwell Geismar seems to feel
that "it was from . . . Pío Baroja that Dos Passos gained his early
intellectual concepts," [27] a more recent critic, Charles W. Bernardin,
in an article on Dos Passos' Harvard years, does not mention Baroja
when he refers to the young author's reading interests.[28] Wrenn

seems to disagree with Geismar's implication and points out that "Baroja was more nearly a corroboration and an example than a source." [29] Dos Passos, with ideas so parallel to those of Baroja already vaguely forming in his mind, found himself in Spain in 1916 as a compromise with his father who did not wish his son to lose his life too soon. The esthetic purpose that was to bring him to Seville to study architecture eventually led him to the reinforcement of his social concepts in the rich medium in which he was to find himself and also led him to grow more freely than in the stifling milieu he had abandoned.

If Dos Passos was to find the corroboration of his concepts in Baroja's Spain, he was also to strengthen the dichotomy that had been growing within him and which was to bring about the same desperation and pessimism it had earlier brought to Baroja. By 1916, Dos Passos had already begun to realize the potentially nefarious effects of the industrialization of America. He had asked: "Are we not like men crouching on a runaway engine? And at the same time we insensately shovel in the fuel with no thought as to where we are being taken." [30] The split that Granville Hicks had noted in his analysis of the early Dos Passos was to dominate his literary and intellectual horizon for many years to come, and may account for the apparent change in his political ideology during recent years. [31] In this early period there were two solutions for his loathing of our modern way of life. He could take refuge in some escape from unpleasant realities, or he could face the industrial mess and assist in working out some radical change through participation in those organizations which were endeavoring to alter the structure of society. The fact that he was eventually to choose the latter course of action is ample proof of Wrenn's theory of his eternal quest for roots and his rejection of the solution of exile from a limbo to which he had never really belonged. This desire to belong, this wish to participate in the struggle, was far more strong in Dos Passos than it was in Baroja. It was this that was to lead Dos Passos in the opposite direction, away from that of the lonely Basque who preferred to accept a self-imposed exile at the fringe of action, to find the novel as his own theatre of action. The Spanish critic César Barja has aptly described this use of the novel by the members of the Generation of '98:

. . . si Baroja fuese el hombre de voluntad y de acción, el héroe que a cada paso estamos a punto de encontrar en sus novelas, posible es que no hubiera escrito ninguna de las cincuenta y tantas que hasta la fecha lleva publicado. . . . en vez de escribir Baroja, de escribir algo, la novela vivida, tenga que contentarse con vivir la novela escrita. Y esto porque lo que Baroja es ante todo y sobre todo, es hombre de pensamiento, no de acción. Su acción, a falta de impulsos más eficaces, ha debido agotarse en escribir novelas y más novelas.[32]

The struggle within Dos Passos was not to be resolved, even for the moment, for many years. In *One Man's Initiation* in 1917, he had sought refuge from a world gone mad when he asked "if there were somewhere nowadays where you could flee from all this stupidity, from all this cant of governments, and this hideous reiteration of a hatred, this strangling hatred." [33] And yet, his endless desire to belong to something, to participate in the world of conflict, his desire to understand and, if possible, to change the system that made the horror possible, was eventually to triumph. It was in Spain, Hicks adds, that "the two desires lived, side by side, during his travels in Spain, as recorded in *Rosinante to the Road Again,* and in the East, as recorded in *Orient Express,*" [34] the latter published in 1927, and recapturing for the moment that same contradictory world which had existed for Dos Passos more than ten years before. Malcolm Cowley has found this same impression when he writes:

Sometimes in reading Dos Passos you feel that he is two novelists at war with each other. One of them is a late-Romantic, a tender individualist, an esthete traveling about the world in an ivory tower that is mounted on wheels and coupled to the last car of the Orient Express. The other is a hard-minded realist, a collectivist, a radical historian of the class struggle.[35]

The two worlds that divided Dos Passos, and which essentially represent the two phases of his own personality, are depicted in a somewhat different way by John Reid. Drawing mainly from *Rosinante to the Road Again,* Reid describes the life of the peasants in Spain and their attitude toward modern civilization. This view, which is a primary characteristic of one phase of the thinking of Baroja and other members of the Generation of '98, is a defense of the simple and traditional way of life, in contrast to the turmoil of modern industrialized society. Reid notes that Dos Passos, while in Spain, also took an interest in the radical, political movements in Madrid and in the northern provinces. Dos Passos uses a mule driver—also one of the favorite *porte-paroles* of Baroja—to express one facet of the contradiction. "In America," says the mule driver,

"they don't do anything except work and rest so as to get ready to
work again. That's no life for a man. People don't enjoy themselves
there. It's not gold people need, but bread and wine and life." [36]
These might be the exact words of any of a dozen personages in the
novels of Baroja, from the old wagon driver Nicolás Polentinos,
characterized as a King Lear of La Mancha in *Camino de perfección*
to the English painter Bothwell, who has run away from civilized
England to live in a small backward village of Spain, in *El
Mayorazgo de Labraz*. Dos Passos, in a moment reminiscent of a
scene between Fernando Ossorio and the German vagabond
Schultze on a Spanish mountainside in *Camino de perfección,* considers the words of the old man and says: "I had lain back with my
eyes closed and wished that my life were his life." [37] This dream of
the Romantic—to return to the simple, uncomplicated life—was
probably reinforced for Dos Passos during his Spanish experience
and his contact with the work of Baroja. This acceptance of one of
the major aspects of Spanish intellectual thought of the time demonstrates once more Dos Passos' almost intuitive grasp of the essential
concepts of the men of the Generation of '98—the contradiction
between the desire to bring progress to a world of primitive suffering and the discovery of a certain solace in this backwardness and a
misgiving about the many advantages of modern society and industrialization. Spain became for Dos Passos the incarnation of a dilemma already implanted within his mind, and it gave him no key to
a possible solution to it.

The world which Dos Passos found in Spain had certain contrasts
to his own American experience, which were to become a major
force in his later, more important novels. In a moment of nostalgia
and hope, he saw people who were happy and who came out to
welcome him with wine and watermelon. "In the modern world of
America," he muses, ". . . they would come out after us with shot-
guns loaded with rock salt." [38] They are happy people, without fear,
and dependent upon no one. They make love and sing to a guitar,
and when they are old, they tell stories and bring up their children.
But the desperate search for security could not be so naively simple
for either Baroja or Dos Passos. In both cases the double vision of
possible salvation was inevitable, and in both cases—though in
somewhat different ways—it was to make the novelistic creators as
well as their created personages incapable of a truly meaningful
resolution of the dilemma. Both were victims of a "failure of nerve."

According to Reid, Dos Passos had this split vision of Spain: Spanish life is a delightful oasis in a desert of sordid industrialism; a revolutionary feeling is growing among the lower classes of Spain, and Spain, separated by the Pyrenees, may evolve a new society— not overcentralized—and thereby escape "the festering tumult of a Europe where the system that is dying is only strong enough to kill in its death-throes all new growth." [39] Dos Passos was to return to Spain a number of times between 1919 and 1937 when he went with Ernest Hemingway and a number of others to do some film documentaries on the Spanish Civil War. During these years, the contemplative escapist Dos Passos had lost ground to the man of action and the participant in the grand events of these years. The romantic disenchantment was momentarily lost, and the American novelist, now famous, found that the Republic in Spain was not radical enough. As early as 1921, in his commentary on Baroja which was written four years after his first trip to Spain, he had compared Baroja to the Russian Maxim Gorki who, along with Dostoevski, was one of the favorites of the Spanish novelist. "Instead of the tumultuous spring freshet of a new race," writes Dos Passos, "that drones behind every page of the Russian, there is the cold despair of an old race, of a race that has lived long under a formula of life to which it has sacrificed much only to discover in the end that the formula does not hold." [40]

However, the Spanish experience—whether it offered Dos Passos new ideals or simply nourished those already rooted—was to leave scars on the literary creation of the novelist which no later change of ideology could efface. The despair that grew from Baroja's inability to resolve in reality the literary contradiction that made his life a constant "lucha por la vida," or what Unamuno called an eternal "agonía," a purgatory that would last forever, drove the Spanish writer to accept new contradictions to replace old ones, to sweep from one extreme to another, to defend anarchist horror and murder on the one hand and then weep at the sadness and tears of a solitary child. Dos Passos, too, was to find himself in an eternal agony, a victim of lonely despair, tormented by a hunger born of a psychological need to belong, to be a participant in the activities of men, to find new roots in something with a purpose, to give some sense of meaning to an aimless life. This desire for roots, for some ground on which to stand, may have turned the disenchanted radical of the twenties into the modern conservative Republican. Wrenn talks of

Dos Passos as "a bright, sensitive adolescent who 'grew flowers and vegetables and . . . liked books and . . . wanted to go away to sea and to foreign cities . . . and liked things to be beautiful'. . . ." [41] Dos Passos never renounced any of these romantic ideals and was very much like the ever-wandering Baroja, "el hombre humilde y errante." [42]

Dos Passos' closest friend while in Spain, and the man who was later to be his translator, was José Robles Pazos. [43] Together the two men saw so much of the Spanish scene that was to have an extraordinary influence on the later works of the American novelist. Some of the characteristics of Dos Passos' impressions during this period of his life bear a striking similarity to the tastes of both Baroja and the Generation of '98. Their preoccupation with the works of El Greco might be taken as inevitable, but the fact that both men were so impressed by the painting of *El enterramiento del Conde de Orgaz* of El Greco in the city of Toledo cannot be taken as coincidental. This painting pervades a good portion of Baroja's early novel *Camino de perfección* and is discussed by him in several essays. Baroja's use of the work as the background of the story of an artist's search for meaning and purpose brings the Spanish writer ever closer to the young Dos Passos as he wandered through the museums of Spain with Robles Pazos. On his second trip to Spain Dos Passos once again came into contact with this painting, and he describes the experience in this way:

> The infinite gentleness of the saints lowering the Conde de Orgaz into the grave . . . and men concentrated, converging breathlessly on the single flame of their spirit. . . . Every man's life a lonely ruthless quest . . . these generations . . . working to bury with infinite tenderness the gorgeously dressed corpse of the old Spain. [44]

The other symbol of the Generation of '98 did not elude the young American either, and he captures its meaning in his report of his first trip to Spain in his article "Young Spain." He saw in the *Quijote* the essence of the Spanish dichotomy that was to fit so well into the contradiction that was growing within him:

> The two great figures that typify Spain for all time were Don Quixote and Sancho Panza. Don Quixote, the individualist who believed in the power of man's soul over all things, whose desire included the whole world in himself. Sancho, the individualist to whom all the world was food for his belly. On the one hand, we have the ecstatic figures . . . in whose minds the universe is but one man standing before his reflection,

God . . . the originals of the glowing, tortured faces in the portraits of El Greco. On the other hand are the jovial materialists. . . . Through all Spanish history and art the threads of these two complementary characters can be traced.[45]

The heroes of the Spanish Baroja, the many facets of his complex personality, are the symbols of the contradiction of his generation, the two faces of love and hate, of the reason and the heart, of the spirit and the flesh, of Don Quixote and Sancho Panza. Dos Passos' heroes, from Martin Howe and Tom Randolph in 1917, to the idealists and the materialists—often separated, often two sides of the same individual—in *U.S.A., Most Likely to Succeed,* and even *The Great Days* are variations on the same theme. César Barja has called these Barojan heroes "héroes en movimiento constante, viajeros exploradores de la aventura, vagabundos sempiternos sobre un inacabable *Camino de perfección.*" [46] Dos Passos found in many of these heroes the same failure of nerve, the same aimless worship of action and struggle on the part of men truly incapable of meaningful action, men whose will had been broken both by the society around them and by the inner contradiction of their own personalities. This *abulia,* the breakdown of will so important to the writers of the Generation of '98 in Spain, is best reflected in the characters of the novels of Baroja. One of them, Fernando Ossorio, in *Camino de perfección,* best summarizes the feeling when he says of himself: "Algún resorte se ha roto en mi vida." [47] It is manifested in the futility, the boredom and aimlessness in the characters of Azorín and in the lack of capacity for true purpose on the part of any of the heroes of the Generation. Baroja, in his characterization of his idol Friedrich Nietzsche, had aptly described himself and his heroes when he wrote of the German philosopher as a "pobre diablo, de talento megalómano, y soñador incapaz de matar una mosca y creyéndose más terrible que Atila." [48] In a like manner, Dos Passos, in his characterization of the Spanish Pío Baroja as a "novelist of disintegration" (1921), is at times quite close to a personality which might later have been called his own. Alfred Kazin, in 1942, writes of Dos Passos as one whose

heart has always gone out to the men who are lonely and human in their rebellion, not to the victors and the politicians in the social struggle, but to the great defeated—the impractical but human Spanish Anarchists, the Veblens, the good Mexicans, the Populists and the Wobblies, the Bob La Follettes, the Jack Reeds, the Randolph Bournes, all defeated and uncontrolled to the last, most of them men distrustful of too much power, of centralization, of the glib revolutionary morality which begins with hatred and terror and believes it can end with fraternity. So even the first figure in *U.S.A.*, the itinerant Fenian McCreary, 'Mac,' and the last, 'Vag,' are essentially Wobblies and 'working stiffs'; so even Mary French, the most admirable character in the whole trilogy, is a defeated Bolshevik. And it is only the defeated Bolsheviks whom Dos Passos ever really likes. The undefeated seem really to defeat themselves.[49]

And so Dos Passos writes of Baroja in 1921:

Spain is the classic home of the anarchist . . . where the Iberian race has grown up centerless. In the sixteenth and seventeenth centuries . . . the Spanish genius was forced to ingrow—into the mystical realm where every ego expanded in the solitude of God. The eighteenth century reduced God to an abstraction, and the nineteenth brought pity and the mad hope of righting the wrongs of society. The Spaniard, like his own Don Quijote, mounted the war-horse of his idealism and set out to free the oppressed, alone.

But the anarchism of Baroja is of another sort. He says somewhere that the only part a man of the middle classes can play in the social revolution, is destructive. He has not undergone the discipline necessary for a builder, which can come only from common slavery in the industrial machine. His slavery has been an isolated slavery which has unfitted him forever from becoming truly a part of a community. He can use in only one way the power of knowledge which training has given him. His great mission is to put the acid test to the existing institutions, to strip them of their veils. This does not mean that Baroja writes with his social conscience. He is too much of a novelist for that, too deeply interested in people as such. But it is certain that a profound sense of the evil of existing institutions lies behind every page he has written, and, occasionally, only occasionally, he allows himself to hope that something better may come out of the turmoil of our age of transition.

Only a man who had felt all this very deeply could be so sensitive to the new—if the word were not so threadbare, I should call it religious—spirit which is shaking the foundations of the world's social pyramid, perhaps only another example of the failure of nerve.[50]

Dos Passos' own view of life was equally adamant. "To Dos Passos," writes Malcolm Cowley, "the world seems so vicious that any compromise with its standards turns a hero into a villain. The only characters he seems to like instinctively are those who know they are beaten yet still grit their teeth and try to hold on."[51] Dos Passos' early difficulty in resolving the contradiction which was reinforced through his Spanish experience brought him to the same doubts, the same breakdown of will, the same failure of nerve that had long prevented Baroja from finding some solution to an unanswerable dilemma. César Barja refers to Baroja as a man of thought whose self-image is that of a man of action. To Barja, these Spanish authors were all victims of their own excessive reflection. Baroja was the ideal example of the man of thought whose heroes are failures in *la lucha por la vida.*

Baroja chose to make the concept of action the primary theme of his literature. He would eternally glorify the Nietzschean ideal of action and will in all his created personages. These "pobres abúlicos," men with broken and defeated will, are inevitably failures, men overwhelmed in the struggle and driven to suicide or inaction. These are the "héroes fracasados" that seem to have made so deep an impression on one aspect of the young Dos Passos. The last words spoken by César Moncada, the prototype of the Barojan man of action in *César o nada,* when he considers the possibility of a return to political life after his defeat—a defeat due to his own weakness—are: "I have no idea of going back into politics. What for? I am nothing, nothing." [52]

This same *abulia,* the sickness of will described by Unamuno, Azorín, and many of Baroja's contemporaries as the basic weakness of Spanish society and the cause of her decadence, is epitomized in almost all of the novels of Baroja. It is a reflection of his failure, both as a novelist and as an individual, to find some purpose to life, some solution to the tragedy of his own wretchedness and the aimlessness of man. Barja has said of these heroes of Baroja's novels:

. . . se lanzan a la vida activa, ponen en la voluntad y la acción el sentido de la vida; por un momento intrigan, luchan y triunfan, y, en último término, fracasan. El medio ambiente, el amor, la reflexión, su propia manera de ser, cualquier otra cosa, rompe en ellos el resorte de la voluntad, los paraliza y los aniquila. ¿Nietzsche? ¿El superhombre? Ignoramos lo que habría sido el superhombre de Nietzsche, por no haber jamás existido; pero de Nietzsche mismo sí sabemos que no fué precisamente el superhombre por él concebido, excepto, acaso, como héroe de pensamiento. Fué, en resumen, un alma romántica, harto sentimental. Su nietzscheanismo, evidente en varias cosas, arrastra el contrapeso de un fuerte romanticismo sentimental que lo paraliza a cada instante.[53]

In Baroja's world of *la lucha por la vida,* the Darwinian survival of the fittest, his heroes must choose between two alternatives or they must attempt to reconcile two basically contradictory points of view. They must either accept the challenge of the struggle in order to survive in the amoral world around them, or they must sacrifice their hopes of victory to the inevitable defeat which would result from their compassion and their sentimental and romantic personalities.

It is pity that generally destroys the Barojan "man of action." The one side of the personality is represented by the idea of an elite, of a defense of expediency, of a rejection of humane feeling and an apology for the terrors of power. The hero here is the theoretical superman, all-knowing and all-powerful, the ideal individualist. For him life is a jungle, and he must live by the laws of the animal kingdom. It is this side of Baroja's ideology that has brought him into relationship with the extreme right in Spanish politics. But the rightists failed to recognize the basic anarchistic tendencies in his spirit and in his writings. Baroja, often disconcerted by his own feeling of pity for the tragedy of the masses, would turn against them with vituperative hatred. His individualism is reminiscent of the extraordinary comment: "I love Humanity, but I hate People." [54] Perhaps Sacha, the heroine of *El mundo es ansí* best speaks for the author when she says: "La vida es esto: crueldad, ingratitud, inconciencia, desdén de la fuerza por la debilidad, y así son los hombres y las mujeres y así somos todos." [55] What can we do in this world where all is violence and cruelty? she wonders. We cannot stop living; we cannot stop; we must go on to the very end. Baroja, in his essay *Mi moral*, again speaks for this one aspect of his ideal:

Soy un individualista rabioso, soy un rebelde; la sociedad me parece defectuosa porque no me permite desarrollar mis energías, nada más que eso. . . . Mi noción central de la moralidad es ésta: Todo precepto moral que ayude a la evolución, es bueno; todo precepto que lo dificulte, es malo. . . . Adelante y sin piedad: ésta es buena después de haber vencido. [56]

Again we see a glorification of struggle and action in which Baroja uses a Spencerian analogy—man likened to the animal and vegetable worlds. According to the hero of *César o nada,* man has simply converted the physical struggle of the past into an intellectual and social fight, but if the struggle is colder and more polite, it is equally cruel and vicious.

Alongside this extreme aspect of the Barojan hero stands the alternative, the other facet of the contradiction. The romantic, sentimental, sensitive, and compassionate natures of a great majority of his protagonists form the weight that drags them down. They lead to the same failure of nerve that Dos Passos refers to in his essay on Spain and which he attributes to the rise of pity in the last two centuries of man's history. Baroja, the apparent defender of force and callous indifference to pain, is only hiding his truly humane character in the same way that the protagonists of his creation attempt to do this. Essentially he greatly resembles the young Dos Passos—he is an admirer of all beauty, a lonely figure walking in the early morning over the far corners of the earth, lost on the margins of a world he cannot change, of a world he never made. Baroja, like the young American novelist, found that his pity and his sensitivity could find no solace in a concept of violence and cruelty. While Baroja was to remain a man outside the field of action, separated from all causes and movements, a kind of intellectual anarchist, Dos Passos was to eventually place himself at the very forefront of political activity and become a partisan of such causes as the Sacco and Vanzetti case; he became a man who almost considered his literary talent to be a weapon on the battlefield. And yet, Dos Passos became in his later years a victim of the same disenchantment that had paralyzed Baroja, as well as the members of his generation. Only the extraordinary power of his desire to be incessantly active and to be a part of some cause brought the novelist from the disillusion with the left to the defense of the extreme right.

The dilemma that faced Baroja's heroes is, in the end, one that has no solution. Simone de Beauvoir, in *The Mandarins,* places one of her characters in the same predicament when he finds himself defending the murder of hundreds of thousands of human beings as a necessary condition to the progress of some political ideology. Baroja could never practically accept this condition; he has said many times that he would not permit a single child to weep in order to bring about the progress of humanity. The protagonists of the novels of writers such as Baroja are usually victims of the same tragic failure which affects the theoretical Superman in Nietzsche's works. Those who are aware of the deficiencies of society and who realize what must be done to improve it are incapable of the kind of action they feel is necessary to advancement. Those who are callous and indifferent enough to function well in an amoral society are generally devoid of a vision of the good life and are content to satisfy their own unlimited egotistical desires. William Butler Yeats refers to this when he writes: "The best lack all conviction, while the worst / Are full of passionate intensity." [57]

Baroja's real failure is not only a personal one, in that he failed to realize the dreams which he and his contemporaries had envisioned for the revival of a new spirit in Spain; it is very much deeper than that, and it set the pattern for a number of writers who were greatly influenced by his work. His fictional creations—the heroes to whom he literally gave life and into whom he breathed wills of their own—were all failures. He gave them an independence and a free will to determine their own fates, to establish their own destinies. He was so honest in his conscience and so plainly pessimistic that he could not bring himself to self-deception, even at this level. As in the case of his fellow Basque, Unamuno, Baroja offered the ultimate pessimism. "Even if I were God," as the literary creator of the Generation of '98 so often was, "I could not resolve this dilemma." The failure was absolute and irrevocable.

All of Baroja's protagonists, Juan in *El Mayorazgo de Labraz,* Andrés Hurtado in *El árbol de la ciencia,* Dr. Iturrioz in *La dama errante,* César Moncada in *César o nada,* Juan Alcázar in *Aurora roja,* Manuel Alcázar in *La busca* and *Mala hierba,* to mention some of the earlier ones, are variations of the stereotyped reflection of their author. All are sensitive to the problems of society and yet are unable to do anything meaningful to change it. Some do not even try. Andrés Hurtado says that "la vida en general . . . le parecía una cosa fea, turbia, dolorosa e indominable." [58] He adds in a tone of despair that "el mundo le parecía una mezcla de manicomio y de hospital; ser inteligente constituía una desgracia, y sólo la felicidad podía venir de la inconciencia y de la locura." [59] Andrés is eventually driven to suicide and is called a precursor by one of his friends. Andrés' view of the impossibility of a meaningful life is described in this way:

> Pensaba que en la vida ni había ni podía haber justicia. La vida era un corriente tumultuoso e inconciente donde los actores representaban una comedia que no comprendían; y los hombres, llegados a un estado de intelectualidad, contemplaban la escena con una mirada compasiva y piadosa.[60]

Dr. Iturrioz understands the means which are necessary for a program of action, but he is unable to use them. He cannot be the performer; he must remain the teacher. He is the most cynical of all Baroja's heroes and best approximates the author himself. He speaks for one aspect of Baroja when he argues for the Darwinian concept of the survival of the fittest:

> Vivir dentro de la vida natural, dentro de la realidad, por dura que sea; dejar libre la brutalidad nativa del hombre. Si sirve para vigorizar la sociedad, mejor: si no, había por lo menos mejorado el individuo. Yo creo que hay que levantar, aunque sea sobre ruinas, una oligarquía, una

aristocracia individual, nueva, brutal, fuerte, áspera, violenta, que perturbe la sociedad y que inmediatamente que empiece a decaer sea destrozada. Hay que echar el perro al monte para que se fortifique, aunque se convierte en chacal.[61]

While Dr. Iturrioz represents the man of theory, César Moncada becomes the "man of action" and actually attempts to execute a program which Dr. Iturrioz might have accepted. Moncada is the ideal Machiavellian hero, the idealist who uses political expedients to achieve his ends. Not only does this activity partially corrupt his ideals, but he eventually demonstrates that he has never truly accepted the arbitrary methods he cites, and he is inevitably destroyed. His ideology reads almost as if it were from a manual of the expedient 'prince': "No puedo elegir mis medios," he says. "La política es eso: hacer algo con nada, hacer mucho con algo, basar un castillo en un grano de arena." [62] Of life he says: "La vida es dura y hay que ser tambíen duro como ella para triunfar." [63] Of politics in Spain he says: "La política española es como un estanque; un trozo de madera fuerte y densa se va al fondo; un pedazo de corteza o de corcho . . . se queda en la superficie. Hay que disfrazarse de corcho." [64] His comment on patriotism is a model of idealism and expediency in an uneasy combination:

> Las posiciones políticas tienen eso; con la cabeza tocan con lo más noble, la salvación de la patria y de la raza; con los pies con lo más miserable. . . . Hoy todavía un político tiene que mezclarse entre los reptiles, aunque sea un hombre honrado.[65]

In 1917, in the midst of one of the most terrible struggles that man had known up to that time, Baroja wrote what might be termed a personal resolution of his dilemma. It is very reminiscent of Gilbert Murray's somewhat romantic hope for mankind.

> Pensando estoy por la fuerza y me inclino a creer que el mundo es un circo de atletas, en donde no se debe hacer más que vencer, vencer de cualquiera manera; sintiendo estoy por la piedad y entonces me parece la vida algo caótico, absurdo y enfermizo.
> Quizás en el porvenir los hombres sepan armonizar la fuerza y la piedad, pero hoy, que todavía la fuerza es dura, brutal y atropelladora, hay que tener piedad; piedad por los desheredados, por los desquiciados, por los enfermos, por los ególatras, cuya vida es sólo vanidad y aflicción de espíritu.
> Y además hay que tener esperanza.
> Dentro de lo posible está el que la Ciencia encuentra la finalidad de nuestro mundo, que ahora nos parece una bola inútil y estúpida repleta de carne dolorida, que anda paseándose por los espacios.

Y aunque tengamos la evidencia de que hemos de vivir constantemente en la oscuridad y en las tinieblas, sin objeto y sin fin, hay que tener esperanza, hay que hacer que nuestro corazón sea como el ruiseñor que canta en la soledad de la noche negra y sin estrellas o la alondra que levanta su vuelo sobre la desolación de los campos a la luz pudorosa y cándida de la mañana.[66]

Baroja's preoccupation with many of the same problems that had long troubled Dos Passos was, perhaps, one of the leading factors in accounting for his attraction to Baroja when he first came to Spain in 1916. Dos Passos had reached a crucial point in his life and was undoubtedly open to an influence of this type. He wrote of Baroja some years after his first visit: "He was too timid in the face of pain and too skeptical of science as of everything else to acquire the cocksure brutality of a country doctor."[67] It must be pointed out that Dos Passos found in the work of Baroja something more than a contradictory ideology and view of life similar to his own. He discovered a quality that many critics have found to be one of the more enduring aspects of the novels of the Spanish writer—a panorama of Spain and its people, with special emphasis on the lower depths of Spanish life. Baroja offers the reader a gigantic view of an entire century, and in this respect he follows in the footsteps of the great writers of picaresque novels who had made their view of life in Spain so well known. Dos Passos was more influenced by the trilogy *La lucha por la vida* than any other work, and it was to play a major role in the creation of *U.S.A.* and many other novels. The world of Madrid as Baroja saw it in the late nineteenth and early twentieth centuries was to become Dos Passos' own depiction of an America in disintegration. He writes of Baroja's depiction with a warmth and affection which betray an extraordinary admiration for both the man and his work:

Baroja's world is dismal, ironic, the streets of towns where industrial life sits heavy on the neck of a race as little adapted to it as any in Europe. No one has ever described better than Baroja the shaggy badlands and cabbage patches round the edges of a city, where the debris of civilization piles up ramshackle suburbs in which starve and scheme all manner of human detritus. Back lots where men and women live fantastically in shelters patched out of rotten boards, of old tin cans and bits of chairs and tables that have stood for years in bright, pleasant rooms. Grassy patches behind crumbling walls where on sunny days starving children spread their fleshless limbs and run about in the sun. Miserable wine shops where the winds whine through broken panes to chill men with ever-empty stomachs who sit about gambling and find furious drunkenness in a sip of *aguardiente*. Courtyards of barracks where painters who have not a cent in the world mix with beggars and guttersnipes to cajole a little hot food out of soft-hearted soldiers at mess-time. Convent doors where ragged lines shiver for hours in the shrill wind that blows across the bare Castilian plain waiting for the nuns to throw out bread for them to fight over like dogs. And through it all moves the great crowd of the outcast, sneak thieves, burglars, beggars of every description, rich beggars with a flourishing clientele and poor devils who have given up the struggle to exist, homeless children, prostitutes, people who live a half-honest existence selling knick-knacks, penniless students, inventors who while they are dying of starvation pass away the time telling everybody of the riches they might have had; all who have failed on the daily treadmill of bread-making, or who have never had a chance to enjoy even the doubtful privilege of industrial slavery. Outside of Russia there has never been a novelist so taken up with all that society and respectability reject.[68]

What one can say of the novels of Baroja may be said, to some extent, of the novels of Dos Passos. César Barja quotes Baroja's own concept of his novel as "un saco donde cabe todo." [69] The impact of Baroja's novelistic form on Dos Passos led the latter to call them "descriptions of places and people more than of anything else. . . . natural history rather than dramatic creation." [70] He feels that the novels are filled with pictures etched with vitriol of Spanish life and adds: "If we could inject into American writers some of the virus of Baroja's intense sense of reality, it would be worth giving up all those stale conquests of form we inherited from Poe and O. Henry." [71] Barja's view of the novel of Baroja carries the same impression:

> Puede comparársela a un viaje en el que lo de menos es el fin, y hasta el camino, en cuanto conducente a un fin. En efecto, lo importante en ella es el camino en sí y de por sí, y poco más que un camino es la novela. En él, más que en el fin, radica el interés máximo, y por recorrerlo leemos el libro. Porque se trata de un camino en extremo pintoresco, por supuesto. A lo largo de él va el novelista saludando y despidiendo personajes, personajes que, como el novelista mismo, van y vienen de viaje; narrando aventuras, discutiendo ideas, teorías y sistemas; haciendo reflexiones, describiendo paisajes, contando chistosas y extrañas anécdotas e historias de todas clases.[72]

Malcolm Cowley has captured this very aspect of the novel of Dos Passos without any allusion to Baroja when he says:

> His real hero is society itself—American society as embodied in 40 or 50 more or less typical characters who drift along with it, struggle to change its course, or merely to find a secure footing—perhaps they build a raft of wreckage and grow fat on the refuse floating about them; per-

haps they go under in some obscure eddy—while always the current sweeps them onward toward new social horizons. In this sense, Dos Passos has written the first American collective novel.[73]

Dos Passos, like Baroja, was content to be a novelist of the moment. He quotes from Baroja in his work "A Novelist of Disintegration," about the Spanish writer's indifference to enduring fame and his feeling that his work was very ephemeral.[74] Referring to his work *La dama errante,* Baroja writes:

Probablemente, un libro como LA DAMA ERRANTE no tiene condiciones para vivir mucho tiempo; no es un cuadro con pretensiones de museo, sino una tela impresionista; es, quizá, como obra, demasiado rápida, dura, poco serenada. . . .
Este carácter efímero de mi obra no me disgusta. Somos los hombres del día, gentes enamoradas del momento que pasa, de lo fugaz, de lo transitorio, y la perdurabilidad o no de nuestra obra nos preocupa poco, tan poco, que casi no nos preocupa nada.[75]

Like the ephemeral character of the works of the man he admired so much, Dos Passos himself was a man of the moment. In his early works one is impressed by the similarity of his concept of life and his panoramic depiction of a society in decay to the work of the early Baroja. Dos Passos found in novels like *La lucha por la vida* both inspiration and the corroboration of ideas that had long been stirring within his troubled mind. His description of the early life of Glenn Spottswood in *Adventures of a Young Man* seems to be an American version of the Spanish brothers in the Barojan novel. The hero's wasted and tragic destruction on the battlefields of Spain during the Civil War is much like the useless sacrifice of Juan Alcázar's life in the street-fighting in Madrid during an anarchist uprising. Both men are sacrificed in vain, betrayed by their friends, misunderstood by everyone, and doomed to destruction from the very beginning. The protagonists of Baroja's novels find new forms in the American novels of Dos Passos, but they are variations on the same basic theme. There are geographical differences, and Dos Passos' works were written against the background of a new and somewhat different age. Baroja had sought for meaning and order in an essentially chaotic world; he could not find it, nor were his heroes able to find it. He had cried for peace of mind and a rest from his eternal wandering, and this could not be granted to him. By 1936 he had surrendered to the forces around him, and he retired even deeper into the shell of his subjectivity and began to work on his memoirs. This was the least meaningful period of his creative life. He retreated to that lonely and personal world he knew so intimately. He turned his back on the preoccupations of war and peace, life and death, in the hope that he might find some small consolation in a smaller arena of life's struggle. During these years of disenchantment and exile he wrote, in 1936, a final testament to his loss of faith, a confession imbued with pessimism and despair:

Neither Communism, nor Socialism, nor anarchism, can do anything at the moment to calm and give confidence to the people and the bourgeoisie. And this holds whether their followers proclaim the wisdom of military discipline or attend processions with wax candles in their hands.

At this moment, when Whites and Reds are fighting with desperate courage in Spain, it seems that there can be no midway solution. That is the worst of it: either a Red or a White dictatorship. There is no alternative. I am not a reactionary or a conservative. Neither have I any selfish interests in one faction or the other. I have no fortune, nor have I ever received any benefits from the State. I have been an odd enough Spaniard, with a desire to make a living by writing, something rather difficult and illusory in Spain. In spite of everything I believe that today a White dictatorship is preferable for Spain. A dictatorship of White Republicans one supposes it will be. With more or less serenity in it, but with some sense, too. A Red dictatorship is the same everywhere—a government which makes mistakes, whose intentions are obscure and confused.

Someone will perhaps say that my preference is that of an old man who, as the saying goes, prefers the ill he knows to the good he does not know. It is possible, but at least my opinion is sincere and disinterested.

Kierkegaard used to say, with uncompromising puritanism: 'One thing or the other.' I, if my opinion were of any consequence in this matter of Spanish politics, would parody his words, and say: 'Neither one thing nor the other.' [76]

Whereas Baroja had placed his faith neither in any movement nor political ideology and remained free of attachment until his death in 1957, Dos Passos had turned from his earlier confusion, torn between two contradictory poles, to accept—even if with great reservation—a position within a specific theory of action and a prevalent ideology. Although Wrenn tries to make it appear that Dos Passos had not accepted such a position because of his unwillingness to accept without question, there remains little doubt as to where the American author stood in those trying days more than thirty-five years ago. Dos Passos, like Baroja, had spoken for an era. He attempted to find what Wrenn calls "pattern and form and unity which would give meaning to the apparently chaotic world in which he grew up." [77] In what might almost be called an apology for the author Wrenn adds: "If he has lost the cool detachment essential to the artist, he has retained the warm humanity essential to the man. If his readers regret the passing of the artist, they may applaud the enlightenment of the historian and the triumph of the man." [78] An analysis of the early influences on Dos Passos and his work makes an acceptance of this view impossible. The same factors which moved him to alignment with the left are probably responsible for his recent alignment with the right. Then as now, it was a desire for roots, a need to belong to some movement, however unpopular, however ineffective. "Continually seeking new ground on which to stand," [79] Dos Passos rejected the solution of nonalignment and chose to remain on the field of conflict. As an artist, he created a literary impression of a world which was an integral part of his life and experience. Now he finds himself, some thirty years later, anxious to return to those same impressions, to those same people and places, and to see them through new critical eyes, and to interpret them in light of a new age and a new perspective. This is impossible. Like Baroja, he was a man of his time. Like him, he spoke for the moment. And the moment of Baroja and of Dos Passos has long since passed. All else is repetition, re-evaluation, an attempt to return to the past and revise one's ideology in the light of new insights. Baroja never felt the need to do this because he never sought new attachments. He remained eternally aloof—a figure on the margins of society, an anarchist in spirit to the very end, watching from the wings of the stage of life. Like his heroes, he dreamed of a possibility that fantastic powers would be given to him for one brief moment. In that moment he might annihilate all mankind, regarding the species as a lost hope. The deep-rooted pessimism and the strong sense of individualism never permitted him the opportunity to find some force to which he could attach himself. Baroja, like Dos Passos, came on the scene at a moment of transition, when an old world was in decay. Both were able to represent this world as admirably as any of their contemporaries. Dos Passos found in Baroja a kindred spirit, and he found in his writing a view of life he could accept as his own. The contradiction was to remain for both men. Dos Passos, in all his attempts at re-evaluation, in all his rationalizations, can never remove the deep roots implanted within him so many years ago when he found in Pío Baroja a man like himself—a man of the moment who was proud of the ephemeral nature of his work. In his depiction of Baroja, after his return from Spain, Dos Passos chose a selection from the Spaniard's own work which might indicate the essential romantic—if somewhat hopeless—dream that both men knew. Speaking of Manuel, one of the characters in *Mala hierba*, Baroja writes:

And he continued talking of a vague ideal of love and justice, of energy and pity; and those words of his, chaotic, incoherent, fell like balm on his ulcerated spirit. Then they were silent, lost in their thoughts, looking at the night. An august joy shone in the sky, and the vague sensations of space, of the infinity of those imponderable worlds filled their spirits with a delicious calm.[80]

The dreams of their heroes could never be reconciled with reality. The result of the contradiction could lead to but impotence, futility, and despair—to a failure of nerve.

*LEWIS P. SIMPSON*

# ISAAC McCASLIN AND TEMPLE DRAKE
## The Fall of New World Man

THE SOURCE OF William Faulkner's powerful vision of the American South, duly allowing for his innate genius, was fundamentally not the accident of birth which made him a Southerner but the accident of birth which made him a modern. Unlike Southerners of the last century and, unfortunately, many of this century, Faulkner knew that the history of American Southern culture is an integral part of the crisis of modern Western civilization. This crisis—which by now seems to have assumed total proportions—announced itself in one significant way in 1751, when Jean-Jacques Rousseau won a prize from the Academy of Dijon for his essay asserting that the arts and sciences have done more to corrupt than to aid human beings. Rousseau's attitude prophesied the aftermath of the Enlightenment, indicating that in the very midst of the century which coined the word "civilization" a profound discontent with civilization had begun to arise. From that time until the present the existence of this element of dissatisfaction has been a major characteristic of the literary and artistic expression of Western culture. Indeed Western literature may be said to have become modern only when this virulent discontent began to get into the central nervous systems of its writers. "It seems to me," Lionel Trilling observes, "that the characteristic element of modern literature, or at least of the most highly developed modern literature, is the bitter line of hostility to civilization which runs through it." [1]

Why did a deep unhappiness with civilization become manifest at the moment when Voltaire thought that Europe, in spite of all its

88

political and religious differences, had achieved intellectual unity; and when the French Encyclopedists believed that the advancement of human knowledge was going to create an almost perfect world? Many answers have been ventured, one of the least satisfactory being the oversimplified notion of "the rise of romanticism." Romanticism was only superficially a cause. Basically it was a symptom of a drastic historical displacement of the individual in relation to the world. This dislocation occurred, Hannah Arendt argues in her brilliant work entitled *The Human Condition,* when the ancient distinction between the "public realm" (the realm of the *polis* in Greece and of the *res publica* in Rome—the realm in which the individual person could be seen and heard and through his actions and words achieve a kind of permanence) and the "private realm" (the realm of the family—the undisclosed, impermanent area dominated by the sustenance of the physical life process) began to be reversed and finally more or less erased by "the rise of society." By the twentieth century, society—a great, utilitarian mass world dominated by abstract scientific and technological processes—has absorbed the realms through which Western man traditionally ordered his existence and maintained his world. "What makes mass society so difficult to bear," Professor Arendt points out, "is not the number of people involved, at least not primarily, but the fact that the world between them has lost its power to gather them together, to relate and to separate them." [2]

As the traditional world was replaced by modern society, a typical response of the sensitive mind to the loss of order was "romantic individualism." This emphatic, introspective individualism tended to center on a longing to discover or to rediscover the primal, instinctual sources of life. If mankind could begin over again! The translation of this impulse into possibility was no more than a wishful hope in the congested European metropolis. But out on what Walter Prescott Webb calls "the great frontier," especially on that portion of it existing in what is now the continental United States, modern man could express his frustration with the civilized condition in an actual search for new ways of defining and ordering his existence to be developed out of a vitalizing new relationship between the individual and nature in a virgin wilderness.

Lewis Mumford has an interesting theory in this regard that, I think, can be adapted to the argument I am attempting to set forth here. According to this theory, Old World man began in the eighteenth century to try "to find a new way out from the repetitive impasses of 'civilization' by making a fresh start on a more primitive basis. This effort, imposed by the very need to survive in the raw American wilderness, brought modern man face to face with the ancient realities of paleolithic and neolithic culture, on which the life of the indigenous Indian was based: in the New World modern man turned to . . . pre-civilized existence . . . and lived on this older level with a new intensity, as a conscious *release* from civilization—though fortified both with many civilized skills and with infiltrations of . . . Christian morality." [3] But New World man had in a sense too many civilized skills, in particular his rapidly increasing mechanical ones. The opening of the New World, Mumford remarks, was accomplished with the help of many technological innovations—the navigation chart, the chronometer, the rifle, the railroad. In his desire to conquer the land, New World man destroyed the possibility of making a truly fresh beginning in mankind's social and moral history by allowing his mechanical side to take precedence over his romantic inclinations. He did not, in other words, effect a "synthesis of the romantic and utilitarian elements." He did not keep "alive the new values that he had experienced" in his contact with a virgin world. Instead "once he had conquered the wilderness he surrendered abjectly to the instruments that had made his conquest so swift—and his life so rootless. . . ." Mumford declares, "Properly interpreted the rise and fall of New World man is a more significant drama than anyone has yet portrayed, though the pioneer himself was doubtless only partly aware of the significance of his actions and the implied goal of his efforts." [4]

I

One way, it seems to me, to look at Faulkner's great saga about the South is to examine the complex relation it bears to the drama of the abortive New World man. The setting of the Yoknapatawpha stories is the frontier South and this same South after the frontier passed away. Of all the frontiers that offered the chance of a fresh start— the hope of a new relationship with nature—to Old World man, the territory of the American South was surely one of the most promising. It offered a beneficent climate, much rich soil, an abundance of water, many forests, and a great variety of game. Here, if anywhere, the discontented Old World man might seek to bring the utilitarian and the romantic into a creative synthesis.

But this did not happen. The Southern frontier was early saddled with the anachronistic institution of chattel slavery. A chance to throw off this labor system at the end of the eighteenth century was lost when certain technological inventions made slavery indispensable to the rapid expansion of the South. First came the cotton gin, soon the steamboat, and then the railroad. Together slavery and technology began the task of destroying the vast wilderness world, and technology finished the job. Among many other things Faulkner in his chronicles of Yoknapatawpha County tells us the story of this massive destruction and its consequences.

In telling the pre-Civil War portion of his saga he emphasizes the damnation of slavery more than the damnation of technology. Still, more than once, both implicitly and explicitly, he dramatizes the ironic relationship between the two. For example, we may consider a wonderfully suggestive scene in "Red Leaves," when Issetibbeha, the Indian chief, is discussing with his fellows what to do with a parcel of African slaves they have on their hands. Their discussion of "the Negro question" takes place while they are "squatting profoundly" beneath the gilded names above the doors of the staterooms of a steamboat. Long ago, Issetibbeha's father, the man called Doom, had had his Negroes spend five months moving a deck house across the wilderness, after removing it from a steamboat which had run aground, so that he could make it his house. The Indians talk:

"We cannot eat them," one said.
"Why not?"
"There are too many of them."

Finally, they decide—as they meditate beside the relic of the white man's mercenary technological invasion of the woods—that they must do as the white men do. They must "raise more Negroes by clearing more land to make corn to feed them, then sell them. We will clear the land and plant it with food and raise Negroes and sell them to the white men for money." One asks:

"But what will we do with this money?"
They thought for a while.
"We will see."

The implications of this situation in "Red Leaves"—that is, the corruption of the paleolithic culture of the Indians—might be considered at some length. Let us let it stand simply as a preface to a consideration of Faulkner's most profound treatment of the conquest of the wilderness by slavery and technology. This is to be found in the long version of "The Bear."

## II

In this complicated and difficult story Isaac McCaslin comes closer than any of Faulkner's characters to realizing the idea of the development in the New World of a new version of man. Tutored by the old half Indian, half Negro, Sam Fathers, he enters into a relationship with the wilderness which clearly suggests Mumford's notion of modern man returning in the New World to a more primitive level of existence and living on this "older level with a new intensity, as a *conscious* release from civilization," although deriving support both from civilized skills and Christian morality.

Following his initiation into manhood when he kills his first deer and Sam Fathers ritualistically smears his face with the blood, Ike completes his induction into not only the skills but the mystique of the hunter when he first sees Old Ben, the great bear, who is a kind of primal god. To see the bear Ike has to divest himself, Sam Fathers tells him, of his gun—the gun being of course a prime symbol of civilized man's technological domination of the woods. "You will have to choose," Sam tells him. Ike makes his choice one morning before daylight and leaves the hunting camp without his gun and enters the forest. He takes with him nonetheless two major devices of modern civilization: a compass and a watch. After nine hours during which he goes far deeper into the wild country than he has ever gone before, he still has not seen Old Ben. And he thinks: "It was the watch and the compass. He was still tainted." "A child, alien and lost in the green and soaring gloom of the markless wilderness," Ike brings himself to relinquish "completely to it."

Having abandoned the watch and the compass and even a stick he has carried along for protection against the numerous snakes, the boy loses all sense of direction. But he does not panic. "He did . . . as Sam had coached and drilled him: made this next circle in the opposite direction and much larger, so that the pattern of the two of them would bisect his track somewhere. . . ." At the same moment he discovers the bush on which he had hung his compass and watch, he sees the fresh tracks of the bear. Then he sees the animal itself:

It did not emerge, appear: it was just there, immobile, fixed in the green and windless noon's hot dappling, not as big as he had dreamed it but as big as he had expected, bigger, dimensionless against the dappled obscurity, looking at him. Then it moved. It crossed the glade without haste, walking for an instant into the sun's full glare and out of it, and stopped again and looked back at him across one shoulder. Then it was gone. It didn't walk into the woods. It faded, sank back into the wilderness without any motion as he had watched a fish, a huge old bass, sink back into the dark depths of its pool and vanish without even any movement of its fins.

Having thus "released" himself from civilization and having entered with proper respect and humility into a living relationship with the wilderness, Ike has achieved newness of life. He has won for himself the right to moral freedom. Now he can use his gun throughout a long career as a hunter in Yoknapatawpha County prudently and wisely. In his hands mechanical power will not destroy the great values of the human heart: "courage and honor and pride, and pity and love of justice and liberty." Is, then, Ike the New World man redeemed from the impasses of civilization?

One distinguished student of modern literature, R. W. B. Lewis, attempts in an essay on "The Bear" to prove that Ike becomes something like a new man in a new world, that he is a key to salvation. In a long and arresting argument which I cannot reproduce in the limited space of this essay, Lewis contends that Ike is "the hero of the New World" and that in his "honorable long career" he "moves in a world of light—a light still meagre but definite; a new world in which values have been confirmed by being raised to a higher power; not the new world beyond the frontier—that is precisely what is transcended—but a world so perpetually new that Ike sometimes seems to be its only living inhabitant." Lewis carries the parallel between Jesus and McCaslin far enough to suggest that the Yoknapatawpha hunter possibly is a new incarnation, "a miracle of moral regeneration." [5]

This is hardly so. Although Ike voluntarily gives up his title to the property of his family because the land has been cursed by slavery, he is, I would agree with Robert D. Jacobs, in his total aspect "a pathetic figure, slightly comic, certainly ineffectual." He represents only the nostalgic possibility of modern man rising in the guise of New World man to a new and better moral condition. In reality

New World man in his effort to follow Rousseauesque discontent
into a new condition was creating another Fall of Man and binding
himself more securely by the fetters of society than ever before. In
Faulkner's works Ike serves not, I believe, as a hero. He is a witness,
the primary witness in Faulkner, to what Stephen Spender has
described as the "Second Fall of Man." The English poet, commenting on theories of modern culture like Eliot's famous idea of a
"dissociation of sensibility," says:

In all these theories there is perhaps concealed the idea of a Second
Fall of Man in the industrial age. The operative cause of this Second
Fall was the concept of individualism [in contrast, Spender apparently
means, to the feudal concept of community], which led from the
Renaissance onward, to the scientific era. Knowledge of science and
industry here plays the role of eating of the tree of knowledge. The
Second Fall is considered so much worse than the first one that Original
Sin can be looked back on as the sign of man's comparative innocence,
whilst it is precisely the loss of the sense of Original Sin which is the
peculiar worse-than-damned condition of men in the period of exile
which is the Second Fall. For the sense of Original Sin offers man the
possibility of redemption whereas the loss of this sense condemns him
to a life deprived of all moral significance.[6]

When I say that Ike is Faulkner's chief witness to the Second Fall,
I do not mean to suggest that he is a fully aware witness. I mean that
through his perspective as a kind of moral philosopher he affords us
an ironic and dramatic commentary on the Second Fall. About God's
intention in revealing the New World to mankind Ike theorizes:

Dispossessed of Eden, Dispossessed of Canaan, and those who dispossessed him dispossessed him dispossessed, and the five hundred years of
absentee landlords in the Roman bagnios, and the thousand years of wild
men from the northern woods who dispossessed them and devoured their
ravished substance ravished in turn again and then snarled in what you
call the old world's worthless twilight over the world's gnawed bones,
blasphemous in His name until He used a simple egg to discover to them
a new world where a nation of people could be founded in humility and
pity and sufferance and pride of one to another.

But the spiritual redemption of the New World was prevented by
greed and pride. These sins inspired the effort to possess and to
exploit the virgin land by means of chattel slavery, which is the
subject of the fourth section of "The Bear," and by the
ever-increasing use of the instruments invented by the technological-
industrial revolution. More especially by the last. For—and I state
what I think Faulkner implies—slavery was a curse, but a curse
bears a moral significance rooted in man's original sinfulness. Tech-

nology masks greed and pride in the amorality of scientific and industrial "progress." It separates man from both his sense of involvement with his fellow man and with nature and dehumanizes him.

Do we not see this in the last section of "The Bear"? Did not Faulkner choose, among other reasons, to place the story of the eighteen-year-old Ike's return to the wilderness rather than that of the twenty-one-year-old Ike's meditation on slavery in the plantation commissary at the end of "The Bear" for the sake of emphasis? In any event in the final section Ike sees with his own eyes the coming doom of the wilderness after the end of slavery in the form of a new planing mill. He sees the mill already half completed, covering two or three acres of what had been untouched forest land. He sees "what looked like miles and miles of stacked steel rails red with the light bright rust of newness and of piled cross ties sharp with creosote, and wire corrals and feeding-troughs for two hundred mules at least and the tents for the men who drove them. . . ." This irrepressible attack on the wilderness had been preceded by the work of an insignificant little locomotive used for several years in a small logging operation:

> It had been harmless then. They would hear the passing log-train sometimes from the camp. . . . They would hear it going out, loaded . . . flinging its bitten laboring miniature puffing into the immemorial woods-face with frantic and bootless vainglory, empty and noisy and puerile, carrying to no destination or purpose sticks which left nowhere any scar or stump. . . . But it was different now. . . . It was as though the train (and not only the train but himself, not only his vision which had seen it and his memory which remembered it but his clothes too, as garments carry back into the clean edgeless blowing of air the lingering effluvium of a sickroom or of death) had brought with it into the doomed wilderness, even before the actual axe, the shadow and portent of the new mill not even finished yet and the rails and ties which were not even laid; and he knew now . . . why Major de Spain had not come back, and that after this time he himself, who had had to see it one time other, would return no more.

At the conclusion of "The Bear" Ike is walking through the woods when he comes upon a large rattlesnake. Not only does he see the snake, but with the acute sensory perception of the woodsman he smells him: "the thin sick smell of rotting cucumbers and something else which had no name, evocative of all knowledge and of pariahhood and of death." As the snake glides away, Ike addresses him in the primal tongue he had heard Sam Fathers use six years ago when they had confronted a large buck deer in the wilderness: "Chief," he

said: "Grandfather." Shortly after this mystical moment with the
snake, Ike hears "a sound as though someone were hammering a
gunbarrel against a piece of railroad iron, a sound loud and heavy
and not rapid yet with something frenzied about it, as the hammerer
were not only a strong man and an earnest one but a little hysterical
too." He comes upon a gum tree where he is to meet Boon Hogganbeck, the more or less irresponsible hunter who two years earlier had
finally put an end to the legendary bear, Old Ben, and had thereby,
as Robert D. Jacobs says, symbolized "the abrogation of the old
relationship between man and nature." In the years before, Major de
Spain and the others had hunted Old Ben each year as a ritual rather
than as an act of depredation. Ike witnesses this scene:

> At first glance the tree seemed to be alive with frantic squirrels. There
> appeared to be forty or fifty of them leaping and darting from branch to
> branch until the whole tree had become one green maelstrom of mad
> leaves, while from time to time, singly or in twos and threes, squirrels
> would dart down the trunk and then whirl without stopping and rush
> back up again as though sucked violently back by the vacuum of their
> fellows' frenzied vortex. Then he saw Boon, sitting, his back against the
> trunk, his head bent, hammering furiously at something on his lap. What
> he hammered with was the barrel of his dismembered gun, what he
> hammered at was the breech of it. The rest of the gun lay scattered
> about him in a half-dozen pieces while he bent over the piece on his
> lap his scarlet and streaming walnut-face, hammering the disjointed
> barrel against the gun breech with the frantic abandon of a madman.
> He didn't even look up to see who it was. Still hammering, he merely
> shouted back at the boy in a hoarse strangled voice: "Get out of here!
> Don't touch them! Don't touch a one of them! They're mine."

We remember the story of Eli Whitney, the inventor of the cotton
gin: how he sent the rifles the Army had ordered from him—a box of
barrels, a box of triggers, etc.—and thus announced the invention of
interchangeable parts. Or we may remember this story. Whether or
not Boon's confounding is linked specifically with the history of
technology, it effectively symbolizes the combination of greed and
mechanical power which destroyed the wilderness and its creatures.
That the power has momentarily failed only makes Boon a more
striking example of the Second Fall.

In "Delta Autumn," a tale about Ike in his old age, he is a witness
to one of the ultimate results of the Second Fall, the creation of a
wasteland out of the great Delta forests of Mississippi:

> Now a man drove two hundred miles from Jefferson before he found
> wilderness to hunt in. Now the land lay open from the cradling hills on

the east to the rampart levee on the west, standing horseman-tall with cotton for the world's looms . . . —the land in which neon flashed past them from the little countless towns, and countless shining this-year's automobiles sped past them on the broad plumb-ruled highway, yet in which the only permanent mark of man's occupation seemed to be the tremendous gins, constructed in sections of sheet iron and in a week's time . . . —the land across which there came no scream of panther but instead the long hooting locomotives; trains of incredible length and drawn by a single engine, since there was no gradient anywhere and no elevation save those raised by forgotten aboriginal hands as refuges from the yearly water and used by their Indian successors to sepulchre their fathers' bones, and all that remained of that old time were Indian names on the little towns. . . .

Lying in his tent alone, old Ike conceives of the judgment upon the Second Fall of man:

This Delta. *This land which man has deswamped and denuded and derivered in two generations so that white men can own plantations and commute every night to Memphis and black men own plantations and ride in Jim Crow cars to Chicago to live in millionaire's mansions on Lake Shore Drive; where white men rent farms and live like niggers and niggers crop on shares and live like animals.* . . . No wonder the ruined woods I used to know don't cry for retribution! . . . The people who have destroyed it will accomplish its revenge.

Ike's bitterness assumes that the Second Fall has not completely obliterated the element of Rousseauesque discontent that drove modern man to seek to return to nature. It may be, however, that Faulkner is one of the last writers to experience fully the Rousseauesque tradition of discontent—that is to say, a writer who really feels what it means for modern man to have lost the chance to enter into a living, instead of a bull-dozing, relationship with nature. We may now be entering the age of "post-modern man." A major characteristic of this age will be the full acceptance of a mass-technological society as the one and only way of existence. No doubt the people who live in the post-modern world will accomplish the revenge of "the ruined woods," but will they realize it? Punishment is meaningless when the punished have no moral norm to which they can relate their punishment, and nature as a moral or ethical norm has become almost meaningless.

### III

Faulkner was always aware of this ironic dilemma. Not, I would emphasize, as a dilemma or a problem as such. He was aware of it in the complexity of his feeling for the drama of modern Southerners who are modern human beings. His awareness is strongly implied in that strange early work he called *Sanctuary* and in that stranger later work, a play, he called *Requiem for a Nun*. Published in 1951, *Requiem for a Nun* is a sequel to the story of Temple Drake as this is related in *Sanctuary*, a novel published twenty years before.

*Sanctuary*, the most notorious of Faulkner's novels, has been reprinted more often than any of his other works. It has been analyzed in many ways. In my opinion, it is surely one of the most telling reflections on the fall of New World man (which is more generally speaking the Second Fall) in modern literature. The chief character, Temple Drake, is the daughter of an aristocratic Mississippi family. How "bad" she is at the beginning of the story is not clear; but the fact that her name is inscribed on the "foul, stained wall" of the men's room in the railway station at Oxford suggests that her reputation is not unblemished. When she agrees to slip off a train taking students to a baseball game at Starkville in order to take a trip in a risqué manner with Gowan Stevens, a spoiled youngster who cannot hold his liquor, she ends up in a bootlegger's nest. Here she is raped by a gangster named Popeye Vitelli, violated in a way that even the most sophisticated will agree is intriguing. Subsequently she is taken to a Memphis house of prostitution by Popeye, who, because he has no sexual capacity at all, supplies her with a lover named Alabama Red, another gangster, and enjoys himself watching them make love. This scandalizes even Miss Reba Rivers, the madam and high priestess of the house, but it goes on until Red is killed when he tries to slip into Temple's room without Popeye. Popeye is a jealous lover even though he has to make love by proxy. In the ins and outs of the story that follow, Red is buried after one of the wildest funerals imaginable. It is held in a road house. When the orchestra becomes solemn enough to play "Nearer, My God to Thee," a drunken woman in a red dress comes in yelling, "Whoopee . . . so long, Red. He'll be in hell before I could even reach Little Rock." Lee Goodwin, a bootlegger, is charged with the rape of Temple at the beginning of her adventure. Temple allows her false testimony to send Goodwin to his death at the hands of a lynch mob. The mob sets him on fire after drenching him with gasoline. Popeye is apprehended for a murder he did not commit and is hanged in Alabama.

Wherein does the peculiar power of this lurid tale lie? We do not have to follow the allegorical interpretation of George Marion O'Donnell in which Popeye is said to represent literally "Amoral Modernism," but, I would insist, *Sanctuary* develops, perhaps to some extent in a concealed way, the controlling image of modern literature: the wasteland of modern industrial, mechanical society. Look at the scene, for instance, which Temple sees when she arrives in Memphis in Popeye's automobile:

At the foot of the bluff below Main Street Popeye turned into a narrow street of smoke-grimed frame houses with tiers of wooden galleries set a little back in grassless plots, and now and then a forlorn and hardy tree of some shabby species—gaunt, lop branched magnolias, a stunted elm or a locust in grayish, cadaverous bloom—interspersed by rear ends of garages; a scrap-heap in a vacant lot; a low doored cavern of an equivocal appearance where an oilcloth-covered counter and a row of backless stools, a metal coffee-urn and a fat man in a dirty apron with a toothpick in his mouth stood for an instant out of the gloom with an effect as of a sinister and meaningless photograph poorly made. From the bluff, beyond a line of office buildings terraced sharply against the sunfilled sky, came a sound of traffic—motor horns, trolleys—passing high overhead on the river breeze; at the end of the street a trolley materialised in the narrow gap with an effect as of magic and vanished with a stupendous clatter. On a second storey gallery a young negress in her underclothes smoked a cigarette sullenly, her arms on the balustrade.

Popeye drew up before one of the dingy three-storey houses, the entrance of which was hidden by a dingy lattice cubicle leaning a little awry. In the grimy grassplot before it two of those small, woolly, white, worm-like dogs, one with a pink, the other a blue, ribbon about its neck, moved about with an air of sluggish and obscene paradox. In the sunlight their coats looked as though they had been cleaned with gasoline.

This is the world of Popeye Vitelli, who fears the sights and sounds of nature, wears a hat resembling a modernistic lampshade, has eyes like rubber knobs, and, in his black suit, seems to be stamped out of tin. Sexually impotent, he is further isolated from sensory experience by his allergy to alcohol. None of the terrible things he does can be blamed on drunkenness. He is a sheer horror, representing a stage in the Second Fall of Man a good many degrees below that represented by poor old Boon Hogganbeck. He is the complete reversal of the idea of the New World man living in new connection with nature; he is the entire perversion of the value of the instinctual life.

But Temple is the greater horror in *Sanctuary*. If the dream of the rise of New World man developed in its purest form in the mystique of American girlhood, we have in the story of Temple Drake the

record of the absolute defilement of this mystique—a defilement all
the more absolute because Temple is a violation of the mystique of
Southern American girlhood, and, still more absolute, because she is
a violation of Southern American Mississippi girlhood. The full
picture of Temple does not emerge in *Sanctuary*. Her motivation is
not made explicit until she appears, eight years older, in *Requiem
for a Nun*. The reason for this may be that Faulkner was not fully
cognizant of her motives himself. But the careful reader may find
her motivation strongly implied. She wants Popeye to assault her;
she tells the sordid tale to Horace Benbow, the lawyer, "with actual
pride." She could escape from the Memphis house, but she doesn't
because she loves life there. She could save Goodwin's life. She does
not because she has no compassion whatsoever. At the end of
*Sanctuary* Temple and her aristocratic father are in the Old World,
in Paris, in the Luxembourg Gardens. In what may well be reckoned
one of the key scenes in American literature, Faulkner describes the
scene:

It had been a gray day, a gray summer, a gray year. On the street men
wore overcoats and in the Luxembourg Gardens as Temple and her
father passed the women sat knitting in shawls and even the men playing
croquet played in coats and capes, and in the sad gloom of the chestnut
trees the dry click of the balls, the random shouts of children, had that
quality of autumn, gallant and evanescent and forlorn. From beyond the
circle, with its spurious Greek balustrade, clotted with movement, filled
with a gray light of the same color and texture as the water which the
fountain played into the pool, came a steady crash of music. They went
on, passed the pool where the children and old man in a shabby brown
overcoat sailed toy boats, and entered the trees again and found seats.
Immediately an old woman came with decrepit promptitude and collected
four sous.

In the pavilion a band in the horizon blue of the army played Massenet
and Scriabine, and Berlioz like a thin coating of tortured Tschaikovsky
on a slice of stale bread, while the twilight dissolved in wet gleams
from the branches, onto the pavilion and the sombre toadstools of um-
brellas. Rich and resonant the brasses crashed and died in the thick
green twilight, rolling over them in rich sad waves. Temple yawned
behind her hand, then she took out a compact and opened it upon a
face in miniature sullen and discontented and sad. Beside her her father
sat, his hands crossed on the head of his stick, the rigid bar of his
moustache beaded with moisture like frosted silver. She closed the
compact and from beneath the smart new hat she seemed to follow with
her eyes the waves of music, to dissolve into the dying brasses, across
the pool and the opposite semicircle of trees where at sombre intervals

the dead tranquil queens mused, and on into the sky lying prone and vanquished in the embrace of the season of rain and death.

We recall other American girls in our fiction who go to Europe. One is Henry James's Daisy Miller, the "little American flirt," who in her American innocence is victimized by corrupt European manners, yet who in dying wins a moral triumph over this corruption. We think, more especially, of Milly Theale. The highest reaches of James's mystique of American girlhood are glimpsed in this beautiful, frail girl, the sacrificial victim who in death spreads her wings of love over the Old World schemers who have destroyed her. Both Daisy and Milly are redeemers sent from the New World to save the Old World; or, at least, to show it up for what it is. Seated in Luxembourg Gardens—listening indifferently to the music of the last great romantics crashing about her, wholly sensate, wholly amoral, and completely isolated in the present, for she has no sense of the past—Temple symbolizes the utter end of the dream of the moral regeneration of mankind in the beautiful and fertile Garden of the New World. For her there is no salvation.

Twenty years after he left Temple in the Luxembourg Gardens, Faulkner came forth with his second work about her, *Requiem for a Nun*. Why did he write this drama? He said that he got interested in the question of what would happen if Gowan Stevens, the boy who was too drunk to help Temple when they were stranded in the bootlegger's lair, falsely sacrificed his vanity by marrying her. A more compelling reason Faulkner had in writing *Requiem for a Nun* may have been his compulsion, not to save Temple's soul, but to give her one that might be saved. He does this in a bizarre manner; yet the melodrama makes explicit the logic underlying it: namely, if man is to be saved from the Second Fall, he must once again be persuaded of the First Fall, or of the necessity of believing in Original Sin and in mankind's community in sin.

In the second story about Temple, duly and properly married, she lives in Jefferson with Gowan in a modern suburban bungalow. She and Gowan enjoy the pleasures of the local cocktail set, who like to believe they are liberal in their social and political opinions while they sweat out their hangovers every Sunday morning in their church pews. The group Temple now belongs to believes that the enlightened opinions of her and her husband have led her to bring into their home as a nurse for their two children an ex-dope fiend and ex-prostitute Negro named Nancy Mannigoe. Actually Temple has employed Nancy because she can speak the language Temple still yearns to hear, the language she learned in Miss Reba's sporting house in Memphis. "You know," Temple tells the Governor in the confessional scene when she futilely seeks a pardon for Nancy, "you know: the long afternoons, with the last electric button pressed on the last cooking or washing or sweeping gadget and the baby safely asleep for awhile, and the two sisters in sin swapping trade or anyway avocational secrets over Coca-Colas in the kitchen. Somebody to talk to. . . ." Nancy, however, does not cure Temple's boredom with the role of middle class mother and wife. So, when Pete, a younger brother of her dead lover, Alabama Red, shows up to blackmail her with some obscene letters she had written years ago to Red, she tells him that she will pay his price if he will take her away with him. Seeing the situation, Nancy—in what one critic terms "the most insane solution to the problem of a broken home ever presented in fiction"—strangles Temple's baby in a last desperate effort to keep the family together. The basic motive of the solution is more fundamental. The lawyer Gavin Stevens puts it this way: Nancy murdered the baby because she believes that "little children, as long as they are little children, shall be intact, unanguished, untorn, and unterrified." This is what Christ meant when he said, "Suffer the little children to come unto me." He would protect them as long as they were children from the universal and necessary sinning and suffering of all mankind. When Gavin asks Nancy, "The salvation of the world is in man's suffering. Is that it?" She replies, "Yes, sir." And when he asks, "you have got to sin, too?" she says, "You aint *got* to. You cant help it. . . . He dont tell you not to sin. He just asks you not to. And He dont tell you to suffer. But he gives you the chance. He gives you the best He can think of, that you are capable of doing. And He will save you." At the end of the play Temple, who has expressed doubts about whether or not there is a God, still appears to be in a labyrinth of doubt. She has come to the point of saying in effect that if she has a soul and nobody wants it, then she is "sunk." And, "We all are. Doomed. Damned." Temple realizes what she is incapable of realizing at the end of *Sanctuary*. Man is a fallen creature who longs for salvation.

What may be called, albeit somewhat loosely, the Christian theme is prominent in the dialogue portions of the three acts into which *Requiem for a Nun* is divided. The dialogue, it is important to recognize, is only part of the play. Each act is preceded by a long prologue about the history of Yoknapatawpha County done in some of the most elusive rhetoric Faulkner achieved in a long career of writing slippery rhetoric.

The ironic theme of the prologues might be said to be "was" in relation to "progress." What they emphasize—Faulkner said he intended them to be contrapuntal to the dialogue sections—is the overwhelming rapidity of the Second Fall of Man. "There was no time." This is a major note in the prologues. It reaches a climax in the last one, which is devoted to the meaning of the jail in Jefferson, the oldest building in the town, somehow surviving, even though re-modeled, and although inevitably doomed to be replaced:

And still—the old jail—endured, sitting in its rumorless cul-de-sac, its almost seasonless backwater in the middle of that rush and roar of civic progress and social alteration and change like a collarless (and reasonably clean: merely dingy: with a days' stubble and no garters to his socks) old man sitting in his suspenders and stocking feet, on the back kitchen steps inside a walled courtyard; actually not isolated by location so much as insulated by obsolescence: on the way out of course (to dis-appear from the surface of the earth along with the rest of the town on the day when all America, after cutting down all the trees and leveling the hills and mountains with bulldozers, would have to move under-ground to make room for, get out of the way of, the motor cars) but like the track-walker in the tunnel, the thunder of the express mounting behind him, who finds himself opposite a niche or a crack exactly his size in the wall's living and impregnable rock, and steps into it, inviolable and secure while destruction roars past and on and away, grooved ineluctably to the spidery rails of its destiny and destination; not even— the jail—worth selling to the United States for some matching allocation out of the federal treasury; not even (so fast, so far, was Progress) any more a real pawn, let alone knight or rook, on the county's political board, not even a plum in true worth of the word: simply a modest sinecure for the husband of someone's cousin, who had failed not as a father but merely as a fourth-rate farmer or day-laborer.

The "new people" in Jefferson—"outlanders, living in new minute glass-walled houses set as neat and orderly and antiseptic as cribs in a nursery ward, in new subdivisions named Fairfield or Longwood or Halcyon Acres"—have no contact with the jail. Only the "in-tractable and obsolescent of the town who still insist on wood-burning ranges and cows and vegetable gardens and handymen who had to be taken out of hock on the mornings after Saturday nights and holidays" know the jail. That is, "until suddenly *you*, a stranger, an outlander, from say some suburbia in the East or the North or the

Far West," happening to pass through Jefferson, go with one of the townspeople to see the jail. You are somewhat embarrassed because the jailer's wife is preparing a meal; but you go into the kitchen anyway to see one of the jail's best known historical features: a name and a date scratched thinly on a window pane—"Cecilia Farmer April 16th 1861." Who was this name? She was, the old people of the community know, a "frail and useless" girl, daughter of the jailer of nearly a century before. During a battle in and around Jefferson during the Civil War, she was standing, as usual, musing at the window on which with her grandmother's diamond ring she had some time earlier etched her name. A Confederate soldier saw her for a moment. There was no communication between them. He did not speak to her; nor did he find out her identity. But after the war he came all the way back from Virginia to take this "maiden muse" for his bride—not, however, to the Virgin West, unravaged by war, where they would be "engaged only with wilderness and shoeless savages and the tender hand of God." Their destiny is with a farm in Alabama, a land "rendered into a desert . . . by the iron and fire of civilization." What became of this girl of "invincible inviolable ineptitude"? You wonder. Did she have a "long peaceful connubial progress toward matriarchy in a rocking chair nobody else was allowed to sit in, then a headstone in a country churchyard"? This, you decide, was not enough for that face. "No symbol there of connubial matriarchy, but fatal instead with all insatiate and death-less sterility; spouseless, barren, and undescended; not even de-manding more than that; simply requiring it, requiring all—Lilith's lost and insatiable face drawing the substance, the will and hope and dream and imagination—of all men (you too: yourself and the host too) into that one bright fragile net and snare; not even to be caught, overflung, by one single unerring cast of it, but drawn to watch in patient and thronging turn the very weaving of the stran-gling golden strands. . . ." Was Cecilia Farmer actually Lilith, in Hebraic lore the first wife of Adam, who became a demon, the en-emy of children, and merciless seducer and murderer of men? Or was she a "demon-nun and angel-witch," or a siren? You feel com-pelled staring at the scratching on the window pane, which seems "to have entered into another sense than vision," to decide who this "frail and workless girl" was—"not *might* have been, nor even *could* have been, but *was:* so vast, so limitless in capacity is man's imagina-tion to disperse and burn away the rubble-dross of fact and proba-

bility, leaving only truth and dream. . . ." Then you are gone "to
unfumble among the road signs and filling stations to get back onto
a highway you know, back into the United States; not that it matters, since you know again now that there is no time: no space: no
distance. . . ." You have heard a voice "across the vast instantaneous
intervention, from the long time ago: *'Listen, stranger; this was myself: this was I.'"*

The human imagination, Faulkner appears to be saying, although
it may be diverted from contemplating the nature of man in the time
of the Second Fall, when even "little lonely lost farmhouses" glitter
and gleam with "automatic stoves and washing machines and television antennae," can still "burn away the rubble-dross of fact and
probability" to discover "truth and dream." This is what happens to
you, the outlander, when you leave the booming, industrial-
technological United States and go into the obsolescent jail, where
Cecilia musing at the window marked her identity upon it so that
you could see it nearly a century later and wonder what she was like.
So that *you* could decide that she might have been a primal demon.
Not just idly wonder but be compelled to wonder, because, as the
description of Cecilia keeps emphasizing, she was, or is, a muse, a
source of wisdom. We are not divorced from her by our illusory
absorption in the present, for the human brain carries in it all
time.

What happens if we seek a more specific interpretation of the
meaning of Cecilia by connecting her with Temple? I am not sure at
all. Yet Faulkner apparently intended to suggest at least the possibility of an implied comparison between the two. Cecilia, a Mississippi girl, may have been in some sense the demon Lilith, killer of
children and devourer of men. (Compare a comment on Eula
Varner in *The Town:* "that damned incredible woman, that Frenchman Bend's Helen, Semiramis—no: not Helen nor Semiramis:
Lilith: the one before Eve herself whom earth's Creator had per-
force in desperate and amazed alarm in person to efface, remove,
obliterate, that Adam might create a progeny to populate it. . . .")
In *Requiem for a Nun* Temple says it was she, not Nancy, who killed
her baby. She committed the murder eight years earlier when she
kept her illicit tryst with Gowan. Gavin Stevens observes to the
Governor that Red, Pete, and Gowan were all drawn to Temple
"enough to accept, risk, almost incredible conditions." Does there
survive in Temple the ancient destructive power of the insatiable,

sterile Lilith? Through Cecilia Farmer, a blonde muse whose presence is still felt in the jail, is Temple brought into the realm of the myth of the White Goddess, who according to Robert Graves in his book about her is the ultimate source of Truth? Surely no firm answer can be given. Yet it may well be that Faulkner with his inclination to multi-dimensional complexity and his vision of single human lives projected against the background of all human history intended in the concluding act of *Requiem for a Nun* to juxtapose the myth of the White Goddess and the myth of the usurping male God of Christianity. If man is to find his way out of the modern wasteland, if he is to find salvation for the Second Fall and to achieve a life of moral significance, he must understand how his nature comprehends both the destructive lust of Lilith and the merciful love of God represented by the Christ embodied in Nancy.

*JOHN WILLIAM CORRINGTON*

# LAWRENCE FERLINGHETTI
# AND THE PAINTER'S EYE

WITH THE GRADUAL ebb of publicity concerning "The Beat Generation," it has become possible, in the last year or so, to read the poetry
of Lawrence Ferlinghetti as literature rather than as a portion of an
attenuated and faintly ludicrous social documentary. The "Beat"
tag, so long an active element, arousing a surprising degree of
partisanship among otherwise astute readers, has lapsed at last into
the same kind of literary irrelevance as have such relatively meaningless terms as "The Auden Circle" and "The Imagistes." Having
survived the onslaughts of *Life* and the *Saturday Review,* the praise
of Kenneth Rexroth and the blame of J. Donald Adams, this most
recent of literary phenomena and the figures connected with it have
become the proper matter of literary criticism. One can, with some
hope of objectivity, attempt to discover what meaningful sound may
persist in certain "Beat" writing, now that the fury has subsided.

It becomes apparent, I think, to even the most casual reader, that
those writers lumped together by news media and popular review-
ers under the "Beat" label are, in fact, as distinct from one another as
was Baudelaire from Rimbaud, Verlaine from Mallarmé. In the case
of Ferlinghetti, one finds it difficult to understand why he has been
considered of a kind with his more celebrated contemporaries, Allen
Ginsberg and Gregory Corso. While there are marked differences
between Ginsberg's poetry and that of Corso, a veritable chasm
separates their work from Ferlinghetti's.[1] If Ginsberg can be said to
possess form, it is a form based on rhetorical repetition—a form
reminiscent of Sears catalogues. Corso's shorter poems are loosely

107

unified even considered as lyrics, and his long poems, for the most part, make use of the same Whitmanesque periods common to Ginsberg's "Howl." But in Ferlinghetti's poetry, one finds a consistent and subtly developed sense of form based not upon rhetorical devices or repetition, but on the analogies between poetry and painting; on the correspondences between written and graphic style; on the metaphorical and actual unity between major art forms.

In some thirteen poems scattered through *Pictures of the Gone World*[2] and *A Coney Island of the Mind*,[3] Ferlinghetti makes constant reference to painters and sculptors, both ancient and modern.[4] Moreover, even in poems not specifically dealing with or mentioning art and artists, Ferlinghetti betrays his own post-war education in painting and his dependence upon that background by an overwhelming reliance on visual imagery and by creating a series of essentially graphic events which contain little of the ideational and narrative matter expected of a literary work. An example of this nonconceptual poetry is poem *1* from *Pictures*:

<pre>
            Away above a harborful
                        of caulkless houses
        among the charley noble chimneypots
                    of a rooftop rigged with clotheslines
            a woman pastes up sails
                    upon the wind
     hanging out her morning sheets
                    with  wooden  pins
            O lovely mammal
                            her nearly naked teats
                throw taut shadows
                        when she stretches up
        to hang at last the last of her
                        so white washed sins
            but it is wetly amorous
                        and winds itself about her
            clinging to her skin
                            So caught with arms upraised
            she tosses back her head
                        in voiceless laughter
        and in choiceless gesture then
                        shakes out gold hair
     while in the reachless seascape spaces
                        between the blown white shrouds
        stand out the bright steamers
                        to kingdom come
</pre>

Such a poem, when set against the work of a poet like Dylan Thomas, whose whole artistic orientation was essentially verbal, who clearly did not move from image to language but rather conceived in terms of language itself, becomes readily identifiable as a work moving from a visual conception into the matrix of poetic language. Perhaps a concurrent reading of poem *1* from *Pictures* and Thomas's "Altarwise by owl-light" will illustrate the profound distinction between visually and verbally conceived writing.

Ferlinghetti, in his exploitation of the image almost bereft of "idea" as such, follows rather closely upon modern theory developed by major painters. "Subject"—that which a picture is *about*—is of far less significance than composition—what, in fact, because of the painter's shaping genius, the picture *is*. In a sense, the "subject," whether it be a horse, a landscape or a human figure is essentially an excuse for painting, and is hardly to be considered in valuing the picture as a work of art. Speaking of Cézanne, Picasso and the other fathers of Modern Art, Maurice Grosser says, ". . . their subject was art itself—how pictures are built. Their aim was to isolate the essential qualities of character and structure in a picture which make it a work of art." [5]

Grosser mentions James Joyce and Gertrude Stein as poets who, following the painters, took composition as their subject matter. He compares two Stein poems, suggesting that "Portrait of F. B." and "Rooms" have "the same cadences and the same shape." He concludes: "But the actual words used in the two poems are completely different. This is exactly the sort of thing a painter of the time might have done—different versions of the same composition constructed with different still-life objects or with different colors." [6] Had Grosser a wider acquaintance with modern poetry, he might have found more felicitous examples of this similarity in the work of Stephane Mallarmé, certain of Ezra Pound's early poems, or Federico García Lorca's *Poet in New York*. However, Grosser makes clear that "subject" has become increasingly irrelevant in contemporary art. In the case, for example, of abstract expressionism, the subject has, in James Joyce's phrase, been "refined out of existence," leaving behind an artifact, an object which, rather than containing a rational complexus to be comprehended by a viewer, is an esthetic ikon to be apprehended. There is no idea to be extracted from a canvas in the abstract expressionist mode; rather the picture is constructed to produce a response in one looking at it. By analogy, those poems of Ferlinghetti's which we are discussing—like many of

Mallarmé's, Pound's, Lorca's, and Rimbaud's—are not concerned with ideas, themes, narrations, conceptualizations, but rather with the representation of events and entities in such a way as to evoke a response or a series of responses in the reader. After reading poem *1* from *Pictures* it would seem difficult to explicate the poem except in terms of its graphic significance. It is a paean to woman, to unconscious sexuality, to the art of artlessness—but as a vehicle of idea (in the sense, say, that "Dover Beach" is a vehicle for Matthew Arnold's concepts) the poem would appear insignificant.[7]

In poem *5* from *Pictures*, Ferlinghetti speaks of

> . . . this man who was all eyes
>     had no mouth
>             All he could do was show people
>     what he meant
>             And it turned out
>                     he claimed to be
>                 a painter
>                     But anyway
>         this painter
>                 who couldn't talk or tell anything
>                 about what he
>                             meant
>             looked like just about the happiest painter
>                 in all the world
>         standing there
>                 taking it all "in"
>                             and reflecting
>             Everything
>                 in his great big
>                         Hungry Eye. . . .

Departing from the "pure poetry" we have been discussing, Ferlinghetti turns his hand to theoretical matters. This figure who has no mouth, who cannot tell, but must show his meaning, is representative of the painter—and, by logical extension, of the poet as well—who chooses to work outside the limitations of "subject" ordinarily expected and traditionally called for. I suspect the absence of a mouth in Ferlinghetti's "happiest painter" refers not to the muteness of painting, but rather to its refusal to limit its dealings to the logical and narrative, to the merely anecdotal. In this sense, the modern poet, like the painter, frequently has no mouth. Both take in the world through their "Hungry Eyes." But neither limits himself to phenomena: what is taken in is not simply reproduced on canvas or framed in words. The artist's eye is not, in Grosser's phrase, "the innocent eye of the camera." Rather, the world is dissected, sorted, manipulated, and recreated in terms of the artist's vision— which, a Hungry Eye indeed, devours in order to create.

It should be noted that, as I have suggested above, there are numerous figures antedating Ferlinghetti whose work, whether based in the same theory or not, bears considerable resemblance to the "pure poetry" found in *Pictures* and *Coney Island*. To quote a few of these, with the purpose of emphasizing the visual orientation of this earlier work, one might begin with Rimbaud: "The cascade resounds behind light-opera huts. Candelabra extend out through the orchards and alleys of the neighboring labyrinth,—the greens and reds of the setting sun. Horace nymphs with First Empire coif-fures. Siberian rounds, and Boucher's Chinese ladies." [8] Compare the descriptive nature of Rimbaud's brief prose-poem with poem *17* from *Pictures:*

> Terrible
>           a horse at night
>     standing hitched alone
>                in the still street
>       and whinnying
>            as if some sad nude astride him
>   had gripped hot legs on him
>           and sung
>                a sweet high hungry
>       single syllable

In each poem it is the figurative which dominates; both poems function as artifacts to be experienced, to be *seen,* rather than as verbal cognates for ideas impacted within them. Again, precisely the same sort of function is discovered in a number of Pound's early poems—though in less sophisticated and self-conscious form:

> The apparition of these faces in the crowd;
> Petals on a wet, black bough.[9]

Here, as in Rimbaud's poem, as in poem *17*, we find the poet moving from a *seen* reality—a festive sunset occasion in Rimbaud's poem; a group of people awaiting the subway in Pound's; a horse hitched alone in Ferlinghetti's—to an unseen but still visual re-creation of the seen in the poetic imagination. The pictorial nature of the imaginative extensions is not altered by the fact that Pound shapes a kind of one-for-one relation between fact and creation (faces =

petals; station platform = bough) and Ferlinghetti superimposes his "sad nude" simile upon the actual horse.

Charles Mauron, in discussing the poetry of Mallarmé, finds it necessary to use metaphors of painting in order to explain the "obscurity" of the work: "The poet certainly wishes to avoid sharp contours, but, like Renoir, will have rich and full color nonetheless." [10] Again, Mallarmé "had in him something of the great 'baroque' artists: a passion for vast wave-like diagonals, for sentences running from end to end of the work." [11] In the same volume, Roger Fry discusses Mallarmé's creative method:

. . . with Mallarmé the theme is frequently as it were broken to pieces in the process of poetic analysis, and is reconstructed not according to the relations of experience but of pure poetical necessity. In this he anticipated by many years the methods of some Cubist painters.[12]

Thus, Fry suggests, there is no limit to the violence the poet or painter may do to a given "subject." The artist's "Hungry Eye" absorbs, and what is projected by his inner vision will be an autonomous object: ". . . as in painting, so in poetry, you can do as you please," Wallace Stevens puts it.[13]

Continuing this brief chronology of Ferlinghetti's antecedents, one cannot overlook the work of García Lorca. Celebrated by younger writers because of his tragic death in the Spanish Civil War, Lorca's *Poet in New York* has been profoundly influential on contemporary American poetry. And Lorca, like Ferlinghetti, was possessed of a singularly "Hungry Eye":

> Blood fell on the mountains, and angels went in search
>     of it,
> but their chalices held only wind; blood spilled from
>     their shoe-tops, at last.
> Lame dogs puffed at their pipes, and the smell of hot
>     leather
> was gray on the circling lips of those who vomit on
>     street-corners. . . .[14]

Angel del Rio considers Lorca's later poetry as purely visual in form. "In a certain sense," del Rio says, "Lorca was more surrealist than the surrealists." [15] Del Rio is conscious of Lorca's derivations from painting techniques in the poems that make up *Poet in New York:* ". . . the similarity in imagery between some of Lorca's poems and Dali's paintings . . . is such that no better illustrator could have been found for *Poet in New York* than the Catalonian creator of the 'surrealist object.' " [16]

On this question of Ferlinghetti's antecedents among poets whose work was conceived and executed within the frame of modern painting's theory, there remains one further example to point out. It would be difficult to find a piece of modern poetry more completely visual than this:

fandango of shivering owls souse of evil-omended polyps scouring brush of hairs from priest's tonsures standing naked in the middle of the frying-pan—placed upon ice cream cone of codfish fried in the scabs of his lead-ox heart—his mouth full of cinch-bug jelly of his words—sleigh-bells of the plate of snails braiding guts—little finger in erection neither grape nor fig—commedia dell'arte of poor weaving and dyeing of clouds—beauty creams from the garbage wagon—rape of maids in tears and in snivels—on his shoulder the shroud stuffed with sausages and mouths—rage distorting the outline of the shadow which flogs his teeth driven in the sand and the horse open wide to the sun which reads it to the flies that stitch to the knots of the net full of anchovies the sky-rocket of lilies. . . .[17]

It is to be expected that a prose-poem by Pablo Picasso would be a flood of imagery. The poem was written during the Spanish Civil War as Picasso prepared a set of sketches to be called "The Dreams and Lies of Franco." It illustrates, with considerable power, a kind of reversal, a feed-back from artist to poetry. As Ferlinghetti and his predecessors have drawn both method and conception from the graphic arts, so the most distinguished of modern painters makes use of poetry in order to sketch, as it were, a schema for drawings which he plans.

Perhaps none of Ferlinghetti's poems so fully exploits the method and the shape of a modern painting—and at the same time the form of Picasso's poem and subsequent drawings—as does his poem *6* in *Pictures:*

And the Arabs asked terrible questions
and the Pope didn't know what to say and the people
ran around in wooden shoes asking which way was the
head of Midas facing and everyone said
No instead of Yes
While still forever in the Luxembourg
gardens in the fountains of the Medicis were the
fat red goldfish and the fat white goldfish

and the children running around the pool
    pointing and piping
                *Des poissons rouges!*
    *Des poissons rouges!*
             but they ran off
and a leaf unhooked itself
              and fell upon the pool
    and lay like an eye winking
               circles
   and then the pool was very

          still

            and there was a dog
      just standing there
              at the edge of the pool
       looking down
             at the tranced fish
     and not barking
        or waving its funny tail or
               anything
   so that
        for a moment then
     in the late November dusk
  silence hung like a lost idea
        and a statue turned
      its head

It would seem clear that in Ferlinghetti's mind—and perhaps in Picasso's, too—there is no real or substantive distinction between the act of painting and that of making poetry. Technical differences are simply problems to be overcome—but the modern poem, like the modern painting, must be conceived in terms of composition, not in terms of subject matter.[18] The poem is shaped by what Roger Fry, as noted above, calls "poetical necessity"—the poem's form shapes its own requirements. The same holds true of painting. "I have never made trials or experiments," Picasso has said. "Whenever I had something to say, I have said it in the manner in which I felt it ought to be said." [19] Thus we have a poet who calls his poems "Pictures," and a painter who "says" things with his brush.

Insofar as prose statement may be required, Ferlinghetti has not stinted in its use. Indeed, his most recent work has suffered from an almost journalistic flatness, a regrettable lack of the brilliant imagery found in *Pictures* and in much of *Coney Island.* But if the poetry of "reportage," in E. M. Forster's phrase, should fail to match his vision,

Ferlinghetti has had at his command the further resources of the painter's eye and the painter's wide-ranging, inclusive theory:

Don't let that horse
                eat that violin
        cried Chagall's mother
                    But he
            kept right on
                        painting
And became famous
And kept on painting
                The Horse With Violin In Mouth
And when he finally finished it
he jumped up upon the horse
                            and rode away
            waving the violin
And then with a low bow gave it
to the first naked nude he ran across
And there were no strings
                    attached

If Marc Chagall, in poem *14* from *Coney Island,* serves as an epitome of the painter (as does Picasso in another poem—*24* in *Pictures:* "but that night I dreamt of Picasso / opening doors and closing exits / opening doors and closing exits in the world . . ."), then Lawrence Ferlinghetti may well stand as an epitome of the modern poet. Ferlinghetti, like Kenneth Patchen's "impatient explorer who invents a box in which all journeys may be kept," has ranged into the deep space beyond limiting canons of literature and has created a provocative and significant body of poetry which, while based in the tradition extending from the Symbolists through Lorca, manipulating theory and technique born with modern painting, is nevertheless still experimental and tentative. Ferlinghetti has produced a poetry in which handling of object attempts to replace "subject" in significance, a poetry which must be apprehended and experienced as cultural event rather than as subject-verb-object reportage of "reality." Perhaps Ferlinghetti himself has best described the sort of thing he has attempted. In poem *13* from *Coney Island,* he tells how he would "paint" . . . "a different kind / of Paradise,"

    . . . there would be no anxious angels telling them
            how heaven is

the perfect picture of

a monarchy

and there would be no fires burning
in the hellish holes below
in which I might have stepped
nor any altars in the sky except

fountains of imagination

*CALVIN EVANS*

# CINEMATOGRAPHY
# AND ROBBE-GRILLET'S *JEALOUSY*

THE VERY TERM "antinovel" is disarming. By inference the antinovel-
ist is bluntly telling the critic that aesthetic standards of the Western
tradition are misapplied in his case. This is less out of arrogance than
out of a conviction that his particular way of reacting to the data of
life constitutes a radically new artistic experience. It is an experience
whose quality is scarcely congenial to being judged on the basis of
psychology, linear development, social critique, density of plot, and
style (at least in its usual connotation). Indeed, it would be stretch-
ing the point to try to force the antinovel into conformity with these
criteria as none of them seems pertinent to its inner structure. In the
first place the society-psychology equation as it is observed in
nineteenth-century novels is repudiated by the new novelist on the
grounds that it is arbitrarily deterministic. We are for the most part
confronted with an assemblage of social automata who, in a given
set of historical circumstances, evolve towards a logical dénouement
of their problems and frustrations. The trajectory of this evolution is
staked out with appropriate peripeties and vicissitudes in accord-
ance with the author's ingenuity.

The new novelist has no quarrel with this time-honored procedure. He does not impudently, like ingrate progeny, mock or depre-
cate august tradition. Certainly, he is too much of an artist and
human being not to be moved by *Madame Bovary, Père Goriot,
Vanity Fair, L'Assomoir,* etc. But he also seems to have realized that
a novel of social contingency is no longer equal to interpreting the
metaphysical anguish that gnaws at twentieth-century man. It is

neither necessary nor feasible in this essay to reiterate the well-known facts which have led to the social alienation of the modern artist. In truth, it must be owned that the modern literary artist, though admiring the deep-seated genius and dazzling virtuosity of nineteenth-century writers, regards the contents of their works as one vast cliché; perhaps not so much a cliché as an irrelevancy. In an era when a relentless existentialist critique has called into question virtually all the values of the Western ethos, the vanguard artist has turned his back on society and retreated into himself. He is quite content to allow the professional sociologist to bring his Shavian zeal to the problems of the day. For Robbe-Grillet, Ionesco, Beckett, Sarraute, and the like, society is either barely perceptible in the background or is angrily destroyed before our eyes by means of an expressionistic *humour noir*. It would seem from all this that the writer is intent upon cutting the ground from beneath him, for how is it possible, one may ask, to write an "asocial novel," to negate the very element that infuses all human activity? Yet, in his disillusionment the new novelist is patently trying to do just that—to examine the world at precisely the place where actuality and socio-political concerns have abandoned it. Obviously, such a program would imply a total revamping of values commonly associated with novel criticism. All the former hooks and labels having to do with character, plot, and style are suddenly found to be obsolete or invalid. The new novelist is beyond the pale. He must discover new ways of reacting to the metaphysical void that confronts him. In brief, the new or antinovel is a highly subjective exercise that endeavors to observe the immediate impact of phenomena upon a psyche in its isolation—all of which brings us to Robbe-Grillet.

In Alain Robbe-Grillet's *Jealousy,* one of the foremost examples of the *nouveau roman,* an attempt is made to strip the novel of all naturalistic narration as well as of that description which could be termed background embellishment.[1] This procedure represents a logical progression from Joycean and Kafkaesque precedents. However, a decided innovation is the fact that Robbe-Grillet makes no pretense of lending to his work a linear development from either a temporal or psychological point of view. Neither does he choose to penetrate *la vraie vie* by means of a loosely constructed interior monologue or by evoking the nightmarish atmosphere of a mazy bureaucracy. He rather confronts the reader with a series of sensory perceptions consisting of a cycle of objects and other precise data that keep recurring as part of a desultory montage. This is simply the bare account of a tormented mind's reaction to the everyday phenomena that comprise his domestic surroundings. Though the mind is doing the perceiving, it is through the objects that the atmosphere of crisis is created. The author eschews the conventional approach to the situation which would consist of an exhaustive probing into the mind of the perceiver carefully analyzing the psychic rapport with each object, à la Proust. There is no effort to interpret in valid psychological terms the impact of data. Such impact is to be divined by the reader as he is gradually exposed to the visual experience of the narrator. The end result is that a non-verbal language emerges whose special syntax is made up of angle shots, close-ups, dissolves, pans, in short, of cinematographic elements. It is not that the author has willfully striven to simulate camera techniques, but rather that these techniques seem appropriate to present "alliterative" trends of the novel. Nor is one justified in asserting that *Jealousy* would make a more impressive film than novel, considering the barrenness of its style and the lack of direct emotional appeal. To paraphrase Verlaine, what Robbe-Grillet has done is to *reprendre au cinéma son bien.*

In *Jealousy* the sparse plot deals with a man (the narrator or "perceiver") somewhere on a banana plantation in Africa who suspects his wife of infidelity. However, again to emphasize the lack of explicit story detail, the word jealousy is mentioned but once and then in the most casual of contexts. Further in connection with plot, the goings and comings of a certain Franck, amorously involved with A . . . , the wife, receive a great amount of attention. The narrator takes no active part in the proceedings, but since all the scenes occur within the immediate radius of his vision, we are aware of his omnipresence. The events of the book are told so obliquely and in such truncated episodes that the reader never fully understands the exact nature of the anguish and *désarroi* that pervade it. Whether or not ultimately a murder is committed is for the reader to decide. Here are no emotional pyrotechnics of the *crime passionel*, no discursive treatment of a psyche tortured by jealousy and suspicion as in *The Kreutzer Sonata* or the Swann-Odette relationship— only a subdued, indescribable malaise that fluctuates in intensity throughout. Segments of perception are culled at random by a disturbed mind with no previous emotional buildup or motivation. We are, from the outset, suddenly plunged *in medias res* without being apprised of the key incidents lurking in the background of the climax. The author thrusts before us a series of peripheral data, cited always with the same dispassionate exactitude, full of angles and symmetry which suggest a sort of Cartesian camouflage covering a taut subjacent drama.

Before launching into his narrative, the author furnishes a precise contractor's diagram of the floor plan and premises which enables the reader to picture for himself the exact movements and positions of the protagonists. This alone speaks effectively for the importance attached by Robbe-Grillet to purely visual data. A painstaking description of the arrangement of chairs on the veranda is given in order that we may keep accurately in mind the vantage point from which the narrator observes Franck and A . . . who always sit next to each other. Sundry details concerning the texture of the wood of the balustrade, the angle of the shadow from the column, the remains of a crushed scorpion on the wall, a corner of blue stationery that protrudes a fraction of an inch from Franck's shirt pocket, are given in the first part of the novel. This repertory of objects forms a vocabulary and syntax whose fine shadings are wrought by the particular angle or focus in which the object is perceived through the eyes of the narrator.

It would appear that such a style, though admittedly still in the experimental stages, represents the furthest extreme to which the antipsychology of modern writers has been carried. Certainly Robbe-Grillet has nothing to be red-faced about in that respect.[2] Ever since the Goncourt brothers and Zola, the avant-garde of the novel from Proust, Joyce, and Kafka to the present have wondered if there weren't a more effective way of getting at the truth than by depicting the grave psychological repercussions that befall wretched mortals at odds with society. The results of such clinical analysis seemed too pat, too much in conformity with le bon sens, traditional pride of the French. Proust showed that there was something far more deepseated in the conflict between the superficial social animal and the bottomless depths of his interior life than could be sounded by a smug intellectualism.

Perhaps never did we become more acutely aware of the symbolic language that is constantly being forged by the subconscious and by our dreamlife than through the subtle pictorial art of Griffith, Dreyer, and Stroheim. The entire art of these men consisted in suggesting by a mere surface ripple an inner crisis of cataclysmic proportions for the individual. An object photographed within a certain context could jar the very foundations of being. In such a situation words would have been intruders. The simple fact of the matter is that cinematographic art can reproduce the psychic flow of the *durée intérieure* in all its kaleidoscopic manifestations.[3] The camera can bring together in whatever sequence any number of phenomena whose linkage might seem irrational to the intellect. It is only to be expected that the novel would try to find some way of profiting from this new art which made the psychology of the conventional novel appear somewhat superficial in comparison.

The transference of cinematographic montage to the novel required, as we have seen in *Jealousy*, a drastic downgrading of the word as a vehicle for creating mood or for serving as the purveyor of the usual details of sociology, local color, and plot. The word must be completely unobtrusive, even self-effacing in its deference to the image. This is not a matter of poetic imagery which seeks to free itself from rigid connotation and thereby make its appeal to the emotions rather than to cerebration. In such a case, freedom is achieved when the poet, or novelist, succeeds in evoking the meta-phorical vigor of the child or of primitive perceptive processes. These rare moments entrance the reader to the extent that he be-comes virtually oblivious to the literal or practical meaning of the word: the poem or passage is transmuted into pure feeling. Robbe-Grillet also triumphs over the word but not by means of metaphor, at least not verbal metaphor. Geometrical is the term that quite naturally comes to mind where the author's language is concerned. It is, indeed, so denuded and unassuming that it rather resembles the language one would normally use to describe a stage set with its varied props.

The veranda is empty too; none of the armchairs has been brought outside this morning, nor has the low table that is used for cocktails and coffee. But under the open office window, the flagstones show the trace of eight chair legs: two sets of four shiny points, smoother than the stone around them. The two left-hand corners of the right-hand square are scarcely two inches away from the two right-hand corners of the left-hand square.[4]

A great deal of data of this sort is filed away in the subliminal mind, at first as gratuitous detail. The mind in its affliction becomes at once a hypersensitive recorder of minutiae. What in its everyday context seems trivia, such as the crushed scorpion on the wall, the

blue stationery, the tapered hands, the slow chant of the servant
boy, Franck's table manners—are transformed into a gamut of symbols whose orchestration gradually climbs to an hysterical rhythm. It
is the rhythm par excellence of the *durée intérieure*. Adroitly ironi-
cal is this linear precise statement of phenomena which creates at
the outset, with respect to the narrator, a false impression of solidity
and lucidity. The reader begins to sense the precarious footing upon
which this ostensibly stable world is grounded. What seemed to be a
perfectly sane and well-knit set of visual responses is held together
by a tenuous thread. Gradually the corrosion of jealousy causes the
house of intellect to buckle and crumble into the abyss. The mind,
out of kilter, deprived of its rational balance, cedes to those processes, subjacent to waking perception, which follow their own logic.

As in *Albertine disparue,* where in the mind of Marcel all phenomena become inextricably bound up with the memory of the dead
heroine and are thereby transformed into a sort of elegiac lexicon
which alternately returns to comfort or torment the author, so in
*Jealousy* there emerges out of the ceaseless psychic attrition a morbid animism. Even the commonplace objects and situations of day-
to-day existence are arranged into a mute language of hermetic
syntax and style that seem to be composing a poem of dark and
demonic import. As the narrator becomes severed from the sedate
cadence of cortical perception, temporal continuity as well as spatial
logic are submerged in the torrent of the subconscious. Strange
correspondences and juxtapositions assert themselves in this realm
of nightmare. They constitute themes and motifs which form a part
of a dissonant symphonic construction à la Berlioz, reaching, as do
the works of the latter, a paroxysm at which point all rational order
disintegrates.

The prime artistic effect created by this technique is that the
rapport established between reader and author far exceeds what is
normally thought of as empathy. The verbal sorcery by which the
object is disencumbered of its literal identity and restored to its pure
autonomy as object annihilates aesthetic distance and absorbs the
reader into the camera-mind of the narrator. That is to say, we
actually live and participate in his anguish. Of course it is possible to
resist the hypnotic character of the work and to be impervious to its
disquieting rhythm, just as one could conceivably ask, after seeing
*Hiroshima mon amour,* "What did all those scenes of suffering at the
beginning have to do with the love affair?" There is no way for the

artist to force a commitment upon his patron. Under proper circumstances of exposure the reader of *Jealousy* is, indeed, committed to
total involvement. For one thing, as we have seen, the rhetorical wall
of the conventional novel is nonexistent. We cannot sit back in
comfortable detachment while an all-knowing artist keeps whatever
conflicts well in hand and provides for us a pleasant empathy. Even
the moments of febrile intensity to be found in the novels of Dostoevski are kept at bay by the fitting of such moments into an organic
scheme of mercurial development. Things are constantly under
control. We are not allowed to fall prey to a hierarchy of objects into
whose web the narrator himself becomes entangled. Such safe-
guards as provided by a cerebral arbiter are absent in the *nouveau
roman.* The reader is quite as much at the mercy of the dark realm of
the narrator's mind as he would be to the montage of an art film
whose sonic aspect is closely married to the image. Ideally, he would
be weaned away from intellect and transferred to the subthreshold,
oneiric level of being. Herein there can be no control over time or
space, since the author himself has acceded to this same level of
experience. We find ourselves completely helpless before the on-
slaught of objects.

I suggest that it is impossible to read *Jealousy* without suffering a
certain malaise comparable to that ofttimes suffered during the
course of a film on the order of *Wild Strawberries* or *Hiroshima mon
amour,* both of which effectively employ *la durée intérieure.* Every
facet of these seemingly unrelated sensory impressions has a valid
affinity for us, since even though we may be unable to relate them
specifically to something in our personal lives, they are easily within
the range of potential experience. The adulterous situation is
brought to light almost casually through the welter of clinical detail.
It is a delicate shudder dimly seen on the surface of what appears to
be a blueprint of the house and premises drawn to scale. Even the
"protruding islands formed by the last vestiges of paint" on the
balustrade come within the scope of a remarkably acute vision.[5]
Now and then a subtle allusion: the exchange of a fleeting smile
between Franck and A . . . à propos of a certain passage in a book
whose setting is Africa. No, it isn't a smile, merely the fluttering of
evening shadows on A . . .'s face. Or it is a vague innuendo about
Franck's ineptitude as a mechanic, A . . .'s writing a note on blue
stationery, the reluctance with which Franck discusses his wife's
indisposition, the proximity of A . . .'s tapered hand to Franck's as

they sit on the veranda, the sly maneuver of injecting a note into the conversation about a possible trip to the port. But these data, though mentally registered by the husband, receive no subjective processing or interpretation. Everything regarding the Franck-A . . . liaison seems to be mentioned in passing as accessory to the principal part of the inventory. Gradually, the nervous tremor that skims lightly over this roster of drab observations begins to infiltrate into the subconscious where it proceeds to work its effect upon the surface mind. Mingling with normal responses it is catalyzed into a symbolic language that makes abstraction of time and space.

At this point the reader is exposed to a frenzied montage consisting of a disjointed series of flashbacks, close-ups, angle and distortion shots, pans—in short, to a style whose subtlety is based upon camera techniques. With the word reduced to an innocuous appendage of the image, we are immersed in the insanity of the narrator. The motifs so lucidly enumerated in the first few pages break loose from the narrator's control, and he, as well as the reader, is subjected to their caprice. They fall into those patterns and sequences which conform to the hermetic equations resulting from the collision of sanity and deep emotional shock. The slow erosion of jealousy sharpens sensory perception to the extent that phenomena and events are abruptly lumped together in uneven sequence. The whole effect is kaleidoscopic, and though it suggests a morbidly euphoric masochism, the narrator for all his enjoyment of self-torture is nonetheless at the mercy of the "phenomenal" world created by his mind.

The perceptual abnormalities of a mind in crisis are projected onto all the components of the milieu. They are brought to life and become the means by which the story is told. Reality becomes an incubus wherein each gesture, each object fits itself into a sinister fresco. The dark rhythm of the novel appears when temporal continuity begins to disintegrate, when it is clear that the narrator no longer controls event sequence. Things and actions are colored by inner torment. One impression spawns another in accord with some latent design. It is the rapid inexplicable thought transitions that provide the main element comparable to what one might term style.

Perhaps the whole affair is a result of an excruciating reverie indulged in by the husband during the absence of A . . . and Franck. Whether imagination or reality it must be owned that

*Jealousy* presents an extremely authentic picture of the mind's painful peregrinations in stressful circumstances. My theory would be that the husband, having fallen into an anguished half-dream state while Franck and A . . . are at the port, becomes prey to a chaotic parading of domestic phenomena before his mind's eye. Reconstructed in fragmentary flashes, to form a grotesque portrait, are all the elements of his plantation life. Things are in upheaval, and the narrator, obviously a man who has endeavored to cling to order and stability, is powerless to cope with this collapse of his private world. Nevertheless, in a desperate effort to defer the advent of chaos, even towards the end he uses such "stabilizing" words as cylindrical, trapezoid, symmetry, triangular as if by some verbal magic to wish away the menace to his security.

Here is an example of the drastically segmented montage as it begins to occur after the original statement of phenomena: in the first segment a clinical treatment of Franck's khaki shirt from whose "carefully buttoned pocket" protrudes a sheet of blue paper "folded several times, probably in eighths"; transition to conversation fragment concerning alleged car trouble en route back from the port; cut to workmen in the hollow of the valley; revert to "car trouble" theme with Franck's wry comment about being a "bad mechanic"; rapid focus upon Franck's grimace "immediately absorbed, at the same time as the wrinkled white suit, by the shadow of the hallway"; study in perspective of the bottle of soda, the cognac, and the crouching men near the bridge crossing; transition to Franck and A . . . sitting in veranda chairs; cut to Franck's table manners:

The right hand picks up the bread and raises it to the mouth, the right hand sets the bread down on the white cloth and picks up the knife, the left hand picks up the fork, the fork sinks into the meat, the knife cuts off a piece of meat, the right hand sets down the knife on the cloth, the left hand puts the fork in the right hand, which sinks the fork into the piece of meat, which approaches the mouth, which begins to chew with movements of contraction and extension which are reflected all over the face, in the cheekbones, the eyes, the ears, while the right hand again picks up the fork and puts it in the left hand, then picks up the bread, then the knife, then the fork. . . .[6]

So continues the increasingly accelerated flow of mental snapshots which flit across the narrator's mind during his moments of anxious solitude. It is difficult to avoid the genuine impression that the author has somehow completely removed himself from the narrative, even more so than in the case of Flaubert, since the latter at least pursues a rigorously linear development, a story line. Nor is it a matter of stream-of-consciousness, which implies a certain concatenation of thought processes generated by reverie or a semi-wakeful state, not necessarily dependent upon exterior stimuli. Here the feeling is one of suspension and disorientation as if we had been severed from any sort of guiding principle. Data break away from the temporal and spatial continuity of rational arrangement and finally, as tension builds, a law unto themselves, rush headlong towards the narrator. We are in a realm lorded over by objects. The role of words is that of rather frantically seizing the angles, dimensions, the gross bulk of phenomena in a last-ditch effort to anchor the mind to the clearly etched, stable world of Euclidean shapes.

The undeviating use of the present tense heightens both the auditory and visual drama. In his night of agony the narrator hears the sound of a motor in the distance, possibly Franck's car:

> . . . a kind of growling, or rumble, or hum of a motor, the motor of an automobile on the highway rising toward the plateau. It fades for a moment, only to resume all the more clearly. This time it is certainly the sound of a car on the road. It rises in pitch as it draws nearer. It fills the whole valley with its regular, monotonous throbbing, much louder than it seems in daylight. Its importance quickly surpasses what would normally be expected of a mere sedan.[7]

Everything is happening *now*. Reader involvement is increased as the rapid flow of images breaks into his own consciousness. The anarchic fusion of events, the emergence of unsuspected interrelationships between phenomena make for a new and exciting kind of psychic realism. Notably the word "now" introduces most of the chapters, and it is consequently as if the actual exterior flow of time were replaced by the fictional present. We are an active party to what is happening in the novel, since our sensory mechanism has become fully engaged. Words have scarcely time to capture and to intellectualize events, since we are moving about in an unrelenting present. We are prey to a dynamically kinetic style whose grammatical components are images rather than words. What seems an indiscriminate and incoherent mixing of visual and auditory data begins its frantic ascent towards delirium as the

> . . . black, calm, hot night, like all the rest, is occasionally interrupted only by the short, shrill calls of tiny nocturnal carnivores, the sudden buzzing of a beetle, the rustle of a bat's wings. Then a silence. But a fainter sound, something like a hum, makes the ear strain. . . . It stops

at once. And again the lamp's hissing can be heard. Besides, it was more
like a growl than the sound of a car motor. A . . . has not yet returned.
They are a little late, which is quite normal, on these bad roads.[8]

The preceding passage is one of the more explicit examples of
how sensory experience is colored by the absence of A . . . and
Franck. But implicitly all data reflect the effects of jealousy by their
magnification and intensification. Like Roderick Usher, the narrator's nerves have become acutely sensitive to the slightest stimuli.
*Percipi est dolere,* for all stimuli are suffused with the most universal
and elemental of human emotions. At another point in the novel the
sound made by a centipede on the wall becomes associated with the
mental image of Franck's car bursting into flames.[9] The *correspond-
ance* is then extended to the crackling sound of A . . .'s brush "now
moving down the loosened hair." [10] These evanescent sensations,
which intertwine and lock together according to their own peculiar
connotative logic, reach their summit as towards the end the transitions become more rapid and choppy. The frenetic orchestration of
the sonic and the visual becomes almost unbearable as the narrator's
psyche is buffeted about now by a crushed Scutigera on the wall
(that Franck had killed earlier with a wadded napkin), now by the
monotonous sound of the crickets in the nocturnal air, now by a
painful inventory of the contents of A . . .'s writing table (with
particular attention given to the "first of these which shows the
evident traces of a word scratched out on the upper right of which
only two tiny lines remain, greatly lightened by the eraser" [11]), and
now by a dining-room window one of whose cracked leaves reflects
the forms of Franck and A . . . as they emerge from the car, until
all disconnected segments of sensation merge into an overwhelming
kaleidoscopic unit. This climactic phase of the novel is perhaps best
epitomized by the image of A . . .'s profile, which in the bright
glare of the lamp is impressed upon the husband's retina so force-
fully that no matter where he looks the profile is seen. "The spot is
on the wall of the house, on the flagstones, against the empty sky. It
is everywhere in the valley, from the garden to the stream and up
the opposite slope. It is in the office too, in the bedroom, in the
courtyard, on the road up to the highway." [12]

It is my belief that an analytical approach to the *nouveau roman*
involving a comparative consideration of cinematographic techniques can help lead to a fruitful assessment of its aesthetic intent.
Much remains to be done in this respect. The foregoing study has

attempted to indicate some of the more obvious points of similarity. Basically, it would appear that the goal of *alittérature* differs little from the one that art has been pursuing since Cro-Magnon man was carving his crude designs on the walls of Breton caves: simply that of depicting the literal world through images, or rather, *replacing* it with images. As it is *homo faber's* ineluctable function to define, literalize, and categorize phenomena, to shape them to utilitarian ends, so is it the role of *homo ludens* to cut across the lines of intellect and to work his transfiguring magic upon the hard-and-fast connotations of everyday reality.

In *Jealousy* objects are more important to the story than the three protagonists. Their prominence is due not to their individual autonomy as civilized artifacts but rather to their interrelatedness, to the rhythmic sequence with which they appear. They form an alphabet of hieroglyphs which has meaning not only for the inner emotional life of the narrator but also unfailingly to that of the reader, since the aliteral montage seeps through abstract thought into the involuntary and inscrutable perceptual patterns of his dream life: As Sergei Eisenstein says of Japanese impressionist poetry: "It is the readers who make the 'haiku's' imperfection a perfection of art." [13] Imperfection in the sense that the "finely ground edges of the intellectually defined concepts formed by the combined ideograms are blurred in these poems." [14] Once again quoting Eisenstein on the ideogram: "By the combination of two 'depictables' is achieved the representation of something that is graphically undepictable." [15] Applying this dictum to *Jealousy*, one finds that Robbe-Grillet has with consummate irony first of all depicted in the language of a surveying engineer the stable world of definite angles and shapes and then, by projecting onto that world jealousy's poison, disintegrates it into a psychic montage whose meanings are at once "graphically undepictable." As we have said before, style sheds its literary nature to become completely *imagiste*. And it is in this sense that the style of *Jealousy* may be called cinematographic. To conclude, Robbe-Grillet has apparently given the lie to Proust's somewhat axiomatic statement denying true realism to a "literature which purports to 'decimate things,' to render only a wretched copy of their lines and surfaces." [16] The author of *Jealousy* has found a way to translate into verbal art the very materialism which threatens to stifle all artistic expression.

*JOHN HAZARD WILDMAN*

# TRANSLATED BY MURIEL SPARK

A GOOD TRANSLATION is always an approximation of one thing to another: of language to language, of feeling to feeling, of thought to thought—of one conception as nearly as possible to its parallel. The issue is a matter of degree and suggestiveness; the good translator acknowledges, at least tacitly, that one thing can never *be* another, but that between things there can be a kinship so close as to shrink the margin of difference to very small proportions indeed. He requires from his reader some awareness of this fact, and the ability to achieve comparisons without forgetting distinction and limitation. Cardinal Newman put the situation with beautiful precision when, speaking of the definitions which the Catholics had employed against the fourth-century Arians, he wrote: ". . . still they did not use these formulae for anything beyond shadows of sacred truth." [1] And Muriel Spark, in a series of tightly organized, sharply pointed novels, has achieved, with an amazing degree of illumination, translations of vast abstractions into crisp, containing modern terms, never losing the necessary qualities of suggestiveness and humility. [2]

For she has tackled the most difficult translation of all, one which is seemingly not afraid to forget parallelism and to define itself in strange figures—even when bringing light, to look upon itself, in Newman's words, as a shadow. She has obviously set herself the task of bringing good and evil over into concrete objects of consideration and into explicit situations. It is a temptation to say that she is never didactic, but simply investigative, a sentiment of this sort usually being considered loftily complimentary. But actually she

129

maintains firm stands: she is a translator of something objective (and in that sense foreign); she has the born translator's compulsion to make it accessible, and for the work which she loves, she entertains an undeviating conviction of the rightness of its terms.

Her frame of reference is the Catholic moral universe; her translations of its terms are into the language, actions, and above all, frames of mind of present-day England and derivative cultures. There must be an obstinate streak in her which insists upon the nearly impossible, as if one were ardently fixed upon turning the ode *To Autumn* over into Iroquois. For the English novel, born in the Age of Reason and continually exploring the many streams from that one source, yet nevertheless, when cutting across into other, unfamiliar channels, does strange things—chopping about in odd nervous ways, taking refuge in ambiguous underground dives, or even drying up.[3] The achievements of Mrs. Spark are many, but surely the most striking is her totally successful air of unself-consciousness. She gives an impression of moving in an atmosphere rather than creating it. She is not a voice crying in the wilderness; rather, she perceives effortlessly the real not only under the apparent, but permeating it.[4] To her the connection admits of no strain. "Mrs. Spark offers no comfortably secular explanation for any of these events," writes Samuel Hynes; "her stories are more likely to create mystery than to explicate it, and she is content to leave the supernatural that way— Mysterious. The world of human experience is complex, and not ultimately explicable; evil, her demons remind us, is as actual as nasty servants and telephone calls, and reality is odder than you think." [5]

But there are firm intentions moving through these novels; they become apparent at the best time of all when, the story completed, the reader examines himself and perceives there the way in which the novel grew to its total effect.

## II

André Gide was concerned about the bondage to surface reality of the English, French, and Russian novels; and in *The Counterfeiters* he causes one of the characters, Edouard, to inveigh against this deceptive limitation:

Is it because the novel, of all literary *genres,* is the freest, the most lawless . . . that the novel has always clung to reality with such timidity? . . . The only progress it looks to is to get still nearer to nature. The novel has never known that "formidable erosion of contours," as Nietszche calls it; that deliberate avoidance of life, which gave style to the works of the Greek dramatists, for instance, or to the tragedies of the French XVIIth century. Is there anything more perfectly and deeply human than these works? But that's just it—they are human only in their depths. . . .[6]

This is, however, an issue which Muriel Spark not so much faces as absorbs, for in her work the surfaces of life are both conductors to its depths and also—with the apparent inconsistency of existence— deceptive camouflage for its deeper reaches. In *Memento Mori,* she encompasses both extremes. Here, in a novel where almost all of the characters are belligerently old, she uses their apparent indestructibility as an ironic contrast with their frail tenure of mortality and also as a means of access to their fears. The stoutly barred door advertizes the terror within at the same time that it conceals it. And usually it includes the reason for the terror, for the murderer has entered long ago in the innocent glare of midday and lies happily hidden, waiting for his moment to come to him. Dame Lettie Colston, lifetime visitor of prisons, shrewd, hard starer at human defeat, professional humanitarian, receives threatening telephone calls, announcing her approaching death. It is characteristic of Dame Lettie (as it is of the many other characters who receive similar calls, but in differing voices) that she avoids the obvious explanation, which is also for her world the impossible one. It is Death who is calling. Only one character in the novel realizes this simple fact, a character who is both reconciled to the terms of her own life and yet (maybe for this very fact) unimprisoned by them.

Dame Lettie has recourse to all of the weapons of that world whose use she has studied in the very best manuals and with tightly reasoned logic has put to good practical service. She demands her rights from the police; she calls upon the services of the influential, who have good reason to know who she is; and after they have demonstrated their futility, she dies, murdered, concluding a scene of suspense which rises to the level of Shakespeare and even of a good murder mystery.

It is both unreasonable and yet right to expect of Dame Lettie that she should recognize the dimensions of existence and reckon with them—unreasonable because of the tight cocoon which holds her in; right, because she herself has spun it. "It *is* a troublesome remark," she cries, referring to the reminder of her death, demonstrating the point.[7]

But it is a grim list, this, as Mrs. Spark ticks off the types whose neat but adamantine self-sufficiency is the engine of their failure. In her method, there is a Kafka-like devotion to the point of contact between extremes. Possibly the chief note of distinction between the two, however, is that whereas Kafka uses disgust as the junction from which his many lines of meaning radiate, it is a sort of engagingness from which the trains go out in Mrs. Spark's interpretations. Alec Warner, in *Memento Mori*, is a far-from-lovable character, but there are in his composition those elements which cause a reader to warm to a character—which make the unregenerate Scrooge someone to collect in a way that no one ever wanted to collect a character from Theodore Dreiser. And yet Alec Warner is an ugly, basically repulsive person. His chief interest in life is compiling a dossier on everybody he knows. "If I have been successful in being the first to convey this [good] news to you, will you kindly oblige me by taking your pulse and your temperature immediately upon reading this letter," he requests, "and again one hour afterwards, and again the following morning, and inform me of the same, together with your normal pulse-rate and temperature if you know it? This will be invaluable for my records."[8] One is tempted to see in him an archetype of the corrupters of present-day society, the personality-measurement-men, absolute over a small self-manufactured universe. But actually Alec Warner is infinitely wider than this sort: he is capable of tentativeness; in this attitude there is an ample curiosity existing for its own sake which wars against small dogmatism, even if it is a malicious curiosity; and when his lifetime's harvest of card catalogues about human nature is burned up, he shows a bitter self-contained dignity which is as beyond the measurement-men as is his command of English prose.

But evil, welcomed, moves within him, as it does within Dame Lettie; and old age emphasizes the process and seems progressively to be getting it, safely, into protective deep freeze.

Perhaps, though, evil moves with its greatest ease within the old minor poet Percy Mannering: here smallness reaches large .dimensions, and an epic pettiness is attained through lifelong unobstructed devotion. Here also the Kafka-like proneness of Mrs. Spark to convey large issues through familiar smallness comes to high achievement, for his pitifully futile remarks about a doddering critic, Guy Leet, flow with a poisonous ease and an opulent flowering of evil. "Guy was never a good theatre critic," he sneers, pointing his steady intentions, "and he was a worse novel critic. . . . [He wrote] a lot of superficiality about how he attacked a novel of Henry James's and then met James outside the Atheneum one day and James was talking about his conscience as an artist and Guy's conscience as an artist. . . ." [9] And on it goes. Indeed, the steadying influence of evil was never better brought home.

But here is no doomed universe. Mrs. Spark is as far from the authorized versions of predestination, newly revised, as she is from sentimental evasion. She would probably agree with Frank Sheed that the action of a novel should ultimately rest on a realistic conception of existence; and her conception obviously contains the answer as well as the problem. [10] There is, for instance, Charmion, the aged writer of what would long ago have been called railway fiction. She has so long outdistanced her fame that she has swum into a revival of it. She is also frequently senile and batty; but there is a pervasive quality of goodness that holds together the odd fragmentations of her life. It is she who, progressively made more of a captive in her daily round by a ruthless woman, escapes the encirclement by the superior tactic of putting the battle on another field. There is no sentimentality here, but there is an elusive delicacy in charming, unexpected union with charity; and as with the saints, so with Charmion, the achievement goes beyond the explanation. One sees only the more tangible aspects of the supernatural virtue of charity; its vaster reaches are felt in the vibrations of its touchable part.

But in this novel, filled with the spiteful minutiae of upper-middle-class British existence, Mrs. Spark has traced with Horatian concealment of artistry the flow of grace, and its absence.

III

There is also in these translations of Muriel Spark a happy fusion of setting and people. As there is growth of personality and theme within her novels, so also as an integral part of this process, there is a progressive self-fulfillment of her setting. If there is none of the romantic proneness to treat the setting as opulent scenery before which the characters act, neither is there that self-consciously thematic treatment of setting which, in Thomas Hardy, makes the reader feel as though he were being managed with the kindly condescension due to the slow-witted and having indicated to him, with a slow patient forefinger, the philosophical dimensions of the landscape. Mrs. Spark in this respect fits in admirably with Elizabeth Bowen's conception of setting brought to its ideal function: "Nothing can happen nowhere. The locale of the happening always colours the happening, and often, to a degree, shapes it.

Plot having pre-decided what is to happen, scene, scenes, must be so found, so chosen, as to give the happening the desired force." [11]

Possibly in *The Ballad of Peckham Rye* this admirable treatment of setting is most observable, although not any more skillfully used than in her other novels. Here, however, the devil walks in unlikely haunts. Why it should be unusual for him to circulate among the drab energetic ways of British middle-class to lower-middle-class existence is not clear, but somehow he is usually expected to function within greater ceremonial blaze.[12] Nor is one definitely authorized by Mrs. Spark's treatment to call Dougal Douglas, the central figure of *The Ballad of Peckham Rye*, the devil; rather, one has suspicions in that direction. By the end of the novel, however, there is no doubt whatsoever as to the evil which he has so joyfully welcomed into himself and even more joyfully dispensed.

Yet Mrs. Spark has much of the mystery writer about her: she knows the importance of gathering effects. These she has invested with thematic significance far beyond the dimensions of the typical mystery; also, the truth progressively dawns rather than bursts at the end of things. But she knows the narrative importance of a growth of light, and the uses of tension in that respect.[13]

Therefore, the slick achievements of Dougal in the world of factory and plant are beautiful to behold, provided that one does not come within his orbit. As for the evil nature of the thing, no one denies to evil its own peculiar beauty, the archangelic splendor dying but not yet dead, especially when the beauty is transferred to a process, to a career, to rounded shape and fluent line. Otherwise, in recent decades, how could so many smelly political careers have been so successfully translated into novels carrying the enthusiastic approbation of author and readers? Mrs. Spark, however, has the cruel ability of certain ancient ballad writers to recognize marks and signs and to be shocked but not surprised when the diabolic eye grows drumly. There is an appropriate grimness with which she follows Dougal Douglas in his rise to clerkly importance and beyond, and retails his crescent ways. There is also a grim economy about her treatment of the bitterness, even to the point of death, which he causes.

Nor is one allowed the satisfaction of Dougal's failures; for when these occur, his manipulation of them is confident and authoritative, his transitions to something better easily within his own control. It is true that at the end when he is left writing successful autobiographical novels on the Riviera, all does not seem to be too entirely well with him, in the light of hints that previously he has slipped successfully out of so many fields of endeavor that almost no careers are any longer open to his talents. But nevertheless he remains a threat beyond the point of the novel's conclusion.

And this threat remains because his presence remains in the lunchrooms of large establishments, in the successfully evoked atmosphere of rooming houses, in the offices of vice-presidents, and in entertainments of purely local dimensions: these were the fields over which he ranged and on which he left his dead.[14] One brief look at his room gives the measure of Mrs. Spark's ability to evoke setting:

He sat down among his belongings, which were partly in and out of his zipper bag. There was a handsome brass bedstead with a tall railed head along which was gathered a muslin curtain. It was the type of bed which was becoming fashionable again, but Miss Frierne did not know this. It was the only item of furniture in the room for which she had apologized; she had explained it was only temporary and would soon be replaced by a new single divan. Dougal detected in this little speech a good intention, repeated to each newcomer, which never came off. He assured her that he liked the brass bed with its railings and knobs. Could he remove, perhaps, the curtain? Miss Frierne said, no, it needed the bit of curtain, and before long would be replaced by a single divan. But no, Dougal said, I like the bed. Miss Frierne smiled to herself that she had found such an obliging client. "Really, I do like it," Dougal said, "more than anything else in the room." [15]

Considering the grim destiny of Miss Frierne in her relationship with Dougal, this is strange and interesting, but it is not kind. It is also an emphatically successful mingling of setting, character, and ironically foreboded theme.

Even more obvious, though less impressive, is Mrs. Spark's use of setting in *Robinson*. Here a plane has fallen on a small Atlantic island; and Mrs. Spark does an admirable job of not sounding like all other authors on a similar subject.

But the virtues are also positive, and in this novel evil moves more obliquely than it does in her other works. That is, its early ways are oblique; when it comes into direct attack, it becomes massively apparent, but always couched in human terms: when her effects come out of the foggy eeriness of adumbration, there is a sort of tropical glare lighting up their significance, the one exception being Robinson himself, the misanthrope. He stalks through the setting of his island, always alone, a trifle melodramatic in his lonely satisfactions, in his paradoxical pride that he has not allowed his three unwanted guests, sole survivors of the plane crash, to break through into the isolation of himself. His attitude is paradoxical, for there is a small note of surliness within it which contradicts his main point and which suggests that there has been an intrusion into his aloofness. But if his attitude is illogical in a minor way, it is even more impressively human.

For there is about Robinson that air of discontent which drives many people of refined sensibilities to life upon some sort of an island, there movingly to attempt a kind of inner and outer methodical hardening, the sort of protectiveness that so many of Mrs. Spark's characters flee to both as a refuge from and a substitute for religion. However, Robinson, like all of her major (and many minor) characters, is never imprisoned within a dominant trait. In his case, as in many others, it is a kind of central elusiveness—suggestive, but never admitting, of final definition, that provokes probing rather than cataloguing. And it is through the deserted island, over which Robinson nevertheless seems to rule so absolutely (and at least in the manner of crops, so inefficiently) that Mrs. Spark establishes his mysterious loneliness. It is in this way rather than through his somewhat conventional disdain of religion that we move toward the essence of the man.

Above all other places, it is the dangerous crater of the volcano that Mrs. Spark uses to convey some of the dangerous ambiguity of Robinson and the chuckling note of evil in him, as though he enjoyed tempting his guests through fear.

"How awful to fall in," I said. "No-one would survive it."
Robinson said, "The body would be sucked under immediately. There is a continuous action of suction and rejection going on down there." He

added, "Curiously, if you throw in anything sizeable the eruption gives out a sort of scream . . . the suction action through this narrow pipe causes the sound, do you see?" I didn't see, but I lifted the biggest stone I could manage, and sent it rolling into the milling mud. It gave out a very dreadful scream.

"Sometimes," said Robinson, "without provocation it sighs." [16]

The other characters too are revealed through their new habitat. The narrator, especially, feels the contrast between the new ways and those of her former life in England. With that air of disengagement and commitment which Mrs. Spark strikes off so easily, she weaves her attitude out of reminiscence and current reactions. She searches for small comforts, particularly tea, but her mind's eyes range far beyond the caddy. They go laterally in space too and back in time; they are avid for analogy, and Robinson's general dislike of religion brings to mind a brother-in-law's antiseptic hatred of religion's gaudier moments, especially Marian devotions in Latin countries. But why should Mary, defender against heresies—thinks January Marlowe, the narrator—promote heresy in her own name? This bit of logic is hard and tight in tone, coming immediately after a meditation on the brother-in-law's hopeful quest of finding the narrator on adulterous vacation. And this, in turn, brings her to a consideration of her two fellow plane travelers, both becoming alarmingly themselves during the apparently permanent disappearance of Robinson.

Conrad's narrators, especially the over-helpful Marlow, maintain a firm control over characters and setting, and their cigar-smoky insistence on Everyman's irony is of its nature obtrusive. But January, like the approved-of characters in Mrs. Spark's other novels, is an open-minded investigator of existence, not a thematic chorus. It is not part of Mrs. Spark's convictions, however, that the open mind is *sui generis* closed to grace and can be identified by that happy state of adamantine lock-up. Indeed, she believes quite the contrary. January, who is a sizable distance from sainthood, nevertheless enjoys an illuminating calm minor brilliance which translates so easily into humor, into shrewd appraisal, into confident unboastful action that one inevitably remembers the theological dictum that grace works through nature. "Most of all, I love to compare faces," she says. "I have seen a bus conductor who resembles a woman don of my acquaintance, I have seen the face of Agnes throwing itself from side to side in a pulpit; I make a meal of these." [17]

Roaming the landscape of the island, freed from both the restraints of life in England and from the presence of Robinson, are January's two fellow survivors of the plane crash, Jimmie Waterford and Tom Wells. In the case of each of them there is an ambiguity of intention in which evil may possibly have a full hold, as it most certainly does stand in part possession. Here, the probability of violence impinges; and there is a certain affinity with Graham Greene in the easy confluence of mystery suspense with theological conviction except that in Greene, mental action is matched with external movement; in Mrs. Spark, the second is emphatically subordinate to the first. In this respect, she is closer to the frame of mind of Joyce in *Ulysses* and Faulkner in *The Sound and the Fury* than she is to the Aristotelian conception of tragedy as an action. Suspense gathers mightily in her novel, but the approach is still more meditative than it is dramatic. The matter is, however, hierarchical, not competitive: psychological examination and spiritual examination have the upper hand.[18]

Nevertheless, the obvious catalyst is the setting, the nature of the island. Particularly is this so in the case of Tom Wells, blackmailer and dealer in the occult, one profession supplementing the other, and both carried out on the lowest, dullest, meanest, and most substantial of levels. It was almost inevitable that he should edit a cheap magazine and from the lucrative source of letters from the lonely build himself a brisk-moving blackmail trade. This we do not know for a long stretch of the novel. Companionship breeds a common atmosphere, and we must have a small nasty climate of Tom within ourselves before the specific nature of Tom can bloom in its encouraging sympathetic temperature. But it is the island whose oppressive rural charms lower upon him and compress secretiveness until its tightness must out. Nor can one evil fail in so obvious a situation to seek out another: the mysteriousness of Robinson demands a blackmailer's focused attention.

Jimmie also brings to the island a past that prefers wider places for freer circulation and that sort of concealment part of whose basic nature is circuitousness. His is a more amiable aptitude for perversity; his appetite for evil uses the pointed complaisance of the freeloader. It is a more pleasant brand than Tom's of the same general invention.

Her stay upon the island is both a revelation and a confirmation to January. As in all of Mrs. Spark's novels, examination reveals an interesting world in which grace wars with evil. The former is intrinsically invincible; but the latter flourishes where welcomed, and luxuriant groves of green bay trees cast a dense indicative shade appropriate also to islands other than those found in the most conscientious atlas. From her stay with Robinson, January has learned nothing new, but she has vastly extended the implications of a steady unsentimental Catholic view. Robinson, above all, has not escaped her estimates; and she has the good sense and humility to realize that much of him goes beyond her comprehension. There seems to be something of the supernatural indicating itself through one of Newman's shadows, indicating but not totally revealing.

## IV

Humor is the essential ingredient of a Muriel Spark novel, the pattern of mind which suffuses her translations. Even in her weakest (and her first) novel, *The Comforters,* it sustains the self-consciousness of her apologetics ("Caroline quoted . . . what she had heard said of someone else: 'He exhausted his capacity for conversion when he became an Englishman' " [19]); and in *The Bachelors* it flows rich in an arid land, causing a frighteningly nimble luxuriance of growth in the evil medium Patrick Seton, but producing also a contrasting, slow, maturing movement of realization in other bachelors—the roots perhaps of grace gradually engaging an unlikely soil.

In *The Bachelors,* the humor flows easily into the word choice and the figures of speech, knowing where to stop and insinuate; for Mrs. Spark, like Lawrence Sterne and Lewis Carroll, knows that humor is never stronger than when it is suggestive. Her goal is not theirs, and the feeling of her humorous universe is quite different from theirs, but there is an identity of over-all control. "It is all demonology and to do with creatures of the air," thinks Robert Bridges, the epileptic, at the conclusion of *The Bachelors,* translating futility, thinking of other bachelors and of himself, a bachelor, "and there are others besides ourselves, he thought, who lie in their beds like happy countries that have no history. Others ferment in prison; some rot, maimed; some lean over the bannisters of presbyteries to see if anyone is going to answer the telephone." [20]

In *The Comforters,* where Mrs. Spark's Catholicism is artistically worn just slightly at an angle or maybe with its collar needing a barely perceptible straightening, the humor of shrewd observation and neat dialogue perform a corrective task.[21] In this novel she is a bit prone to make characters (especially the central one, Caroline Rose) explain religion, rather than move happily or otherwise within its paradoxically demanding liberty. So it is with relief and release, as at the resumption of Mass after the intrusion of a sermon, that one reads such dialogue as this:

> "But Caroline isn't a Catholic."
> "She's just become one."
> "I *thought* she was looking thin. . . ."[22]

Or one comes with a feeling of reward upon the shrewd, tight, witty little sketch of Mrs. Jepp: "Louisa Jepp did everything very slowly but with extreme attention, as some do when they know they are slightly drunk. Lawrence heard a clink and a pause, and tinkle and a pause, breakfast being laid. Her footsteps clicked like a clock that is running down as she moved between the scullery and the little hot kitchen; she refused to shuffle."[23]

The chief delight in this novel, though, is the tantalizing nature of its humor when it becomes mixed in with happenings defying an obvious explanation—Mrs. Hogg's disappearance from the back seat of a moving car and her casual rematerializing; the novel which is writing itself through Caroline Rose, herself a humble authority on the novel, as is evidenced by the work on which she is currently engaged—*Form in the Modern Novel*. And yet she probably has more of a control over the novel than she thinks. The reader is twisted and put upon, but enjoys the amiable sadism of the thing. Mrs. Hogg is certainly an evil woman: she has no private life; all of her malevolence is expended in public effort. Is she also a witch? Why can she appear and disappear? How often has this happened without being noticed? She is an expert in reporting unsavory facts: has she had more opportunities in this respect than the reader knows? How can the novel write itself through Caroline? Surely, at the most, foreknowledge, not predestination.

Mrs. Spark handles her most vital insinuations in the language, if not the century, of Lawrence Sterne.

In *The Bachelors*, the grimness of her humor enjoys special attention: she studies her bachelors when they are physically alone, and she watches them take this aloneness into company. Often they compare, but they never share. They never give up this totally central possession. It is both their chief pleasure and their source of pathetic isolation.[24] Above all, our own point of view remains investigative and even sympathetic, but we are denied an empathy that would confuse our critical faculties. "But detachment," writes John Updike, "is the genius of her fiction. We are lifted above the characters, and though they are reduced in size and cryptically foreshortened, they are all seen at once, and their busy interactions are as plain and pleasing as a solved problem." [25]

## V

What constitutes the prime of life? In British civilization it is certainly most accessible in those hearty, fortyish gentlemen from Charles Dickens or *Punch,* red-cheeked, joyous, and upright. Ideally, in their legend, there runs an insinuation of broad acres and constitutional goodness, but actually their real prototype is Hogarth's industrious apprentice grown rotund in belly and bank account, both swellings being virtue's behavior under active encouragement. Under this former apprentice work many apprentices.

The irony of *The Prime of Miss Jean Brodie* lies in superficial affinity with this legend, adapted to the terms and figure of an instructor in a successful girl's school, and in sharp inner distinction. One is tempted to see a commentary on the whole legend, but Mrs. Spark is primarily an analyzer of particular situations, not a satirist. The searching spotlight is very definitely on Miss Jean Brodie in particular, rather than on successfully domineering instructors in general. Indeed, so carefully is it focused on her ways and motives, shrewdly viewed, that the supernatural is relegated to the power behind an insinuated approach, in unawareness of which Miss Brodie moves, rather than something which touches down into the action.

Her ideal is the formation of her girls; and she has come to her prime in this central respect. "Give me a girl at an impressionable age," she says, "and she is mine for life." [26] The formation of the open mind is achieved by coursing the zigzagging trails previously blazed by Miss Brodie. "Hold up your books," she commands her girls, so that they will have thrown up an academic protective cover against someone like the headmistress. "Meantime I will tell you about my last summer holiday in Egypt . . . I will tell you about the care of the skin, and of the hands . . . about the Frenchman I met in the train to Biarritz . . . and I must tell you about the Italian painting I saw. Who is the greatest Italian painter?"

"Leonardo da Vinci, Miss Brodie."

"That is incorrect. The answer is Giotto, he is my favorite." [27]

But a tight-closed fist of an intention, reposing centrally within all other intentions, is a ruthless holding-on to the importance of herself. This is both understood and not understood by her; but there is enough consciousness of it to bring an attendant awareness of emptiness, a realization that nothing grows out of nothing. We realize, more than Miss Brodie, that this can never be a purely negative process, especially in the sense that the perversions of evil bring, at least humanly viewed, positive results. In this sense, emptiness has brought bleakly positive results.

Hans Castorp, in Thomas Mann's *Magic Mountain,* veered toward his prime in strange unintended ways; but his bewilderment eventually became fruitful in regard to evil and death: he found the first in mystical affinity with good, and death an integral part of life. This attitude may have its inadequacies in the light of a fuller truth, but it seems not to have been a bad prop with which to stalk out into World War I. Miss Brodie's pointed life left no room for fruitful bewilderment until it was too late. Like others in Mrs. Spark's works, she suffered from self-enclosure. Sandy Stranger, one of Miss Brodie's set of girls, now grown through the years into reminiscence and assessment, has thoughts on the subject: ". . . she began to sense what went to the makings of Miss Brodie who had elected herself to grace in so particular a way and with more exotic suicidal enchantment than if she had simply taken to drink like other spinsters who couldn't stand it any more." [28]

## VI

In her study of Mary Wollstonecraft Shelley, Muriel Spark wrote: "I would suggest that an individual may maintain a satisfactory fellowship with the world who is intellectually pessimistic—today, in fact, this type is quite common—but the emotional pessimist is rarely at ease in personal relationships." [29]

In summarizing the effect of her novels to date, one feels that, without embarrassing her reader with underlines, she has shown the intellectual pessimist's self-cooled poise and his emotional counterpart's perhaps more hopeful days in the desert. Just as impressively, she has sleuthed the neat path of those who are neither one thing nor the other, but a third; and with an objectivity that does not hesitate to lean cantingly from its own definition she follows the trail of even-pulsed, practical evil, confident of its ways. In her short story "The Black Madonna" she records with a lively clinical exactitude the ruthless efficiency of a novena-faithful woman in giving away her embarrassingly dark child, who seems possibly to be the eventual result of many prayers to the Black Madonna.[30]

Perhaps we have here the indication of whatever weakness Mrs. Spark bears as an artist. Like every other artist, she emphasizes—and in doing so, necessarily omits. There is kindness in here, a brisk sort of kindness, as in her approach to old Mrs. Jepp in *The Comforters*, but little sustained tenderness. There is also the penalty that has to be paid for that air of competence that surrounds all of her characters, but especially the wicked ones or the failures, who march so surely under their respective banners: their briskness lacks leisurely psychological curves. And perhaps even loneliness is too sure of its own nature and never gets lost in fearful informal curiosity about itself.

But this is to cavil.

In these novels, there lie translated from the supernatural world into the natural sphere of demonstration not only Newman's "shadows of sacred truth" but also his remark, made descriptively but in no sense despairingly, that there can be no sinless literature about sinful man. Neither, concludingly, can one find despair, but rather a lively, indeed joyful, sense of involvement in the human condition in Muriel Spark's own lines:

> I therefore resign
> The seven-league line
> In footwear of super-cosmic design
> To the global hops
> Of wizards and wops;
> Hoping that if Byzantium
> Should appear in Kensington
> The city will fit the size
> Of the perimeter of my eyes

And of the span of my hand:
Hands and eyes that understand
This law of which the third
Text is the thing defined,
The flesh made word.[31]

Here, indeed, is more than cue.

*RICHARD J. O'DEA*

# THE POETRY OF ALLEN TATE
## ( *intellectus quaerens fidem* )

TIME AND ALLEN TATE are old enemies; and like a modern Jacob long and often has he wrestled with it in prose and in poetry. And as it did to Jacob, the battle has left its limp, for after years of being the victim of Tatean irony, Time has effected its own ironic twists. The young fugitive has become the venerable and respected "sixty-year-old smiling public man." The man of letters who had regarded professors of English literature with something less than approval ("Prospero serves humanity in steam-heated universities, three / Thousand dollars a year") is himself now lecturing to steam-heated students at, we may hope, slightly better than three thousand a year. The man of no faith ("For the drying God above. . . . No longer bears for us / The living wound of love") has become a member of one of the least flexible creeds. But perhaps the most offensive irony is that the critic who viewed scientism and romanticism as two of the gravest curses of the modern age, has begun to be regarded as a romantic himself. Miss Vivienne Koch seems first to have pointed the finger in this direction,[1] and Richard Foster has developed the thesis to book length.[2]

It is not, however, the intention of this study to point out the inconsistencies in Allen Tate's life and poetry. Growth, of necessity, means change. Few men in our age have more consistently probed, challenged, and analyzed the modern human situation. Few, if any, have spoken out in more withering scorn and moral indignation against the false panaceas, the slippery theory, the dangerous half-truth, the abstractionism that would render man something less than

145

man. If then there has been a change in Tate's poetry and criticism, it has not been an inconsistent one, but rather a growth of a questing intellect, systematically and with severe logic rejecting as untenable various philosophic, social, and aesthetic positions until he arrived finally both with intellect and sensibility at the existential wholeness that had been Dante's. Both Tate's criticism and his poetry have almost from his earliest fugitive years had a certain moral tenor. His search, perhaps subconscious, has been a reversal of that of the medieval scholastics. They thought within a tradition of faith and strove to understand what they had already accepted—*fides quaerens intellectum*. Tate in his poetry has been a microcosm of the modern age, skeptical intellect with dissociated sensibility striving to rediscover for himself and for his age a faith—*intellectus quaerens fidem*. It is this tone of almost desperate intellectuality that gives to his poetry its toughness of fiber and philosophic density. And while Tate's poetry and criticism are a disturbingly creative and critical analysis of the modern ego of the thirties and forties, it is the deeply rational content of this vision that raises it above topicality and because of which both poetry and criticism will endure.

In spite of Miss Koch's admonition of approaching Tate's poetry by way of the "doctrinal fallacy," some general grasp of his ideas is, I think, necessary to an understanding of his poetry.[3] Without this, his personalized symbols remain meaningless. Even so good a contextualist critic as Cleanth Brooks seems in method, at least, to support this judgment.[4] Tate himself, however, would demand but two requisites for the comprehension of modern poetry: "If we wish to understand anything, there is only the hard way; if we wish to understand Donne and Eliot, perhaps we had better begin young, to read the classical languages, and a little later the philosophers. There is probably no other way." [5]

But before violating Mr. Tate's own canon of comprehension, it might be well to consider but briefly a rather consistent criticism of his poetry. Kenneth Burke first implied it when he wrote of a lack of "physicality" in it.[6] John Bradbury, in a more recent critique, discovers "the absence of the pulsing blood that warms Donne's wit-play into moving expression." [7] Both critics are most probably correct; but they may be demanding an univocal genus of poetry when in reality there are many species. Tate's poetry is highly cerebral, but it is not without passion, a savage indignation of the intellectual viewing chaos. It possesses, at its best, a cold rational fury that is quite unique, is immediately identified, and achieves an almost prophetic grandeur. At its worst, it becomes querulous and irritable. But it is by the poet's success not by his failure that he is to be judged.

Tate's philosophy is perhaps not so complex as both he and his critics sometimes make it. The core of his thought seems to revolve around epistemology and ethics rather than metaphysics. It is the modern crisis of culture in decay, a culture in which there is no teleological unity, only a multiplicity of ends that prompts his reexamination of Western man's origins. Like Maritain and other more systematic thinkers, he sees the modern fissure between life and action, contemplation and knowledge for use to begin with Descartes and mathematical abstractionism. This partial knowledge gives rise to the modern scientific method—even criticism has fallen victim to it—that knows only to use.[8] Science imposes its will upon nature and even upon man, not to understand, not to contemplate the existential whole, but to manipulate observable laws for positivistic results. The romantic poet, revolting against science, falls into this same imposition of thesis by will upon uncontemplated, nongrasped reality. But the real villain of modern society is science, not the poet, and the quantitative abstraction that passes for a demireligion, a methodology that looks to positivistic means, never to the final end which is total truth. In history this method abstracts causes and effects from concrete tradition. It gives modern man quantity when he is starved for the quality that is time, that can exist only in tradition.

The problem then of the poet, of modern man, is somehow to recapture the total grasp of reality, of time past existing in time present. Can this be done? In the unfragmented cultures of the past it was accomplished either by the greater myth of religion or by the lesser myth of history. The South once possessed such a lesser myth until the abstractionism of the North destroyed it as scientific skepticism has destroyed the greater. The prototype of modern, abstract man was Henry Adams, who determined to arrive at each moral decision by way of a system of abstract deduction. The prototype of the unified society was Jefferson, in whom morality, manners, even rhetoric were fused in tradition.

In the face of the modern crisis, Tate seems at times almost to despair. Some of his fury arises from the hopelessness of the situation. And if this atomization of man by science were not enough, both poet and reader are faced with the decay of rhetoric that renders "communion" impossible. Only an abstract and behavioristic system of "communication" remains.

What is the modern poet to do? He must shun pure poetry that revels in sensation; allegory and romanticism that are rhetorical motivations to action, that do not possess a self-contained end and existential whole to be contemplated. It is his duty to salvage something from tradition that is more than mere repetition, more than the clothes that recall the sweet memory of dead grandmother. He must create grandmother living. "The living person is the traditional poet, the convention plus the individual experience; the clothes in the attic are the convention alone." [9]

For a long time Tate's thinking seemed dangerously near to the Socratic fallacy, that some kind of existential knowledge alone might save man and the poet. Later he arrived at the conclusion that the will must be joined to the intellect, that vision without charity is not enough. "Neither the artist nor the statesman will communicate fully again until the rule of love, added to the rule of law, has liberated him." [10] The greater myth has become for him a personal reality. If the hell which is modern society, ". . . the society of means without ends, in which nobody participated with the full substance of his humanity" . . . not "our ancestors and our brothers . . . Julien Sorel, Emma Bovary, Captain Ahab, Hepzibah Pyncheon, Roderick Usher, Lambert Strether, Baron de Charlus, Stephen Dedalus, Joe Christmas" has been viewed and reported by modern literature, Tate has discovered for that same society a redemption, "that in order to love, he must have a medium even less palpable than air." Social salvation, liberation from communication, and participation in communion comes "only through the love of God." [11]

Tate's former solution to the modern crisis of fragmented society had been a qualitative culture not unlike Arnold's or Newman's. At present, like Newman, he realizes that a traditional culture is not enough unless that culture be Christian. "For men in the Christian tradition, perhaps for all men in advanced societies, the simplicity of natural grace is inadequate; we require as the dynamic synthesizer of our dual nature the activity of a higher power Divine Grace, which can be fully known only through the Christian Revelation." [12] To create the vision of dissociated man, Tate may once have believed that the best means was a poetry that achieved a tension midway between that of the metaphysicals, a poetry of extension, and that of the great Romantics and Symbolists, a poetry of intension.[13] His acceptance of the Christian vision may explain the change in his more recent poetry. A new rhetoric becomes necessary to express a higher truth. "But the other, higher meanings of poetry might well be true, in spite of the fictional plot, if the poet had the gift of anagogic, or spiritual insight." [14] Perhaps Tate now possesses that gift.

Of necessity, this is an incomplete summary. It has tended to stress the problem of knowledge and of morality that seems central to Tate's poetry. Delmore Schwartz has made a more metaphysical and more comprehensive summary.[15] But inadequate though the foregoing may be, it will, I hope, make clearer the recurring images and tensions in the poems: Plato's cave image, a symbol of the shadow world of abstraction; the continuous use of light for the quantitative vision of science, of night for despair, of twilight for the partial vision of modern man, of the sea as an almost Arnoldian symbol of faith or wholeness. The recurrent Christ image as "drying," "long-gestating," "the Holy Runt," "Year after year the blood of Christ will sleep / In the holy tree," "every son-of-a-bitch is Christ," "mummy Christ," retains its shock value but in the context of Tate's thought emphasizes the modern lack of faith. Aeneas, the symbol of a rich culture plundered by a barbaric culture, is at once the South and the progenitor of Western man. Motion is a frequent symbol for aimless action, for modern life directed by means not ends. Water, like the sea, is used as an almost sacramental symbol of regeneration; but its use can be ironic as in Eliot's "Waste Land." The water that could save, drowns or becomes a frozen hell of ice. The last image, "Both damned in eternal ice," with its explicit allusion to Dante's *Inferno,* but manifests an ever increasing influence of Dante upon Tate in allusion, in form ( the *terza rima*), and in allegory.

Nearly all studies of Tate's poetry have followed chronological order. These excellent and comprehensive critiques have the very worthwhile advantage of studying the poet's growth in technique and in theme. On the other hand, even in his earliest volume, *Mr. Pope and Other Poems,* Tate bids us read his poems according to the divisions of space, time, and history.[16] He divides his final, carefully deleted canon (*Poems: 1922–1947* reissued as *Poems* in 1960 to which he has added "The Swimmers" and "The Buried Lake") into nine sections.

A less inclusive but perhaps more emphatic division of time, death, fragmentation, and religion will be followed in this study. It has the advantage of viewing the poetic expression of Tate's core ideas without reference to chronology and without too many confusing subdivisions. Tate himself can conceive of an infinite catalogue of the fragmentations of the modern mind. "There is literally no end to this list of dissociations because there is no end, yet in sight, to the fragmenting of the western mind." [17] Under each divison one poem judged particularly expressive of the division, will be considered in detail with allusion to similar ideas in other poems.

Gavin Stevens in Faulkner's *Requiem for a Nun* tersely defines what might be the theme of "The Mediterranean": "The past is never dead. It's not even past." In this poem, Tate dramatically presents his idea of qualitative time and the problem it creates. The concretely visual imagery of the poem becomes a symbol of intellectual vision. The actual motion of the boat is symbolic of a movement back into the past. The modern protagonists, "we," move from the quantitative present, "time's monotone," through the "margin" into "antiquity's delay." The "secret need" of rootless, modern man is nourished by the past, by "the very plates Aeneas bore." The aimless motion of a society without purpose is "derelict" and the protagonists from this society having at last discovered the past, "Drop sail, and hastening to drink all night / Eat dish and bowl to take that sweet land in!" Aeneas and his men by devouring the plates removed the curse of the Harpies. Momentarily the curse is removed from the men out of "time's monotone." But the curse is only briefly lifted: "We for that time might taste the famous age / Eternal here yet hidden from our eyes." The protagonist of the "Ode to the Confederate Dead" cannot taste the past even briefly; he can but praise the vision of the dead, can but see the present, "Cursing only the leaves crying / Like an old man in a storm." He, modern man, "a mummy in time," cannot see for he too is cursed; "the patient curse / That stones the eyes." This inability of man to fuse present and past in one "smooth essential flow" is a frequent theme in Tate's poetry. "Ditty" discovers that nature is somehow a continuum; it is only "men, who fail." In the "Horation Epode" the poet has escaped the monotone of the present by way of Webster's vision of good and evil, but the present reasserts itself, "And the katharsis fades in the warm water of a yawn." In the "Autumn" section of "Seasons of the Soul" the poet cannot even regain his own past. In a dream-like vision, he sees father, mother, and others like ghosts who cannot see him, "Who had no look or voice / For him whose vision froze / Him in the empty hall." Like the lover on the train in "Retroduction to American History," the locked-in-ego has no spiritual vision, "His very eyeballs fixed in disarticulation."

In "The Mediterranean," however, the "landless Wanderers" have escaped, have achieved the unification, if but passingly, of tradition. As a result their forefathers "live" and the "Ocean" is "breathing," a living symbol of spiritual communion. But as in Keats's "Ode to the Nightingale" the vision fades, so too does this vision falter and the stanza which began in sound and image with such joyous tranquility, "Let us lie down once more by the breathing side / Of Ocean, where our live forefathers sleep / As if the Known Sea still were a month wide," suddenly halts with, "Atlantis howls but is no longer steep!" The sibilants, the sharp caesura, the final bathetic "steep" all bring an end to the vision. The protagonists face the present with a question, and it seems that "the fair land" that will "unman our conquest" does so because modern science has "cracked the hemispheres with careless hand." The final stanza ends with a richness of imagery, a heaviness of vowels, and a smooth forward flow that is almost Keatsian. But again the sharp caesura, the internal rhyme, and punctuation bring the languid movement to a violent halt. The final "in that land were we born" is a lament.

Louis Rubin sees in this concluding stanza a harmony between poet and nature: "A scene has been described; the ultimate act is one of contemplation."[18] Vivienne Koch has a different view: "The poem ends with a vision of the fecund and luxurious exhaustion of the South—the South conceived as the inheritor of classical culture by a kind of mystical primogeniture."[19] Both readings have a certain validity. However, the last two lines of stanza eight and the whole of stanza nine seem to come as a forlorn answer to the question asked in the caption, "*Quem das finem, rex magne, dolorum?*" There has been a momentary escape from sorrow but the final answer of the poem is "*numquam!*" Because modern man has shattered the union of past and present by destroying the myth of history, there will be no end to his sorrows. The "barbarous brine / Whelms us to the tired land." The momentary vision fled, we return to a world where history gives no vision but "pares / The nails of Catullus, sniffs his sheets, restores / His 'passionate underwear.'"

In form, "The Mediterranean" exemplifies Tate at his best. The first four quatrains are one descriptive sentence. The fifth asks a question; the sixth and seventh present a partial answer. The first two lines of the eighth interrogate the present; the third line explains the impossibility of solution, and the final line and concluding quatrain in one unbroken sweep give the woeful answer to the central problem of the poem. There seems little need to belabor the metrics. They are handled with consummate skill. Caesural pause, rhetorical and metrical stress, the variation of vowel sounds—all this makes one wonder why critics have spoken of Tate's rough and tortured verse. What does seem to emerge from the form is that Tate is most successful when he confines his subject matter to strict and careful pattern. The dramatic quality of the poem, the accurate visual imagery which functions, as does Joyce's, on a realistic and symbolic level, the action itself again achieving a dual function, the classical allusions to Aeneas and to Odysseus fuse into an amazingly concrete and complex whole. This is, perhaps, as close as art can come to the concrete universal.

Like Time, the grinning skull too haunts Tate's poetry. One has but to scan the titles of his poems to see what a preponderant proportion treat this subject. Even in the poems that do not treat it directly, death is introduced in the figures of speech: "as if the sleepy dead / Had never fallen to drowse" ("To a Romantic"); "And the sapphire corpse undressed by Donne" ("Progress of Oenia"); "A corpse is your bedfellow" ("Retroduction to American History"). The ever-present allusion direct or otherwise to death or to death-in-life may be the quality in his poetry that encourages critics to compare Tate to Donne.

What, one might ask, is the reason for this morbid concentration? Death in Tate's poetry seems to have at least three functions: It shocks the reader into an awareness of the inadequacy of his philosophy; it is the beginning of reality, "Time begins to elucidate her bones"; and it is used to emphasize the life-in-death theme: "Our property in fire is death in life." The answer to the question in "The Oath": "Who are the dead?" is "Then Lytle turned with an oath—By God it's true!" "The Meaning of Death" is a life of shadow without substance; "In a long night when learned arteries / Mounting the ice and sum of barbarous time / Shall yield, without essence, perfect accident. / We are the eyelids of defeated caves." In "The Anabasis" the fear is lest we "Should join, before our place, / Death's long anabasis." In "To a Romantic" the reader is told "The dead are those whose lies / Were doors to a narrow house."

It is the first use primarily that Tate makes of death in his early (1924) and much admired "Death of Little Boys." Seemingly the poem presents the dilemma caused by the death of a little boy—the universal "boys" becomes singular in the third stanza—but as we might suspect, the crisis centers upon the observer's loss of emotional control, of his inability to grasp and to comprehend the "event." Like the lover on the train "his metaphors are dead."

The first quatrain might be deceptive were it not for the title. The death that little boys "patient at last" accept like sleep has a shocking effect upon the committed observer. It "will rage terrific as the sea; / Their bodies fill a crumbling room with light." The event can be, if understood, a cause of enlightenment. The observer becomes one with the dead boy, "Gold curls now deftly intricate with gray," and he stares in fear through the window upon "one peeled aster," the universal symbol of death. The third stanza limits the death to one boy in concrete detail, "the ultimate dream" creeping upwards but leaving "round his sturdy belly gleam / Suspended breaths, white spars above the wreck." In the fourth stanza as the "guests, come in to look" and manifest stereotyped sorrow, "turn down / Their palms," the protagonist loses all control; his world totters about him, "Reels like a sailor drunk in a rotten skiff." Whatever the allusion here is—many possibilities have been suggested: Hamlet, Milton, Poe, Hans Anderson, Rimbaud—the total disintegration of the observer is obvious. A kind of idiot response follows: "The bleak sunshine shrieks its chipped music then / Out to the milkweed amid the fields of wheat." Then the answer that is no answer, insane incomprehension is followed by inane motion: "There is a calm for you where men and women / Unroll the chill precision of moving feet." From the first stanza the poet has established an ironic antithesis. The single source of tranquility, of light, of solidity is the dead boy. But the observer's world is "crumbling," "torn in two," "fear," and the final "delirium." The modern protagonist cannot comprehend death; he has no answer to its question. He can only escape from it by routine motion, "the chill precision of moving feet." Without the greater myth of religion or the lesser of history, even the most significant event is incomprehensible.

The form—pentameter quatrains—is strictly controlled. The use of diction is highly concentrated and demands the closest attention. For example, the little boys "surrender their eyes immeasurably to the night." The unexpected use of the adverb concentrates the reader's attention upon the act of dying and away from the expected but vaguer "night." It prepares the reader for the final irony, that the act of death immeasurable in the best of circumstances can certainly not be measured by turned-down palms and chill, precise movement. Each line demands its context: "Gold curls now deftly intricate with gray" is meaningless without "you . . . torn in two," which reveals personal involvement and is further explained by "extends a fear to you." Tate never makes the abstract statement that Yvor Winters demands but the poem is no less intellectual for all that. The density and compression of the imagery forces the universal into the concrete dramatic situation. If abstract clarification is to be had, it must be earned by the reader's contemplation of the experienced poem.

By now the reader must be more and more aware that in Tate's tragic vision all problems are one vast problem. Life in modern society is hell, but hell has a variety of tortures and increasing depths of misery. Tate, like Dante, would lead us by descending circles to the very core of hell. He will not mislead "the banker and the statesman into the illusion that they have no hell, because as secularists, they have lacked the language to report it." Nor will he spare himself; he too is trapped in the modern dilemma, "his hell has not been for those other people: he has reported his own." [20]

Part of this hell is modern man's horrible inner fragmentation. With no inner principle of unity, he is like an idiot with no values, with nothing but timeless, unrelated (because there is nothing to relate to) sense experience. "The idiot greens the meadow with his eyes, / The meadow creeps implacable and still; / A dog barks, the hammock swings, he lies. / One two three the cows bulge on the hill." Benjy Compson is modern man, the living dead; "now in the idiot's heart a chamber stinks / Of dead asters." The unreal scientific abstraction has caused this hell; "Being all infinite, function depth and mass / Without figure, a mathematical shroud." Science has turned us into "Plato's kept philosopher, / Albino man bleached from the mortal clay." Our unreal society exists by the logic of hell, by an insane rationality; "In an age of abstract experience, fornication / Is self-expression, adjunct to Christian euphoria, / And whores become delinquents; delinquents, patients; / Patients, wards of society. Whores, by that rule, are precious."

Of the many forceful presentations of this theme, Yvor Winters finds "The Subway" to be one of the best. Of it he writes, "The feeling is quite specific and unparaphrasable, but one may indicate the nature of it briefly by saying that it is a feeling of dignity and of self-control in the face of a situation of major difficulty, a difficulty which the poet fully apprehends." [21]

"The Subway" is a sonnet, and again we note Tate's masterly control of a difficult form. But even the use of this form is a subtle irony, for the problem presented in the octet finds no solution in the sestet. The octet is an imaginative vision of the subway. It begins with an exact detail, "accurate plunger," but the description becomes progressively more hellish and less and less concrete. By the fifth line the "accurate plunger" has become a "musical steel shell / Of angry worship." The direction of the descent is clearly fixed by the closing line of the octet, "Into the iron forestries of hell." The imagery of the octet had become progressively more violent, progressively less controlled, until it achieves the ultimate violence of this final line.

The octet is at once a cause and a symbol—a symbol of the quantitative abstraction of space that is modern society, a mechanism that extends and extends even to hell itself. It is a cause of the state of the protagonist described in the sestet. He is "broken" when the subway emerges from its "iron forestries of hell." The ever expanding quantity without quality has shattered his rationality so that he too has "become geometries, and glut / Expansions. . . . In the cold revery of an idiot." The limitless spacial imagery of the poem until it bursts into the absolute and insane abstraction of mathematics is a use of the sonnet form unusual as it is powerful.

For many years Tate, like some twentieth-century Augustine, has been stalked by the Hound of Heaven. At times he lashes out at a totally secular society to which "every son-of-a-bitch is Christ, at least Rousseau," or for which "The long-gestating Christ" waits in vain. To this society "since the Christian myth is a vegetation rite, varying only in some details from countless other vegetation myths, there is no reason to prefer Christ to Adonis." [22] But the poet has his own personal hell. He is "Unstalked by Christ;" at Christmas when "Ah, Christ, I love you rings to the wild sky," he can but "think a little on the past," all unconscious of "Christ's deep gaze." Eight years later he was to write, "Ten years are time enough to be dismayed / By mummy Christ, head crammed between his knees."

The loss of a sense of moral evil is an oft repeated theme: "Manhood like a lawyer with his formulas / Sesames his youth for innocent acquital." Only at night does the subconscious accuse, but then men rush "To crush this lucent madness" and to "Tuck in their eyes." In this secular society "blessed without sin" the poet can pray, "O God of our flesh, return us to Your wrath, / Let us be evil could we enter in / Your grace, and falter on the stony path!"

In 1944 Tate wrote perhaps one of his greatest poems, "Seasons of the Soul." Both in form and in allusion it reveals the great influence that Dante had begun to exert upon the poet's imagination. The third "Winter" section has been read by some critics as a complete and final rejection of Christianity. In his sensitive and comprehensive study of the poem Mr. R. K. Meiners not only rejects this position but illuminates the entire structure and content of the poem.[23] To his enlightening and satisfying study little if anything can be added.

Tate concludes the "Spring" section with an anguished appeal to a rather ambiguous "mother of silences" who in the fifth stanza, at least, is clearly Monica, the mother of Augustine. The poem ends with a note of irresolution: "Whether your kindness mother, / Is mother of silences." Perhaps the final line of "The Buried Lake" might be read as an answer: "I knew that I had known enduring love."

In 1952–53 Tate published the first, third, and sixth parts of a proposed long poem, "The Maimed Man," "The Swimmers," and "The Buried Lake." Significantly or not, "The Maimed Man" was omitted from *Poems* published in 1960. All three parts are written in *terza rima,* begin with a classical invocation, and are deeply allegorical. Sections I and VI are dream allegories; Section III is the narrative of an event in the poet's boyhood. It seems to be the poet's intention to review the events of his life both actual and aesthetic: "Where Mrytle twines with Laurel," with the eyes of a new vision, that of faith. No longer does intellect seek faith; now there is the reversal of faith seeking to express itself, of *fides quaerens intellectum.* "Teach me to fast / and pray, that I may know the motes that tease skittering sunbeams are dead shells at last. / Then, timeless muse, reverse my time; unfreeze / All that I was in your congenial heat."

Since Tate has excluded "The Maimed Man" from the most recent canon of his poetry, and since the allegory in "The Swimmers" is clear—a boy's introduction to evil through fear and love is his first vision of the continuing Crucifixion in the Mystical Body—a brief consideration of "The Buried Lake" would seem most appropriate.

The caption, *"Ego mater pulchrae dilectionis, et timoris, et agnitionis, et sanctae spei"* (I am the mother of fair love, and of fear, and of knowledge, and of holy hope) is from Ecclesiasticus. The mother of the original is Truth; in the Catholic liturgy it is applied to the Blessed Virgin and is a frequent refrain in the prayers recited on her feast days.

"The Buried Lake" is a dream-allegory of the poet's life dedicated to the "Lady of light." In it the poet reverses the order of the caption. In an unreal hell, the hotel of the dream, into which the poet is admitted by Cerberus, "where a sick dog coughed out a sickly cark / To let me in," he attempts to exercise his art, "to play my violin," but carnal, impure love, "Small dancing girl," silences his art. He then attempts philosophy, "My friend John Locke" (a symbol of false knowledge), but this too fails him, "And went as mist upon the browning air." Another attempt at art, "the grey sonata," is interrupted by a "stately woman." As the poet holds her in his arms, she turns into a "searching skull whose drying teeth / Crumbled me all night long and I was dead." This seems a clear allusion to St. Paul's, "By sin death entered the world." It is also the poet's first encounter with fear. In this condition of spiritual blindness, "while sight within me, caved," deprived of grace, "All grace being lost," Santa Lucia, Holy Light comes to him. He first resists her music, then attempts to misinterpret it into a nature or vegetation myth; finally he accepts it, "Light choir upon my shoulder, speaking Dove." The poet has by way of impure love, sin, fear, and death finally attained "fair love, knowledge, and holy hope" through Divine Revelation and grace. "The dream is over and the dark expired. / I knew that I had known enduring love."

"The Buried Lake" was published ten years ago; to it nothing has beed added in the interim. It would appear, then, that Tate's reputation must stand, at least as of now, upon his poetry of unbelief. He is essentially a poet of anger and of anguish whose singularly macabre vision achieves tremendous power when confined and controlled by strict form. "The Mediterranean," "Ode to the Confederate Dead," "Seasons of the Soul," some of his sonnets and his shorter poems are great, if limited, poems. His very resistance to abstract statement, his violent strain to force the abstract idea into the concrete image produce enormous tension. The longer, more discursive poems like "Causerie" have brilliant lines but in the more explicit statement of idea and in the greater freedom of form tend to lose force and tension. Tate is undoubtedly one of the most technically talented, intelligent, and powerful poets of the modern period. In tone and subject he may be one of the most limited.

*MILLER WILLIAMS*

# YVOR WINTERS
## or How To Measure the Wings of a Bumblebee

WINTERS STANDS NOW, as he has stood for twenty-five years, on the periphery of the critics' circle. He has been for so long out of the center of things—eccentric in the true sense of the word—that he has been easy to ignore. It is just as easy, and frighteningly safe, to attack him broadside. It is easy because he makes it so; he leaves himself open to attack so often that he seems to invite it. It is safe because the big boys are doing it. To say why they are, and why and how he leaves himself open to it, and how just or unjust the attacks are requires an examination not only of Winters' views, but also of the method by which he presents those views and his application of them and perhaps without being out of order, even a glance at Winters' own poetry.

I realize that I am basing what I say here on essays Winters has written over a period of many years, and I assume that since it is clear that he has changed from an earlier position into the one he now champions, he has not become static but continues to alter his views with experience and error. I have no way of knowing what views he would want to express differently now, however, or perhaps not express at all, and I can work only with what he has put on record.

Any good look at that record should begin, I think, with Winters' own statement of his position. He says, in an essay on Eliot, "My own view of poetry, which I have already indicated, is a simple one: I believe that the feeling expressed by the work is, or should be, motivated by the artist's comprehension of his subject, which is

159

drawn from human experience; and that the value of the work depends upon the justness of the motivation, in whole and in detail." [1] He informs us, though, in *In Defense of Reason,* that the view is not so simple as this:

> The theory of literature which I defend in these essays is absolutist. I believe that the work of literature, in so far as it is valuable, approximates a real apprehension and communication of a particular kind of objective truth. The form of literature with which I am for the most part concerned is the poem; but since the poem exhausts more fully than any other literary form the inherent possibilities of language, what I say about poetry can be extended to include other literary forms with relatively unimportant qualifications, and in point of fact I devote considerable space to other literary forms. The poem is a statement in words about a human experience. Words are primarily conceptual but through use and because human experience is not purely conceptual, they have acquired connotations of feeling. The poet makes his statement in such a way as to employ both concept and connotations as efficiently as possible. The poem is good in so far as it makes a defensible rational statement about a given human experience (the experience need not be real but must be in some sense possible) and at the same time communicates the emotion which ought to be motivated by that rational understanding of that experience. This notion of poetry, whatever its defects, will account both for the power of poetry, and of artistic literature in general over its readers and for the seriousness with which the great poets have taken their art. Milton, for example, did not write *Paradise Lost* to give pleasure to Professor So-and-So, nor did he write it to give free rein to his emotions; he wrote it in order to justify the ways of God to men, and the justification involved not merely a statement of theory but a conformity of the emotional nature of men with the theory. [2]

As we read more of Winters, we find the ideal of morality in poetry becoming or seeming to become broader. The idea takes on new dimensions. Some of the uses to which it is put are, while probably not contradictory, vague to anyone but Winters himself, and certainly something other than a matter of motive-emotion propriety. Keith McKean writes as if he understands the import of all of them, but I have not been convinced of this from McKean's own writing.

Winters attacks Frost's "A Masque of Reason" on the basis that it gives us "no understanding of good and evil in themselves." [3] In discussing Crane's "The Dance," he points out "the difficulty of the pantheistic doctrine." [4] In connection with Stevens' "Sunday Morning," he speaks of "the defects of the hedonistic theme." [5] At other times he writes esoterically of Ransom's failure to offer a "principle of rightness" [6] and Bryant's loss of "the old moral intelligence." [7] And in discussing Shakespeare's reason for writing *Macbeth* and *Othello*, he speaks of "theoretic morality," a grasp of which he says is necessary to an understanding of the nature of sin.[8] Winters makes it clear—and these principles he believes are inextricably involved in the view of the poem as a moral act—that we should enter a poem by way of paraphrase; that the best poetry is poetry of abstract thought; that the morality of a poem lies partly in the metrics of the poem.

His fondness for the paraphrase is apparent in his approach to almost all the poems he considers and is understandable in a critic who believes that the feeling expressed by a work should be motivated by the poet's comprehension of his subject. The subject, then, of the poem, comes first, is primary, and the feeling is secondary. This bears on some of the most important critical discussions of recent years, including those of Eliot, who, Winters says, "sometimes adopts this view, but in the main . . . prefers to assume the emotion as initial: the result is his famous and widely influential theory of the objective correlative." [9]

If Winters finds little glad company in Eliot (I do not intend to imply that Winters is looking for company, or would himself be glad to have it!), he does have at least a more committed compadre—committed, at least, to the paraphrase—in Ransom. And in most of the English teachers of the world. It is not in this that Winters is alone.

But any common ground between Winters and Ransom disappears as soon as the idea of the idea comes up. From "Thunder Without God," Winters' much-read essay on Ransom:

> The difficulty with Ransom's position is this: that he knows, finally, that he cannot get rid of abstractions, yet he has an abhorrence of the rational processes which is less related to that of Ockham than to that of the romantics; it is a traditional feeling—I refer to romantic tradition —which makes him abhor words such as *moral, ideal,* or *rational* without troubling really to understand what they mean.[10]

Winters does not care for the truth-in-a-blade-of-grass idea, unless one says clearly that truth is there. He is apparently not given to finding universals in the concrete specific and does not take much to poetry that does.

This position is important to him, and it bears talking about. I will come back to it a little later. For now, I am establishing the essential points of Winters' critical position, so that it might be examined in the same order, point by point.

Here is his own explanation of the moral significance of meter:

It is for this reason that I have spoken of meter as having moral significance. Meter has certain phonetic values of its own, and it clarifies, identifies, and even modifies the phonetic values of unmetered language. And the total phonetic value of metrical language has the power to qualify the expression of feeling through language. Since the expression of feeling is a part of the moral judgment as I have defined it, the meter has moral significance, for it renders possible a refinement in the adjustment of feeling to motive which would not otherwise be possible. This being true, the poet is not likely to find it embarrassingly easy to write in the "smooth" meters of Shakespeare and Jonson: those meters are difficult in proportion to their smoothness, for they achieve a maximum of effect with a minimum of variation. Every movement in such meter is perceptible, and, in the hands of the good poet, makes its contribution to the total poem. In the lurching meter employed for the most part by Tate, Ransom, and their group, the effectiveness of meter is at a minimum; the meter staggers for the sake of staggering. It is quite as difficult to be Shakespeare today as it was in the year 1600.[11]

I think I have given a fair gist of Winters' critical thinking, and I have given it insofar as possible in his own words. It is never quite fair to set a man's statements up, out of context, and take shots at them, but there is no other way, so far as I know, to be critic, level III.

To begin with, we must decide what to do with Winters' statement that the "primary function of criticism is evaluation," and that "unless criticism succeeds in providing a usable system of evaluation it is worth very little." [12] While Winters sometimes seems to feel that it is this point on which much of the attack against him is based, I don't think it is. The cause for almost all of the objection to his work, I think, is his use of the word "moral," and even more his application of his principle of morality to the work of particular poets. This has caused anger, confusion, and ridicule. But the belief in the importance of evaluation in itself has not. We know that when we examine a poem or any part of it to see what makes it work we are finding out, actually, why it is a good poem, or why it isn't. The difference between most of us and Winters is that we know before we go into the poem whether it is any good or not, and we examine it to find out why we know it. Winters, I believe, examines the poem to decide what he thinks of it, to decide empirically whether it is good or bad, or how good it is.

But we are still evaluating poems. We are saying, intuitively or analytically, "this one is better than that one." And if we can say that "Sunday Morning" is a better poem than "A House by the Side of the Road," then unless we are dealing with some logical trick and an excluded middle we must be able to place other poems—if we should want to—in some more or less certain order along a range between the two, and then perhaps we will place some above "Sunday Morning" and some beside it, so that by refinement of our perception we come to the point where we can say that *Hyperion* is better than *Childe Harold.*

The point of contention is not whether we are going to evaluate poems, but in what terms we are going to evaluate them.

We may judge a poem in terms of what it sets out to do, in terms of how well it does what a poem is supposed to do, of how true it is to itself, or we may judge it in terms of extrapoetic criteria. Now Winters claims at one time or another to consider the poem almost as a new critic—the relation of motive to emotion, all within the framework of the poem; the propriety of object to feeling, all within the framework of the poem. But then he talks about rational acceptability, which, if it has any meaning in terms of poetry, has a very special meaning, and not at all what it has in prose. And he talks about the dangers and weaknesses of hedonism and pantheism and romanticism and determinism as human ideas, and in his mind the presence of such concepts in poetry is an intrusion, and they must by their nature do the poem harm.

In Winters' critical system everything fits together. It is a many-armed body with one head, and that head is the concept of a poem as an evaluation of experience and therefore a moral judgment. It is a pervasive concept, running through every part of the peom, determining the efficacy of every device and the acceptability of every phrase.

This objection to poems whose viewpoint is disapproved of is an objection made from the moralist position—Winters says "theoretic moralists," but I do not know what that means, so I will not try to use it. The point is that if anything will clarify for us what Winters is talking about whenever he talks about poetry, it is an understanding of this concept of poetry as moral judgment.

In my opinion Winters sees two ways in which a poem can fail on moral grounds. These are: by a false wedding of emotion and the object or idea which is supposed to evoke that emotion; and by expressing a theme or general philosophical viewpoint which is morally or rationally unacceptable.

In connection with the first of these, he has categorized several types of unacceptable practices, the most important of which are what he calls the "pseudo-experimental" and the "pseudo-referent." Pseudo-experimental poetry is "the work of a poet who confuses tradition with convention, and who, desiring to experiment, sees no way to escape from or alter tradition save by the abandonment of convention." [13] Pseudo-reference is the building of a rhetoric which seems to grow from and stand on a theme, when in fact there either is no theme—no plot, perhaps—or one poorly related to the rhetoric employed and the emotion invoked.

I'm not sure what validity there is in the idea of the pseudo-experimental. I too find it difficult to imagine writing untraditional poetry without writing unconventional poetry. Perhaps there is a problem of semantics here. There is a lot of stuff written which is self-consciously rebellious and painfully "difficult," but I don't think this is what Winters is talking about. And such poetry as this is more properly attacked anyway in terms of the pseudo-referent, a concept I do think is valid. This is what we're talking about when we say after reading a man's work, "He didn't really say anything, did he?" We get this not only in some poetry, but in many commencement addresses, political speeches, and television commercials.

I have no objection to judging a poem on moral grounds, once we understand what we mean by moral. I want a poem to be honest; I want a poet not to cheat; and I think I know when he has. There are several ways in which a poet can deal in dishonest emotions (which is what we mean when we talk about sentimentalism), and when I say that he has, I'm saying too that he has failed on a point of morality, for honesty is a moral concept.

I can accept—and believed before I heard of Winters—that there should be a proper wedding of idea and emotion. The emotion a poet attempts to evoke *is* an indication of what he interprets the *quality* of an idea to be. This is a moral act, this interpretation and the indication of it, in the simple sense that a man is bound to tell the truth.

When we attempt to give superficial thoughts, shallow ideas, the shape of importance, to give ephemeral things the shape of profundity, we are being dishonest. When we use "instant" emotion—words to which we have been conditioned to respond over so long a period in so many contexts that they have by now so great an emotional impact of their own that it is no longer necessary to say something with the words—but simply to use them: when we do either of these things, we are cheating. I can accept that we are being immoral, if Winters prefers the word, but I'm not at all sure he will accept my explanation—exemplification—of his position throughout this paper. Ransom attempted to make clear what he thought Winters was saying, and had the Red Sea close on him.

Winters' ideas on metrics are strongly proscriptive, traditional, and typical of him. He is not a prophet of tomorrow, but of yesterday, and I think he is proud to have it so. The only two explanations I can imagine for his position on metrics are that his ear cannot hear the subtler movements of so-called free verse, or that when he was converted to moral absolutism he saw the light and looked at everything under it. And this, in that light, is how metrics has to be.

I know too much of Winters' own earlier work to be serious about the first possibility, so I must give him his ear and his honesty. It is when he enters the discussion of thematic criticism that I am unable to go with him, and he seems at times to have some difficulty himself in according it much importance.

Whatever the defects of the hedonistic theme, and with the possible but by no means certain exception of a few short poems by Stevens and of two or three poems by E. A. Robinson, *Sunday Morning* is probably the greatest American poem of the twentieth century and is certainly one of the greatest contemplative poems in English.[14]

And so the "defects of the hedonistic theme" are overcome by the poem's virtues.

But Winters apparently believes—and this I think is basic to his system of criticism—that a poem which makes any statement not in accord with the absolute truth starts out with at least a strike against it. I'm not sure what views are acceptable, but I assume that one would not be in serious trouble talking non-Christian deism, that being the avowed position of Winters.

In order for this sort of criticism to have any merit, one must first make several assumptions:

1 there is an absolute truth;
2 aesthetic experience is weakened if it does not directly reflect this truth; and
3 we know what this truth is.

For the time being I am forced to withhold judgment on the second of these, because I have no idea how to answer the first, and because I know very clearly how to answer the third. I submit that Winters is in the same position. The point of argument here comes to this: In order to decide whether or not a romantic poem is good, it is not necessary to know whether or not romanticism is in accord with the will of God. Will of God aside, Winters says that he finds some themes rationally unacceptable. Here, too, there is the problem of whom we are going to have as a judge of the content of a poem. Eugene V. Debs, no doubt, found capitalism rationally and morally unacceptable. Henry Ford did not. The question is whether a poem expressing the view of Debs is by that fact a better or a worse poem than one expressing the view of Ford. Plato and Aristotle were not in agreement as to what was and was not rationally or morally acceptable. And we have the same question—Eliot and Stevens, Frost and Winters—the same question.

I am, of course, stating the not-very-new belief that a poem must be criticized on its own terms, and that in order to make a valid critical judgment the reader must give the poet his idea. But I am expressing also the belief that a poem is an experience, and that the end of the poem—the end of any experience—is insight; that the thing we have to ask of the poem is that the poet be honest—consistent in idea and true to his focus—that he not mess up the shape of his poem. This is what we can demand of a poet in moral terms. If the poem is not phony, and if the poet knows his stuff, he will draw us into the poem; it will become our experience; through that experience we will come to an insight about people—an insight probably related to the theme but not necessarily confirming it. As a matter of fact, it is quite possible that one might not be able to say what the theme of a poem is in a way that would be fair to the poem.

This brings up another point in Winters' system: the value of paraphrase. Now this also is not new, of course, and is not now exclusively Winters'. But for him it is an essential part of the examination of a poem as a moral act and must be considered here in his terms. And in these terms there is little that can be said to refute him. Given that a peom must first acquit itself thematically, it follows that the theme must be examined as a thing in itself. My objection to this is that a theme rarely exists as a thing in itself. This, too, Winters recognizes at times.

In a discussion of this, he offers this well-developed qualification:

What I have just said should make plain the difficulty of compre-
hending a poem exactly and fully; its total intention may be very different from its paraphrasable, or purely logical content. If one takes, for
example, Mr. Allen Tate's sonnet *The Subway*, and translates it into
good scholarly prose, using nothing but the rational content of the poem
as a reference, one will find the author saying that as a result of his
ideas and of his metropolitan environment, he is going mad. Now as a
matter of fact, the poem says nothing of the sort:

> Dark accurate plunger down the successive knell
> Of arch on arch, where ogives burst a red
> Reverberance of hail upon the dead
> Thunder, like an exploding crucible!
> Harshly articulate, musical steel shell
> Of angry worship, hurled religiously
> Upon your business of humility
> Into the iron forestries of hell!
>
> Till broken in the shift of quieter
> Dense altitudes tangential of your steel,
> I am become geometries—and glut
> Expansions like a blind astronomer
> Dazed, while the worldless heavens bulge and reel
> In the cold revery of an idiot.

The sonnet indicates that the author has faced and defined the possibility of the madness that I have mentioned (a possiblity from the
consideration of which others as well as himself may have found it
impossible to escape) and has arrived at a moral attitude toward it, an
attitude which is at once defined and communicated by the poem. The
attitude is defined only by the entire poem, not by the logical content
alone; it is a matter not only of logical content, but of feeling as well.
The feeling is particular and unparaphrasable, but one may indicate the
nature of it briefly by saying that it is a feeling of dignity, and of
self-control in the face of a situation of major difficulty, a difficulty which
the poet fully apprehends. This feeling is inseparable from what we call
poetic form, or unity, for the creation of a form is nothing more nor less
than the act of evaluating and shaping (that is, controlling) a given
experience. It should be obvious that any attempt to reduce the rational
content of such a poem would tend to confuse or even to eliminate the
feeling: the poem consists in the relationship between the two.[15]

It is difficult to understand how the man who wrote this could also
have written the following lines. They are from an essay on Ransom
and give us cause for belief that Winters for all his absolute knowledge is also human, and can also indulge in the *non-sequitur*, can
also find a clever statement so irresistible that he sacrifices honesty
to it, can also be blinded at times.

If we like the poem without liking its subject, however, in what sense do we like it? The word *like* requires more explanation than Ransom is willing to give. To identify liking with interest is preposterous. We may be interested in communism, cancer, the European war, or Ransom's theories of poetry without liking any of them. According to Ransom's theories, the scientist does not like, in this sense, the objective universe, but that he is desperately interested in the objective there cannot be the slightest doubt. If we like the poem, we like it because of the truth with which it judges its subject, and the judgment is a moral judgment of the kind which I have already described.

Ransom's devout cultivation of sensibility leads him at times to curiously insensitive remarks. In comparing the subject of a poem by Stevens with that of a poem by Tate, he writes:

The deaths of little boys are more exciting than
the sea-surfaces . . .

a remark which seems worthy of a perfumed and elderly cannibal. And in a poem of his own, entitled *Bells for John Whiteside's Daughter*, a poem which deals with the death of a little girl, the dead child herself is treated whimsically, as if she were merely a charming bit of bric-a-brac, and the life of the poem resides in a memory of the little girl driving geese. The memory, as a matter of fact, is very fine, but if the little corpse is merely an occasion for it, the little corpse were better omitted, for once in the poem it demands more serious treatment: the dead child becomes a playful joke, and the geese walk off with the poem.[16]

I have not been able to understand from what Winters draws the dictum, "If we like the poem, we like it because of the truth with which it judges its subject. . . ." He has presented the argument that one can like without approving, but the leap to "we like it because of the truth with which it judges its subject" is a leap of faith. And there is nothing wrong with a leap of faith so long as we know it to be that, and not a duplicatable, logical process.

Winters goes on to cap this bit of illogic with one of his most astounding paragraphs. Ransom uses "exciting" here in the sense in which Amy Lowell used it, saying that the value of poetry is to excite the consciousness. This is consistent with Ransom's views and is not an uncommon use of the word. Winters knows this. To attack the use of it here and to imply thereby that he does not know, when of course he does, is a strange thing for a man whose life is dedicated to the moral implications of the human act.

But the more disturbing is the statement—and I must take it as an honest statement of Winters' belief—that "the dead child herself is treated whimsically, as if she were merely a charming bit of bric-a-brac, and the life of the poem resides in a memory of the little girl driving geese. . . . the dead child becomes a playful joke, and the geese walk off with the poem." I confess that I am at a loss for an answer to anyone who fails to see that the power, the pathos of the scene—the terrible reality of the child's death—lives in living geese, the silly, white geese. Winters' problem here must be that in *paraphrase* the thing does not sound right.

This is not the only problem. Winters is probably offended by the fact that Ransom makes his statement obliquely. Winters, as I have indicated earlier, prefers the abstract, the clearly philosophical statement.

For the past two hundred and fifty years it has been common to assume that abstract language is dead language, that poetry must depict particular actions, or if it be "lyric" that it must be revery over remembered sensory impressions, according to the formula of the associationists. But these assumptions are false. They are our heritage of confusion from Hobbes and Locke, by way of Addison, Hartley, and Alison—and more recently by way of Ezra Pound. A race that has lost the capacity to handle abstractions with discretion and dignity may do well to confine itself to sensory impression, but our ancestors were more fortunate, and we ought to labor to regain what we have lost. The language of metaphysics from Plato onward is a concentration of the theoretical understanding of human experience; and that language as it was refined by the great theologians is even more obviously so. The writings of Aquinas have latent in them the most profound and intense experience of our race. It is the command of scholastic thought, the realization in terms of experience and feeling of the meaning of scholastic language, that gives Shakespeare his peculiar power among dramatists, and Fulke Greville his peculiar power among the English masters of the short poem. I do not mean that other writers of the period were ignorant of these matters, for they were not, and so far as the short poem is concerned there were a good many great poets, four of five of whom wrote one or more poems apiece as great as any by Greville; but the command in these two men is not merely knowledge, it is command, and it gives to three or four tragedies by Shakespeare, and to fifteen or twenty poems by Greville, a concentration of meaning, a kind of sombre power, which one will scarcely find matched elsewhere at such great length in the respective forms.[17]

John Ciardi, in a recent address, brought into focus one of the most cognizant refutations I have heard of the practitioners of paraphrase and abstraction:

The violence I think I see teachers doing to the writing is in the kind of message-hunt they conduct through the poem. They get the kids to paraphrase. This immediately leads away from the form into something called meaning with a capital "M," or "significance" or "larger content"

or "eternal verities"—all dangerous concepts when applied to the poem.
. . . What determines the poem is not the size of the subject, but
the size of the mind that is engaged in the subject.

A fool could look at the universe and see nothing . . . but the most
mind, the most intelligence, could look at an amoeba and project the
universe from it.

I like to say to such students that a better formula, . . . is to fall in
love with some chunky fact of the world, some actuality, and within that
actuality not to make any statements but to let meaning be released
rather than asserted.

Another thing that seems to me to be lost from the essence of the
poetic experience when one tries to start to translate it into examination
terms is its multiplicity. I think a central characteristic of all the arts is
the fact that more than one thing is happening at once—multiplicity
and simultaneity.

. . . if you put anything inside a frame it is no longer just itself but a
force exerting against the frame. The elements of an art work tend, first,
to double on themselves, and secondly, to double against the form. For
example, suppose you want to take a photograph of something you
think of as the Rocky Mountains. Now, as soon as one picks up a
camera and puts a frame around his eye he begins a problem of composition. After all, if all you are thinking of is nature, the whole blessed
business is Rocky Mountains, and all you have to do is aim it over your
shoulder . . . But that does not work inside the frame . . . you see,
as soon as a man picks up a Brownie and starts to look at the Rocky
Mountains, he has a frame and begins to move around because he
wants something in relation to the frame, and something else in relation
to that, and you are off on to something else indispensable in the
experience—the fact is one thing and the form requires or demands
another.[18]

In a *tour de force* of precise analysis which surely even Winters,
who is a master of precise criticism, will admire, Ciardi demonstrates how inextricably theme and form may belong to one another
and how futile their separation must be. He is talking about Keats's
*The Eve of St. Agnes*, the worksheets of which he had studied.

The problem is to get Madeline undressed and into bed and to keep
Porphyro the innocent, high lover. No leer must touch his features.

First Keats seems to have Porphyro just about to faint. That seems to
make him safer, at least it guarantees there will be no violence. But
Porphyro's heart revives:

> Anon his heart revives: her vespers done,
> Of all its wreathed pearls she frees her hair;
> Unclasps her warmed jewels one by one

Warmed jewels has been praised often and justly. How did the jewels
get warmed? By contact with her body, and it is at this one delicate

removal that Keats suggests the presence of her body. It is Keats' kind of
sensory detail—rich, full of suggestion, and yet delicate.

There is the tonality he must preserve, and "wreathed pearls" and
"warmed jewels" have a happy relationship.

Then Keats made a mistake in his next version— "Loosens her bursting
bodice." What happened to the tonalities?

> Of all its wreathed pearls she frees her hair;
> Unclasps her warmed jewels one by one;
> Loosens her bursting bodice . . .

There is no scientific fact any one could adduce to show that Madeline
could not be as buxom as you please and yet be as delicate as you please.
It is not the scientific fact that counts here, but the tonality. "Bursting"
seemed wrong—run for your life, the dam is bursting. It is the flavor of
the word that is wrong.

And here Keats had a lot of trouble. He knew the word was wrong
instantly and he crossed it out. Then he was almost tempted into
cheating. He said: "Loosens her bodice lace-strings." What has he done?
He has neutralized. He has set up a sequence—wreathed pearls, warmed
jewels, and if he is going to observe his own sequence he has to say
"adjective-noun" and "bodice lace-strings" dodges it.

I am sure you find parallels in the composition of any form. A bad
poet would have accepted that cheating, but a good poet never cheats.
He knows when he has cheated—that is why he has to be demanding
upon himself.

Keats crossed out "bodice lace-strings," and after about seventeen
starts he came up with the right answer. You know immediately it is the
right answer. He said: "Loosens her fragrant bodice."

What makes "fragrant" exactly the right choice? "Fragrant" does for
bodice exactly what "warmed" does for jewels. Those are twin words and
at least cousins to "wreathed pearls."

But how far all this is from subject matter. Every poet who has
managed to say a meaningful, good thing about the human condition
has been the sort of person who has been passionately involved in this
kind of sequence in letting the poem build itself out of itself. He has
been involved in the formal elements, and these are precisely the
elements that one cannot get into a final examination paraphrase. They
are also the elements that the approach "Let's appreciate this" does not
reach to unless it gets down to particulars.

The form and the material are the experience.[19]

Winters' defense of the paraphrase, and his preference for the
abstract statement, have brought accusations that he is a didacticist.
He answers firmly that he is not. In his well-known reply to Ransom's attempt to reinterpret the idea of moral judgment, he says:

The subject matter of poetry, on the other hand, is human experience;
it can therefore be understood only in moral terms. The language of

poetry is normal human speech, which was devised for dealing with normal human experience, and I have already indicated the nature of that speech. When Ransom refers to my finding "that ethical interest is as frequent in poetry as any other one," he is again confusing the terms *ethical* and *didactic* and misunderstanding me in his own private fashion.[20]

And, *In Defense of Reason:* "Ransom cannot understand that poetry can have moral content except in the form of didacticism; that is, in the form of purely theoretical statement."[21]

But if, in historical terms, Winters is not a didacticist (since he does pay attention to the texture of a poem), he manages to sound like one, whether he is writing of Shakespeare or Frost.

Shakespeare wrote [*Macbeth* and *Othello*] in order to evaluate the actions truly; and our admiration is for the truth of the evaluations, not for the beauty of the original objects as we see them imitated. And how, one may wonder, can Shakespeare evaluate these actions truly except from the position of a moralist? To evaluate a particular sin, one must understand the nature of sin; and to fix in language the feeling, detailed and total, appropriate to the action portrayed, one must have a profound understanding not only of language, for language cannot be understood without reference to that which it represents, not only of the characters depicted, but of one's own feelings as well; and such understanding will not be cultivated very far without a real grasp of theoretic morality.[22]

. . . [Frost] is the nearest thing we have to a poet laureate, a national poet; and this fact is evidence of the community of thought and feeling between Frost and a very large part of the American literary public. The principles which have saved some part of Frost's talent, the principles of Greek and Christian thought, are principles which are seldom openly defended and of which the implications and ramifications are understood by relatively few of our contemporaries, by Frost least of all; they operate upon Frost at a distance, through social inheritance, and he has done his best to adopt principles which are opposed to them. The principles which have hampered Frost's development, the principles of Emersonian and Thoreauistic Romanticism, are the principles which he has openly espoused, and they are widespread in our culture. Until we understand these last and the dangers inherent in them and so abandon them in favor of better, we are unlikely to produce many poets greater than Frost, although a few poets may have intelligence enough to work clear of such influences; and we are likely to deteriorate more or less rapidly both as individuals and as a nation.[23]

The preceding lines, the conclusion to Winters' essay on Frost, contain not only a warning worthy of any straight-minded and dogmatic didacticist, but a clear implication that poets whose works are essentially romantic may as well resign themselves to second-class citizenship. This is partyline-ism. I do not see how it can be called anything else. And I assume that poets whose images come out of hedonist thoughts, or determinist—and God knows what else—are also relegated to the back of the bus. This is not to say that Winters denies the virtue—perhaps virtue is not the proper word— of certain exceptional poems expressing disapproved philosophies. "Sunday Morning" I have already mentioned. But in order to be a great poem it had to *overcome* its idea!

Now, Hyman and other writers have attacked Winters as if the concept of evaluation in criticism were invented at Stanford University. It should not be necessary to say that nothing Winters preaches is wholly his. Ransom believes in the paraphrase. Frost believed in the efficacy of delicately varied metre. And as far as the idea of evaluation itself is concerned, one might as well turn his guns on such writers as Muller, Farrell, and Weaver:

Like it or not, literature has, in fact, always been a "power of conduct." It has schooled purpose and desire, inculcated values and ideals, which is to say the ideas that men can sing about . . . One may say that the writer should not deliberately aim to instruct or edify: literature should not begin as a criticism of life. But it cannot help ending so.[24]

In providing content, then, art serves an objective function in society. It presents material for the judgment of life and its phenomena; and along with this material it offers judgments on the material. It makes the reader more intensely conscious of the problems of life, of the predicaments of people, the possibilities and the limitations in living, the diversitites in human experience, and some of the meanings, potential and actual, in this human experience. It makes value judgments on conditions, actions, thoughts, situations, environments, hopes, despairs, ideals, dreams, and fantasies. It provides its audience with additional equipment in proceeding with their own lives, and in the outward extension of their interests. It points their emotions, their impulses, their wishes, and their thoughts toward or away from certain goals. It creates, in an ideal and formal sense, the consciousness of an epoch, and is thus one of the instruments that work toward moulding and remoulding the human consciousness.[25]

Thus it can be a sign not only of philosophical ignorance but also of artistic bad taste to treat an object familiarly or from a near proximity. At the risk of appearing fanciful we shall say that objects have not only their natures but their rights, which the orator is bound to respect since he is in large measure the ethical teacher of society.[26]

So why the bother? Why do we fuss so about Yvor Winters? Partly it is because he has taken these views and incorporated them into a single system. Partly it is because he has defended this system in terms of moral absolutism. But primarily, I think, it is because of what he has done finally with the system: it is in great part because we have seen his application of his view that the view is so much discounted.

For one thing, he becomes a psychoanalyst:

> The spiritual control in a poem, then, is simply a manifestation of the spiritual control within the poet, and, as I have already indicated, it may have been an important means by which the poet arrived at a realization of spiritual control. This conception must not be confused with the conception of the poem as a safety valve, by which feeling is diverted from action, by which the writer escapes from an attitude by pouring it into his work and leaving it behind him. The conception which I am trying to define is a conception of poetry as a technique of contemplation, of comprehension, a technique which does not eliminate the need of philosophy or of religion, but which, rather, completes and enriches them.
>
> One feels, whether rightly or wrongly, a correlation between the control evinced within a poem and the control within the poet behind it. The laxity of the one ordinarily appears to involve laxity in the other. The rather limp versification of Mr. Eliot and of Mr. MacLeish is inseparable from the spiritual limpness that one feels behind the poems, as the fragmentary, ejaculatory, and over-excited quality of a great many of the poems of Hart Crane is inseparable from the intellectual confusion upon which these particular poems seem to rest (for examples, *The Dance, Cape Hatteras,* and *Atlantis*). Crane possessed great energy, but his faculties functioned clearly only within a limited range of experience (*Repose of Rivers, Voyages II, Faustus and Helen II*). Outside of that range he was either numb (*My Grandmother's Loveletters* and *Harbor Dawn*) or unsure of himself and hence uncertain in his detail (as in *The River,* a very powerful poem in spite of its poor construction and its quantities of bad writing) or both (see *Indiana,* probably one of the worst poems in modern literature).[27]

But still the main objection is not *that* Winters evaluates, or on what *grounds* he evaluates, or by what *means* he evaluates—but with what *results* he evaluates. We are never able to get far from the feeling that we know where the proof of the pudding lies.

It has given Hyman reason to call Winters a "comic figure," and it has given Winters' defenders some problems they would not have if they were allowed to defend him on the basis of his pronouncements alone. There is a question whether a man's principles should be held accountable for his application of them. Can one, in other words, have a valid conception and yet consistently misapply it? Whatever the answer to this—whether or not the results of Winters' application of his own critical criteria refute the criteria—there is no doubt that the image of Winters as a total critic suffers badly.

Enough has been said about his praise of Adelaide Crapsey, and there is probably more profit for our purpose in looking at a writer whose work is not cast in so special a form.

Elizabeth Daryush has been acclaimed by Winters as "One of the few distinguished poets of our century." [28] She, like Winters, generally writes a poetry peppered with archaisms and poeticisms, and what is even more characteristic of much Winters-approved poetry, it is of so even a temper that a stir of feeling seems like an emotional upheaval. " 'Neath" and "O'er" are not difficult to find—even "O'er seas of time"[!], and such lines as, "Quicklier fall our hearts / than tongue can tell." Exemplifying perfectly what he means by *reactionary* as an honorific critical term, Winters says:

She has something on her mind, she knows it is worth saying, and she tries to say what she means, by employing all the subtlest resources of her art. Poetry as an art is an anomaly at present, and poetry today is rather a debauch, a form of self-indulgence, or a form of self-advertisement. But it was once an art, and it will be again, and I believe that Mrs. Daryush will survive the interval. [29]

Helen Pinkerton writes poems which Winters says are "among the best which I know": they are—like the poems of Elizabeth Daryush and the later works of Winters—remarkable in the sameness of temper, the stone-faced quality, and what seems to be a reverence for glassy-surfaced quietude. [30] This kind of poetry comes naturally out of Winters' strictures. His need for even meter and the abstract statement points to it, and his disaffection for figurative language— which he explains in the following passage—makes it almost inevitable.

Let us examine another figure, this from a speech of Wolsey in Act III, Scene 2, of *Henry VIII*:

> I have touched the highest point of all my greatness;
> And from that full meridian of my glory,
> I haste now to my setting: I shall fall
> Like a bright exhalation in the evening,
> And no man see me more.

The question here, as I see it, is this: to what extent do we have the fall of a star which is irrelevant to the fall of Wolsey? Wolsey's fall is human and therefore spiritual; but it is not visible as a literal fall. The fall of the star is visible. The visibility of the fall derives from the star; the grandeur from Wolsey. A mere falling star could not be described in such a way as to move us as this passage moves us, for we have here the tragedy of a man, the end of a great career; yet the star gives a great sweep of visibility to the image, at the same time that it is kept closely related not merely to the human, but to human grief and helplessness, by being named, in the language of the time, not a star, but an exhalation. That there is an element of Ransom's irrelevance in such a figure is possible, and that the star should be, as it is, as well realized in itself as possible is certain, for the star will accomplish nothing toward reinforcing the tragedy of Wolsey unless it lives in its own right; but the star is introduced for its relevance, and the strength of the figure lies in the similarity between the matters compared. The best poets do not seek such occasions as ends in themselves; they use them when they need them and only when they need them, and they keep them pared as close to the point of relevance as the occasion permits. The occasional margin of decoration that may result from such practice may well be afforded by a strong poem; but to seek to transform the whole poem into decoration is aimless debauchery.[31]

In a study of "The Sixteenth Century Lyric in England," he makes his tastes unmistakably clear:

The wisdom of poetry of this kind lies not in the acceptance of a truism, for anyone can accept a truism, at least formally, but in the realization of the truth of the truism: the realization resides in the feeling, the style. Only a master of style can deal successfully in a plain manner with obvious matter: we are concerned with the type of poetry which is perhaps the hardest to compose and the last to be recognized, a poetry not striking nor original as to subject, but merely true and universal, that is, in a sense commonplace, not striking nor original in rhetorical procedure, but direct and economical, a poetry which permits itself originality, that is the breath of life, only in the most restrained and refined of subtleties in diction and in cadence, but which by virtue of those subtleties inspires its universals with their full value as experience. The best poems in the early school are among the most perfect examples of the classical virtues to be found in English poetry.[32]

So the poem that would please Winters—and, we then assume, the form consistent with his critical views—is pushed from every side to become not a poem, but an essay. The freshman who asks, "If you have something to say, why don't you just come out and *say* it?!" has in Yvor Winters a good friend.

But it must not be forgotten that Winters saw the greatness in Wallace Stevens long before Stevens was noticed by those who think Winters a clown; that he had recognized Crane before most people knew who Crane was. And it must not be forgotten that he has reminded us what precise criticism is; that if he enjoys being alone (and who but Winters can say this?), at least he is not afraid to be;

that no critic can be as generally consistent as Winters without being honest, and that no man can be honest without being at least as inconsistent as Winters in particular ways.

Winters has been of tremendous importance. The world of critics would be poorer without him—poorer because he kept structural analysis alive, and poorer because he has been for twenty-five years throwing firecrackers into the lounge of the Harvard Club—drawing beards on the portraits of famous, pompous, and fat old men. He is important to us partly because he is sometimes right. He is important also because he is a loud and lone dissenter.

I wish that I could agree with him more, but he is a moral absolutist—his views grow out of this position—and one who goes very far with him must start from the same point. So the real contention may be between moral and not critical views, though there are men who claim to be moral absolutists who disagree with Winters' critical principles.

Yet I am unable to debate the moral position, and I am not sure I would like to if I could. I can look only at the criticism that comes out of it and talk about that criticism as if it had no mother. Fallacious as this may be, it is what critics, including Winters, always do, and I do not see how it can be otherwise, or we end talking about politics and religion and philosophy. If it is right that we should end so, then let's stop pretending there is an area of inquiry apart from these and that it is called criticism.

If we are going to write as if there is such a thing, then in those terms there is a further point to be made. That is that we should not turn our backs on one view in turning our attention to another. We have acted as if one must choose between critical views as he would decide whether to become a Baptist or a Catholic—as if any two views were mutually exclusive, as if one must either be didactic, or romantic, or a new critic, and never look on the ritual of another. The Chicago critics have seriously questioned this position, and if they seem to have come out of the questioning as Aristotelians, they are at least unwilling to damn those who are not. There is no critical criterion I am acquainted with which has not brought me some degree of enlightenment in the reading of poetry or which I could deny revealed a source of pleasure which I received from some poem.

We cannot say that all poems must acquit themselves in terms of any particular critical view; we have only to take from the poem what it has to give, and if we are interested, then we can examine the poem to see where the pleasure, the enlightenment, comes from. Winters does this himself now and then in his discussion of a poem. He seems to say, "I like it," and then he proceeds to show wherein it fails. He asks a great many questions of the poem. But a poem also asks questions, and the poem is first. It is criticism, not poetry, which must acquit itself, and it must acquit itself in terms of poetry. We know and usually agree on what is a good poem. When we argue from the standpoint of criticism, we are disagreeing usually about whether it *ought* to have been a good poem. And we disagree because we are critical zealots, because we will not see that good men, intelligent men, are not all moved by by the same thing and because we will not see that all poems do not delight or enlighten or even instruct in the same way, by the same means.

I must say here, and gladly, that Winters has written some very good poems which measure up to his own critical standards and to mine. I am using many words to insist that the greatest fault of Winters' views is that they are exclusive views. But since it is essential to the position of a moral absolutist that his views be exclusive, there is no way to separate this fact from the whole dogmatic system, and I see no way to be fair to the total view in a few words.

For McKean to say, "Literature is important because it can serve as a guide to the good life," is foolish and narrow to the point of blindness.[33] Literature is important for many reasons. If it is important to McKean because it serves him as a guide to the good life, then that's fine. But he is missing a lot.

I would agree that literature—even poetry—might serve this end if I knew what he meant by the good life. The problem here is how it serves, and I think it is because the dogmatic critic, the moralist critic especially, is too limited in this sense, so that he finds himself liking a poem when he knows he shouldn't. To go to a poem that has moved good minds of good men—to go to such a poem with a prepared set of critical standards by which we are going to decide whether or not the poem is any good—is to set out with compass and slide rule to prove whether the bumblebee can fly.

I appreciate the "moral value" of literature, and the idea of honesty is meaningful in a discussion of any poem; but I believe that an aversion to the concrete image and a love for paraphrase do violence to just that "moral value." I find meaning and great men and honesty for reasons not explained by the extricated theme, and I find enlightenment and pure joy in the feel of an image at my fingertips. I believe there is "moral value" in this meaning and honesty, this enlightenment and this joy, and so sometimes, I suspect, does Winters.

# NOTES

BERNARD BENSTOCK

1 All parenthetical numerals refer to pages in James Joyce's *Finnegans Wake* (New York, 1939), with corrections made from Joyce's *Errata*.
2 Henry Fielding, *Joseph Andrews* (New York, 1950), xxxi–xxxii.
3 *Ibid.*, 134.
4 It is interesting to note the comment of Howard Mumford Jones in his introduction to the Modern Library edition of *Joseph Andrews:* "I do not know whether James Joyce was an admirer of Fielding, but it is at least remarkable that after two centuries the English novel in the case of *Ulysses* should recur to a theory of fiction which is outlined in the preface to *Joseph Andrews.*"
5 Myles Dillon, *Early Irish Literature* (Chicago, 1948), 34.
6 Stuart Gilbert (ed.), *Letters of James Joyce* (New York, 1957), 258.

PETROULA KEPHALA RUEHLEN

1 C. P. Cavafy, *Poems (1896–1918)*, G. P. Savidis, ed. (Athens, 1963). The edition is in two volumes, but the second volume had not appeared at the time these lines were written.
2 Cavafy used to publish and distribute each poem in a separate pamphlet; in his own records, he would pin every new pamphlet published to the previous ones in chronological order. Every few years, however, he would bind the pamphlets in slim booklets, in which the order of poems instead of being chronological would be such as to reveal the movement of his creative process. Such booklets Cavafy formed by combining and adding poems successively of the years 1909–11, 1908–14, 1907–17. During the last years of his life he was distributing two booklets containing poems of the years 1905–15 and 1916–18. These booklets Mr. Savidis faithfully reprints in the first volume of his edition, and he follows them with all the older poems of the 1904 and 1910 collections (the only collections in book form proper that Cavafy published during his lifetime). The order of these poems is also thematic. A chronological table is given at the end of the

book, as well as a glossary and various historical and interpretative information. The second volume has been planned to contain the remaining seventy poems from 1919 until 1933 in chronological order, with the addition of his last poem, which the poet did not live to publish. Cavafy did not provide us with the thematic order of these last poems of the second volume, nor with the general thematic order of his whole work.

Mr. Savidis has also announced the forthcoming edition of the *Complete Published Works of Cavafy,* in two volumes, one for poetry and one for prose. This edition will include all the material published by Cavafy himself during his lifetime; special appendices will contain whatever pieces were published posthumously, as well as some pieces which were published during his lifetime and which are attributed to him in part or in whole. This edition will eventually become part of the *Complete Works,* which will include also all the existing unpublished poems, essays, notes, and much biographical material. The edition of the *Complete Works* involves many problems, the most serious of which is the collection of the existing Cavafy papers. A short history of the Cavafy records will elucidate my point.

Cavafy was a very methodical, meticulous man who kept his files in perfect order. He kept copies not only of his own forty letters to E. M. Forster but of the envelopes too, and he left to us the most detailed catalogs of all the poems he has written, complete with dates and all other pertinent information, plus biographical material, notes, essays, etc., all carefully pinned together and classified. Following the poet's death, all this material was moved from the upper to the ground floor of the Cavafy house in Rue Lepsius and subsequently to the house of Mr. Sengopoulos, the poet's heir. The first person to disclose to us the existence of this rich material was Mr. Peridis, who gained access to a small part of the papers and used a number of them in his book on Cavafy. About ten years ago, a part of these papers was entrusted by Mr. Sengopoulos to Mr. Papoutsakis, who has kept them since. The remaining and by far the richest and most valuable part of the material has recently been entrusted to the hands of Mr. Savidis, an enthusiastic scholar who undoubtedly will use it with all the care and respect and attention it demands.

The material in Mr. Savidis' hands comprises approximately five thousand papers, which include some seventy unpublished poems, fifteen to twenty unfinished poems, a number of essays, a great mass of notes on every conceivable topic, from language and metrics to household chores or matters of the poet's private life, biographical material, letters, newspaper clippings, family mementoes, and finally the complete catalogs of his poems mentioned above. Mr. Savidis believes that editing all the material will require approximately five years' work. Of course, the whole matter will finally depend upon the willingness of all people in possession of such papers to cooperate for a common purpose—to restore Cavafy's legacy to its rightful heir, the public.

3  C. P. Cavafy, "Since Nine O'clock," in *Poems* (Athens, 1952), 97. All quotations from the poems are translations by myself.

4  Cavafy, "Caesarion," 89.

5  C. M. Bowra, "Constantine Cavafy and the Greek Past," *The Creative Experiment* (London, 1949), 59.

6  T. S. Eliot, "Goethe as the Sage," *On Poetry and Poets* (London, 1962), 216.

7    *Ibid.*, 219.
8    T. S. Eliot, "East Coker," *Four Quartets* (New York, 1943), 17.
9    T. S. Eliot, "Ulysses, Order, and Myth," in *James Joyce: Two Decades of Criticism,* Seon Givens, ed. (New York, 1948), 201–202.
10   T. S. Eliot, "Yeats," *On Poetry and Poets* (London, 1962), 255.
11   Cavafy, "The God Forsakes Antony," 35.
12   Cavafy, "Theodotus," 58.
13   E. P. Papanoutsos, *Palamas-Cavafy-Sikelianos* (Athens, 1955).
14   T. S. Eliot, *Collected Poems 1909–1935* (London, 1936), 73.
15   Cavafy, "Tomb of Iases," 78.
16   Cavafy, "Those Who Fought for the Achaean League," 129.
17   George Seferis, *Dokimes* (Athens, 1962), 254–59.
18   T. S. Eliot, "What Is a Classic?" *On Poetry and Poets* (London, 1962), 61.
19   *Ibid.*, 56.
20   Edmund Keeley and Philip Sherrard, *Six Poets of Modern Greece* (London and Southampton, 1960), 14–15.
21   Cavafy, "The Displeasure of the Son of Seleucus," 70–71.
22   Cavafy, "King Demetrius," 31.
23   Cavafy, "In the Year 200 B.C.," 189.
24   Cavafy, "Orophernes," 64.
25   Cavafy, "Days of 1901," 157.
26   Cavafy, "The City," 32.
27   Eliot, "Goethe as the Sage," 216.
28   W. H. Auden, introduction to *The Complete Poems of Cavafy,* Rae Dalven, trans. (New York, 1961), vii.
29   Lawrence Durrell, *Clea* (New York, 1961), 11.
30   Durrell, *Balthazar* (New York, 1961), 184.
31   *Ibid.*, 22.
32   Durrell, *Justine* (New York, 1961), 27.
33   Cavafy, "He Came To Read," 140.
34   Durrell, *Justine*, 180.
35   *Ibid.*, 18–19.
36   *Ibid.*, 13.
37   *Ibid.*, 180.
38   Durrell, *Clea*, 223.
39   Cavafy, 32.
40   Durrell, *Justine*, 180.
41   *Ibid.*
42   Cavafy, "The City," 32.
43   Durrell, *Justine*, 114.
44   *Ibid.*, 191.
45   Cavafy, "For Ammones who died 29 years old, in 610," 81.
46   Durrell, *Balthazar*, 225.
47   Durrell, *Justine*, 175.
48   *Ibid.*, 176.
49   Durrell, *Clea*, 231.
50   Durrell, *Justine*, 27.
51   *Ibid.*, 30.
52   *Ibid.*, 112.
53   Durrell, *Clea*, 229–30.
54   George Steiner, "Lawrence Durrell: the Baroque Novel," *The World of Lawrence Durrell,* Harry T. Moore, ed. (Carbondale, 1962), 20.

WALTER BORENSTEIN

1 Ernest Hemingway, in the inscription to *The Sun Also Rises,* uses the phrase: "You are all a lost generation," and attributes it to a conversation with Gertrude Stein. Malcolm Cowley's study, *Exile's Return* (New York, 1934) refers to the writers of this group as exiles. There is some doubt as to whether Dos Passos belongs to either group.

2 Alfred Kazin, *On Native Grounds* (New York, 1956), 267–73.

3 John T. Reid, "Spain as Seen by Some Contemporary American Writers," *Hispania* (May, 1937), 139–50.

4 "People," *Time* (October 29, 1956), 47.

5 Salvador de Madariaga, "The World Weighs a Writer's Influence: Spain," *Saturday Review* (July 29, 1961), 18.

6 Many critics have discussed the concept of *nada* in Hemingway's works and have traced its influences to many Spanish individuals.

7 The so-called "Generation of '98" of which Baroja, Miguel de Unamuno, Ramón del Valle-Inclán, Antonio Machado, and Azorín were leading members.

8 Camilo José Cela, *La colmena* (Buenos Aires, 1951). The first edition of this novel was published abroad because of censorship difficulties encountered in Spain.

9 Gonzalo Torrente Ballester, *Panorama de la literatura española contemporánea* (2nd ed.; Madrid, 1961), I, 420.

10 John R. Dos Passos, "A Novelist of Disintegration," *The Freeman* (October, 1920), 133.

11 Gilbert Murray, *Five Stages of Greek Religion* (New York, 1925), 155.

12 *Ibid.,* 156.

13 *Ibid.,* 206.

14 George Steiner, *The Death of Tragedy* (New York, 1961), 324.

15 Dos Passos, "A Novelist of Disintegration," 132–33.

16 *Ibid.,* 133. It is obvious that Dos Passos almost intuitively grasped the essence of Baroja's ideas through the reading of some of his early novels. Baroja's dissertation in medicine had been on the subject of pain, and his inability to face this aspect of medicine daily had contributed to his early disenchantment. The concept of *abulia* or the breakdown of will power had been an essential characteristic of the heroes of Baroja's novels, and in the novels of his contemporaries. It seems that Dos Passos discovered and admired in Baroja that which was the fundamental character of his philosophy.

17 John H. Wrenn, *John Dos Passos* (New York, 1961), 202.

18 *Ibid.,* 14–15.

19 John M. Brinnin, in *The Third Rose* (Boston, 1959), 232, talks of the interest of both Gertrude Stein and Malcolm Cowley in this group of writers. Brinnin implies that Cowley's reputation, to some extent, was built on this early interest.

20 Wrenn, *John Dos Passos,* 19.

21 *Ibid.*

22 Alfred Kazin has called the Norton-Harjes Ambulance Service "the most distinguished of all the lost generation's finishing schools, . . . subsidized by a Morgan partner." *On Native Grounds,* 270.

23 Wrenn, *John Dos Passos,* 29.

24 Dos Passos, *U.S.A.: The 42nd Parallel* (New York, 1930), 302–303.

25 Wrenn, *John Dos Passos,* 19. The question of Dos Passos' illegitimate birth is somewhat confusing. Only Wrenn and Dan Wakefield in "Dos, Which

Side Are You On?" *Esquire* (April, 1963), 114—who may have taken his information from Wrenn's study—mention this biographical fact. An examination of all other biographical sources brings no evidence for this point. Dos Passos, however, did read and approve the manuscript of Wrenn's work. *Dictionary of American Biography* (New York, 1930), 338–39, in a biography of the author's father, John Randolph Dos Passos, refers to a wife and son, Louis Hays Dos Passos, but makes no reference either to John Roderigo or his mother. The obituary of John Randolph Dos Passos (New York *Times*, January 28, 1917) also omits all reference to the author and his mother. There can be no doubt of his illegitimate birth and of the fact that he took his father's name shortly before his entrance to Harvard. What is surprising is the fact that this has been obscured in the extraordinary quantity of biographical material concerning one of America's leading novelists. Wrenn's theory of Dos Passos' need to belong makes this illegitimate birth even more significant.

26  *Ibid.*, 23.
27  Maxwell Geismar, "A Cycle of Fiction," *Literary History of the United States*, Robert E. Spiller *et al.*, eds. (New York, 1949), 1302.
28  Charles W. Bernardin, "John Dos Passos' Harvard Years," *New England Quarterly* (March, 1954), 214–17.
29  Wrenn, *John Dos Passos*, 195.
30  Reid, "Spain as Seen by Some Contemporary American Writers," 145.
31  Granville Hicks, *The Great Tradition* (New York, 1935), 287.
32  César Barja, *Libros y autores contemporáneos* (New York, 1935), 299.
33  Hicks, *The Great Tradition*, 287.
34  *Ibid.*
35  Malcolm Cowley, *After the Genteel Tradition* (New York, 1936), 168.
36  Reid, "Spain as Seen by Some Contemporary American Writers," 145.
37  *Ibid.*
38  *Ibid.*
39  *Ibid.*
40  Dos Passos, "A Novelist of Disintegration," 133.
41  Wrenn, *John Dos Passos*, 26. The quotation is from Camera Eye 19 in *U.S.A.*
42  This is also the title of an essay by Baroja in *Juventud, egolatría*. The symbol of the wandering Quijote is clear here.
43  Wakefield, "Dos, Which Side Are You On?", 116. Wakefield points out that Robles' death during the Civil War in Spain at the hands of the Communists (according to Dos Passos) contributed to the author's growing distrust of the Communist cause.
44  Wrenn, *John Dos Passos*, 86.
45  *Ibid.*, 87.
46  Barja, *Libros y autores contemporáneos*, 306.
47  Pío Baroja, *Camino de perfección* (Santiago, Chile, 1956), 126.
48  Baroja, "Nietzsche y la filosofía," *Obras completas* (Madrid, 1951), VIII, 853.
49  Kazin, *On Native Grounds*, 270.
50  Dos Passos, "A Novelist of Disintegration," 133.
51  Cowley, *After the Genteel Tradition*, 183–84.
52  Baroja, *Caesar or Nothing*, Louis How, trans. (New York, 1919), 337.
53  Barja, *Libros y autores contemporáneos*, 300–301.
54  The concept is found in many authors and appears in Edna St. Vincent Millay's *Aria da capo*.

55   Baroja, *El mundo es ansí* (Madrid, 1912), 317.
56   Guillermo de Torre, "La generación de 1898 en las revistas del tiempo," *Nosotros* (Buenos Aires, October, 1941), 30.
57   William B. Yeats, "The Second Coming," *The Collected Works of W. B. Yeats* (New York, 1952), 185.
58   Baroja, *El árbol de la ciencia* (Madrid, 1929), 43.
59   *Ibid.,* 67.
60   *Ibid.,* 71.
61   Baroja, *La dama errante* (Madrid, 1908), 59.
62   Baroja, *César o nada* (Madrid, 1910), 14.
63   *Ibid.,* 28.
64   *Ibid.,* 274.
65   *Ibid.,* 394–95.
66   Baroja, *Nuevo tablado de Arlequín* (Madrid, 1917), 58–59.
67   Dos Passos, "A Novelist of Disintegration," 132.
68   *Ibid.*
69   Barja, *Libros y autores contemporáneos,* 337.
70   Dos Passos, "A Novelist of Disintegration," 132.
71   *Ibid.,* 134.
72   Barja, *Libros y autores contemporáneos,* 338.
73   Cowley, *After the Genteel Tradition,* 173–74.
74   Dos Passos, "A Novelist of Disintegration," 134. ·
75   Baroja, *La dama errante,* prólogo.
76   Baroja, "The Mistakes of the Spanish Republic," *The Living Age* (January, 1937), 426–27.
77   Wrenn, *John Dos Passos,* 185.
78   *Ibid.,* 187.
79   *Ibid.* [6].
80   Dos Passos, "A Novelist of Disintegration," 133. The translation of Baroja is by Dos Passos and appeared before the published translation.

LEWIS P. SIMPSON

1   "On the Modern Element in Modern Literature," *The Partisan Review Anthology,* William Phillips and Philip Rahv, eds. (New York, 1962), 264.
2   *The Human Condition* (New York, 1959), 48. Cf. W. H. Auden, "The Poet & the City," in *The Dyer's Hand and Other Essays* (New York, 1962), 80–81.
3   "The Golden Day Revisited," an introduction to the Beacon paperback edition of *The Golden Day: A Study in American Literature and Culture* (Boston, 1957), xx. *The Golden Day* was originally published in 1926.
4   *Ibid.,* xx–xxi.
5   "The Hero in the New World: William Faulkner's The Bear," *Interpretations of American Literature,* Charles Feidelson, Jr., and Paul Brodtkorb, Jr., eds. (New York, 1959), 348.
6   "What Modern Writers Forget," *Saturday Review,* XLV (January 20, 1962), 33.

JOHN WILLIAM CORRINGTON

1   It should be noted that these prefatory remarks refer to the earlier work of all three men. Ginsberg's work, famous at first for its corrosive social criticism and massive use of vulgarism, has tended to become more per-

sonal and, to some degree at least, more controlled in later books. Corso's, originally divided between pure lyric and such abstract social criticism as "Power," "Bomb," and "Army," has lost its whimsy and much of its satiric edge. Ferlinghetti, whose original poetry had little social content except of the most general sort, has become perhaps the most political of the three. It is a commonplace to say that his recent work, "One Thousand Fearful Words for Fidel Castro," and "Tentative Description of a Dinner to Promote the Impeachment of President Eisenhower," marks a catastrophic decline in quality.

2   *Pictures of the Gone World* (San Francisco, 1955).

3   *A Coney Island of the Mind* (New York, 1958).

4   A listing of the artists mentioned in *Pictures of the Gone World* and *A Coney Island of the Mind* includes Praxiteles, Brancusi, Sarolla, Picasso, Goya, Bosch, Chagall, Cellini, and Shahn.

5   Maurice Grosser, *The Painter's Eye* (New York, 1956), 130.

6   Grosser, *The Painter's Eye*, 131.

7   It is worth noting in passing that the general hue and cry against the "Beats" for their supposed anti-intellectualism, at least in Ferlinghetti's case—and one suspects in that of Corso as well—is based, ironically enough, not so much in the purported cultivation of ignorance and repudiation of thought among the "Beats" as in the patent refusal of certain critics (see Norman Podhoretz, "The Know-Nothing Bohemians," *Partisan Review*, XXV [Spring, 1958], 305 ff.) to examine the work in question within its intended context. There is a difference between the anti-intellectual and the nonintellectual, and however incredible it may seem to critics, artistic and literary, there are areas of human experience in which the intellectual is more or less irrelevant.

8   Arthur Rimbaud, *Prose Poems from The Illuminations,* Louise Varèse, trans. (New York, 1946), 47.

9   Ezra Pound, "In a Station of the Metro," *Personae* (New York, 1949), 109.

10  Stephane Mallarmé, *Poems,* Roger Fry, trans., with commentaries by Charles Mauron (New York, 1951), 29.

11  *Ibid.,* 30.

12  *Ibid.,* 301.

13  Wallace Stevens, *Opus Posthumous,* Samuel French Morse, ed. (New York, 1957), 226.

14  Federico García Lorca, *Poet in New York,* Ben Belitt, trans., with an introduction by Angel del Rio (New York, 1955), 109.

15  *Ibid.,* xxxviii.

16  *Ibid.,* xxxiv f.

17  *Picasso: Forty Years of His Art,* Alfred H. Barr, Jr., ed. (New York, 1939), 170.

18  Both Mauron and Fry, in relation to Mallarmé, note that "subject" in art "does not matter." Mauron makes much of Mallarmé's insistence that the value of poetry (and, by extension, one infers, of art itself) consists in a "something else" beyond, above, withdrawn from the nominal matter which serves as apparent subject for the act of creation. While there inevitably exists, in this sort of esthetic theorizing, a certain degree of vagueness, one cannot but call to mind James Joyce's famous "epiphanies," and recall that even Joyce himself, at least insofar as he uses Stephan Dedalus as his mouthpiece, finds the last quality required for beauty, "claritas," almost beyond specification. One suspects that S. Thomas' and Joyce's

"claritas," Mallarmé's "something else," and Ferlinghetti's "fountains of imagination" (*Coney Island*, poem 13) may finally be much the same thing.
19 Barr, *Picasso*, 11.

CALVIN EVANS

1 Alain Robbe-Grillet, *Jealousy*, Richard Howard, trans. (New York, 1959).
2 In *L'Ere du Soupçon*, Nathalie Sarraute states that the word "psychology" is a word that no contemporary author could hear without lowering his eyes and blushing.
3 Henri Bergson describes *durée intérieure* or "pure duration" as, "the form taken by our successive states of consciousness when the self awakens and no longer effects a separation between present and anterior states. Underneath homogeneous duration, extensive symbol of true duration, an attentive psychology disentangles a duration whose heterogeneous moments compenetrate; underneath the numerical multiplicity of well-defined states, exists a self where succession implies fusion and organization." *Essai sur les données immédiates de la conscience* (Paris, 1958), 74.
4 Robbe-Grillet, *Jealousy*, 83.
5 *Ibid.*, 56.
6 *Ibid.*, 71–75.
7 *Ibid.*, 100.
8 *Ibid.*
9 *Ibid.*, 113.
10 *Ibid.*
11 *Ibid.*, 114.
12 *Ibid.*, 139.
13 See *Film: An Anthology*, Daniel Talbot, ed. (New York, 1959), 328.
14 *Ibid.*, 329.
15 *Ibid.*, 326.
16 Marcel Proust, *Le Temp retrouvé* (2 vols.; Paris: Editions de la Nouvelle Revue Française, 1927), II, 34 ". . . la littérature qui se contente de 'décimer les choses', d'en donner seulement un misérable relevé de lignes et de surfaces."

JOHN HAZARD WILDMAN

1 John Henry Newman, *The Arians of the Fourth Century* (New York, 1901), 222.
2 *The Comforters* (1957); *Robinson* (1958); *Memento Mori* (1959); *The Bachelors* (1960); *The Ballad of Peckham Rye* (1960); *The Prime of Miss Jean Brodie* (1961); *The Girls of Slender Means* (1963).
3 Witness, for instance, the clean-handed elaborately innocent suggestiveness of *The Woman in White* or *The Turn of the Screw*, the melodramatic irresponsibility of Mrs. Radcliffe or Bram Stoker's *Dracula*. But also when the supernatural is taken seriously as a system, note the self-conscious whimsy of Bruce Marshall, the defensive diabolism of Graham Greene, or the general uneasiness of Evelyn Waugh in *Brideshead Revisited*.
4 All of her novels except the latest insinuate the presence of the supernatural.

5 Samuel Hynes, "The Prime of Muriel Spark," *Commonweal,* LXXV (1962), 563.
6 André Gide, *The Counterfeiters,* Dorothy Bussy, trans. (New York, 1955), 171.
7 Spark, *Memento Mori* (New York, 1959), 39.
8 *Ibid.,* 139.
9 *Ibid.,* 96.
10 "The novelist is continually in the absurd position of making laws for his characters in a universe that he did not make, and he is forced to this absurdity simply because he does not know the laws of the real universe. Lacking this knowledge, no matter how profound his insight into human character and passion and motive and motivelessness, he is doomed to unreality. A work of art is not composed in order to illustrate the moral law, any more than a cathedral is built to illustrate mechanical laws. But if the builder ignores the laws of mechanics, his cathedral will show its unreality by falling down; and if the artist ignores the moral law, his work will in the long run show its unreality just as certainly." Frank Sheed, *Theology and Sanity* (New York, 1948), 313.
11 Elizabeth Bowen, *Notes on Writing a Novel* (New York, 1950), quoted in Howard E. Hugo, *Aspects of Fiction* (Boston, 1962), 181.
12 Surely the dramatic and thematic impact of Hemingway's *The Killers* is considerably furthered by the fact that the two intensely evil men have the minds and bodies of third-rate vaudeville comics and that the setting offers, ostensibly and ironically, one of the few obvious comforts of naturalism—a sort of dull fly-specked safety, where nothing so suspect of theological associations as evil ever happens.
13 "In a biographical note," writes Samuel Hynes, "Mrs. Spark once listed her favorite occupations as 'Chess and Disguise.' There is something of both visible in her novels: a pleasure in intricately patterned plots, and a pleasure in the concealment of motives and meanings." Hynes, "The Prime of Muriel Spark," 562.
14 Equipped with analogy, *Time* puts this point precisely: "British novelist Spark has been compared to Evelyn Waugh, but the comparison is inexact: she is, in fact, a kind of welfare state Jane Austen, a novelist in whose hands the commonplace becomes mysteriously implausible, the routine eerily irrational." *Time,* LXXVI (August 15, 1960), 82.
15 Spark, *The Ballad of Peckham Rye* (New York, 1960), 23.
16 Spark, *Robinson* (New York, 1958), 77.
17 *Ibid.,* 144.
18 Certainly Anthony Trollope's calm judicial separation of powers is foreign to her approach: "A novel should give a picture of common life enlivened by humour and sweetened by pathos. To make that picture worthy of attention, the canvas should be crowded with real portraits, not of individuals known to the world or to the author, but of created personages impregnated with traits of character which are known. To my thinking, the plot is but the vehicle for all this. . . ." Trollope, *Autobiography* (New York, 1935), 110.
19 Spark, *The Comforters* (London, 1961), 86.
20 Spark, *The Bachelors* (New York, 1961), 219.
21 Humor has apparently carried over to her first play, *Doctors of Philosophy* (1962). J. C. Trewin writes: ". . . during forty minutes I found myself asking whether this was not the wittiest first act in years. I think that in

retrospect it well may be, though later the play dips into a crevasse. . . ."
Trewin, "The World of the Theatre," *Illustrated London News* (October
13, 1962), 574.

22 *The Comforters*, 21.
23 *Ibid.*, 3.
24 This statement from Muriel Spark's edition of the Brontë letters seems to
strike a prophetic note: "It is not until we come to examine these figures
[the Brontës], both in isolation and in correlation, that we can perceive . . . the various distinctive traits of Emily, Charlotte, and Branwell,
and the reasons for these." *The Brontë Letters*, Muriel Spark, ed. (London,
1954), 12.
25 John Updike, "Creatures of the Air," *New Yorker*, XXXVII (September
30, 1961), 161.
26 Spark, *The Prime of Miss Jean Brodie* (London, 1961), 7.
27 *Ibid.*, 9–10.
28 *Ibid.*, 145.
29 Spark, *Child of Light, A Reassessment of Mary Wollstonecraft Shelley*
(Hadleigh, Essex, 1951), 120.
30 Spark, *The Go-Away Bird and Other Stories* (New York, 1958), 74–137.
31 Spark, "Against the Transcendentalists," *The Fanfarlo and Other Verse*
(Ashrod, Kent, 1952), 34–35.

RICHARD J. O'DEA

1 Vivienne Koch, "The Poetry of Allen Tate," *Kenyon Review*, XI (Summer, 1949), 355–78.
2 Richard Foster, *The New Romantics* (Bloomington, 1962), 107–132.
3 Koch, "The Poetry of Allen Tate," 356.
4 Cleanth Brooks, *Modern Poetry and the Tradition* (Chapel Hill, 1939),
95–109.
5 Allen Tate, "Understanding Modern Poetry," *Collected Essays* (Denver, 1959), 128.
6 Kenneth Burke, "Tentative Proposal," *Poetry*, L (May, 1937), 98.
7 John M. Bradbury, *The Fugitives* (Chapel Hill, 1958), 167.
8 Tate, "A Note on Critical 'Autoletism,'" *Collected Essays*, 538.
9 Tate, "Modern Poets and Convention," *Collected Essays*, 545.
10 Tate, "The Man of Letters in the Modern World," *Collected Essays*,
386.
11 *Ibid.*
12 Tate, "Christ and the Unicorn," *Sewanee Review*, LXIII (Spring, 1955),
179.
13 Tate, "Tension in Poetry," *Collected Essays*, 75–90.
14 Tate, "Is Literary Criticism Possible?" *Collected Essays*, 487.
15 Delmore Schwartz, "The Poetry of Allen Tate," *Southern Review*, V
(Winter, 1940), 419–38.
16 Tate, *Mr. Pope and Other Poems* (New York, 1923).
17 Tate, "The Man of Letters in the Modern World," *Collected Essays*, 390.
18 Louis Rubin, "The Concept of Nature in Modern Southern Poetry," *American Quarterly*, IX (Spring, 1957), 65.
19 Koch, "The Poetry of Allen Tate," 367.
20 Tate, "The Man of Letters in the Modern World," *Collected Essays*, 384.
21 Yvor Winters, *Primitivism and Decadence* (New York, 1937), 4.
22 Tate, "Religion and the Old South," *Collected Essays*, 311.

23  R. K. Meiners, "End of History: Allen Tate's Seasons of the Soul," *Sewanee Review,* LXX (Winter, 1962), 34–80.

MILLER WILLIAMS

1  Yvor Winters, "T. S. Eliot or the Illusion of Reaction," *On Modern Poets* (New York, 1959), 41.
2  Winters, *In Defense of Reason* (Denver, 1947), 11–12.
3  Winters, "Robert Frost or the Spiritual Drifter as Poet," *On Modern Poets,* 206.
4  Winters, "The Significance of the Bridge by Hart Crane or What Are We To Think of Professor X," *On Modern Poets,* 134.
5  Winters, "Wallace Stevens or the Hedonist's Progress," *On Modern Poets,* 12.
6  Winters, "John Crowe Ransom or Thunder Without God," *On Modern Poets,* 117.
7  Winters, "Wallace Stevens or the Hedonist's Progress," *On Modern Poets,* 32.
8  Winters, "John Crowe Ransom or Thunder Without God," *On Modern Poets,* 85.
9  Winters, "T. S. Eliot or the Illusion of Reaction," *On Modern Poets,* 41.
10 Winters, "John Crowe Ransom or Thunder Without God," *On Modern Poets,* 73.
11 *Ibid.,* 116.
12 Winters, "Problems of the Modern Critic of Literature," *The Function of Criticism, Problems and Exercises* (Denver, 1957), 17.
13 Winters, "Primitivism and Decadence: A Study of American Experimental Poetry," *In Defense of Reason,* 86.
14 Winters, "Wallace Stevens or the Hedonist's Progress," *On Modern Poets,* 12.
15 Winters, "Primitivism and Decadence: A Study of American Experimental Poetry," *In Defense of Reason,* 19–20.
16 Winters, "John Crowe Ransom or Thunder Without God," *On Modern Poets,* 86–87.
17 Winters, "Problems of the Modern Critic of Literature," *The Function of Criticism,* 61.
18 John Ciardi, "The Form Is the Experience," *Art Education,* XIV (October, 1961), 16–22.
19 *Ibid.*
20 Winters, "John Crowe Ransom or Thunder Without God," *On Modern Poets,* 77.
21 Winters, "The Anatomy of Nonsense," *In Defense of Reason,* 504.
22 Winters, "John Crowe Ransom or Thunder Without God," *On Modern Poets,* 85.
23 Winters, "Robert Frost or the Spiritual Drifter as Poet," *On Modern Poets,* 217.
24 Herbert J. Muller, *Science and Criticism* (New Haven, 1943), 261–62. I am indebted to Keith F. McKean for this passage, and the two following, which he cites in *The Moral Measure of Literature* (Denver, 1961).
25 James T. Farrell, *A Note on Literary Criticism* (New York, 1936), 176–77.
26 Richard M. Weaver, *The Ethics of Rhetoric* (Chicago, 1953), 175.
27 Winters, "Primitivism and Decadence: A Study of American Experimental Poetry," *In Defense of Reason,* 19.

28  Elizabeth Daryush, introduction to *Selected Poems* (Denver, 1948), xiv.
29  *Ibid.*, xiv.
30  Yvor Winters, "The Poetry of Helen Pinkerton," *Sequoia* (Winter, 1961), 31. The mention of Winters' own poetry is not to imply that a man's worth as a poet necessarily affects his worth as a critic. What Winters does with his poems is important, though, because one knows from his early work that he can do whatever he wants to in a poem, and do it well—which means we can assume that he writes as he does now, not because he has to, but because he wants to, and that we can see then in his poem what he thinks a poem ought to be. It is still difficult at times, I admit, not to express doubts concerning Winters' ear, and this has been done often enough, but, as I have said, a look at Winters' early and middle poems will establish quickly that we must go elsewhere for an answer.
31  Winters, "John Crowe Ransom or Thunder Without God," *On Modern Poets*, 106–107.
32  Winters, "The 16th Century Lyric in England," *Poetry, A Magazine of Verse*, LIII (February, 1939), 258–72.
33  McKean, *The Moral Measure of Literature*, 14.

# CONTRIBUTORS

BENSTOCK, BERNARD, assistant professor of English at Louisiana State University, has published articles on Joyce in the *Philological Quarterly*, the *Bucknell Review*, and the *Journal of English Literary History*. His essay "The Quiddity of Shem and the Whatness of Shaun" appeared in the first issue of the *James Joyce Quarterly*. He is the author of a forthcoming book on *Finnegans Wake*.

BORENSTEIN, WALTER, professor of Spanish at Cornell College, Iowa, was formerly associate professor of Spanish at Louisiana State University. He has contributed to *Symposium* and has published translations of Baroja and Azorín.

CORRINGTON, JOHN WILLIAM, instructor in English at Louisiana State University, recently spent a year pursuing studies in modern literature at the University of Sussex, England. His widely published poetry and fiction include the volume of verse *Where We Are*, which won the Charioteer Award for 1961, and a novel of the Civil War period, *And Wait for the Night*. Another volume of verse, *Lines to the South*, will be published in spring of 1965.

EVANS, CALVIN, until his untimely death in June, 1964, was associate professor of French at Louisiana State University. He had published articles on the French avant-garde theater as well as on the cinema. These include "Temporal Aesthetics and the Theater of Jean Tardieu," *Drama Survey*, 1963, and "Mallarméan Antecedents of the Vanguard Theater," *Modern Drama*, 1963.

O'DEA, RICHARD J., who received the Ph.D. degree in English in 1964 at Louisiana State University, is assistant professor of English at Gonzaga University, Spokane, Washington. He has recently completed *To Make the Eye Secure,* a book on Allen Tate.

RUEHLEN, PETROULA KEPHALA, a native of Thessalonika, Greece, was graduated from the Aristotelian University of Thessalonika in 1961. She received her M.A. degree in 1964 at Louisiana State University where she is now a graduate assistant.

SIMPSON, LEWIS P., professor of English at Louisiana State University, edited *The Federalist Literary Mind.* Among his other publications are "Touching 'The Stylus': Notes on Poe's Vision of Literary Order," in *Studies in American Literature,* and essays in *American Literature* and the *Texas Quarterly.*

WILDMAN, JOHN HAZARD, professor of English at Louisiana State University, is the author of the novels *Sing No Sad Songs, Peter Marvell,* and *Fever,* and of a book of poems, *Sun on the Night.* His articles and poems have appeared in the *Sewanee Review,* the New York *Times, Commonweal,* and the *American Institute of Architects Journal.*

WILLIAMS, MILLER, instructor in English at Louisiana State University, recently spent twelve months in Santiago, Chile, on an Amy Lowell Poetry Fellowship. A volume of his poetry, *A Circle of Stone,* was published in 1964. His poems have appeared in such magazines as the *Texas Quarterly,* the *American Scholar,* the *Saturday Review, Poetry,* the *Paris Review,* and *Prairie Schooner.*

# LOUISIANA STATE UNIVERSITY STUDIES

THE STUDIES WAS established to publish the results of research by faculty members, staff, and graduate students of the University. Manuscripts of exceptional merit from sources other than aforementioned are considered for publication provided they deal with subjects of particular interest to Louisiana.

The Studies originally appeared as a unified series consisting of forty-two numbers, published between the years 1931 and 1941. In 1951 the Studies was reactivated, and is now being issued in the following series: Social Sciences, Humanities, Biological Sciences, Physical Sciences, and Coastal Studies. Other series may be established as the need arises.